FLYING
—— THE ——
BLACK FLAG

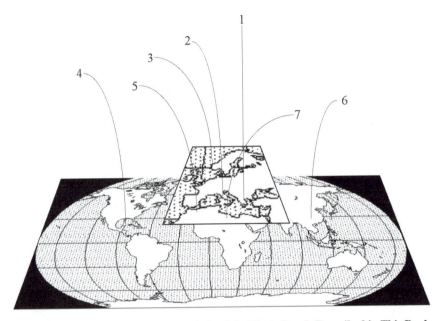

The Locations and Chronological Periods of the Pirate Bands Described in This Book

1. The Greeks (800–146 BC)
2. The Romans (753 BC to AD 476)
3. The Vikings (AD 793–1066)
4. The Buccaneers (1650–1701)
5. The Barbary Pirates (1320–1785)
6. The Tanka Pirates (1790–1820)
7. America and the Barbary Pirates (1785–1815)

FLYING

——— THE ———

BLACK FLAG

A Brief History of Piracy

Alfred S. Bradford

Illustrated by
Pamela M. Bradford

Westport, Connecticut
London

Library of Congress Cataloging-in-Publication Data

Bradford, Alfred S.
    Flying the black flag : a brief history of piracy / Alfred S. Bradford; illustrated by Pamela M. Bradford
        p.   cm.
    Includes bibliographical references and index.
    ISBN 978–0–275–97781–8 (alk. paper)
    1. Pirates—History.   I. Title.
  G535.B73   2007
  910.4′5—dc22   2007003036

British Library Cataloguing in Publication Data is available.

Library of Congress Catalog Card Number: 2007003036
ISBN-13: 978–0–275–97781–8
ISBN-10: 0–275–97781–1

First published in 2007

Praeger Publishers, 88 Post Road West, Westport, CT 06881
An imprint of Greenwood Publishing Group, Inc.
www.praeger.com

Printed in the United States of America

The paper used in this book complies with the Permanent Paper Standard issued by the National Information Standards Organization (Z39.48–1984).

10 9 8 7 6 5 4 3 2 1

To Nils Fredrik Malmstrom

Contents

Preface

Two weeks after September 11, 2001, when the initial shock had passed and the circumstances of the attack seemed to be clear, I began to consider what I, as an historian, could do and it occurred to me that we were in a situation without exact parallels. Terrorists have operated throughout history, but their ability to attack across large distances with devastating effect and to take thousands of lives is a phenomenon of modern technology, and so an historical study of terrorism would not be particularly relevant to our present situation, but when I amended the question and asked, how should we respond to an attack by a group that is neither organized as a regular military force nor openly acknowledged by any formal government, I thought of pirates and the world's response to pirates. Who became pirates? Why? And how did nations respond to attacks upon their citizens by pirates?

Pirates, most simply put, are robbers at sea and by sea. By definition, they—like terrorists—hold "no commission or delegated authority from any sovereign or state empowering them to attack others." Sometimes pirates were just bandits who operated on the water (although they did require a ship, a large enough gang to crew the ship, and sufficient nautical expertise to run the ship) and sometimes they were more than bandits. Whether they operated on a large scale or small, however, all pirates needed a place of refuge where they could refit their ship, sell their booty, celebrate their success—or recover from their failure—and prepare for their next operation. Pirates' motives are clear—others have what they want and they are determined to take it from them—but some pirates (though their primary motivation was still material gain) had secondary motives—to attack and injure those of another religion, another area, or another nationality.

Members of our government have compared terrorists to pirates and have suggested that the worldwide campaign against terrorism bears some resemblance to the worldwide campaign against piracy. I believe that the struggle against piracy does offer historical parallels to the situation we face today: different nations responding to unprovoked attacks upon their citizens by groups neither organized as a regular military nor openly acknowledged by any formal government. I called my publisher and talked to my editor, Heather Staines, and explained my idea to examine pirates throughout history. In conversations with her and her conversations with her fellow editors we clarified the shape and purpose of this book.

This book provides an overview of more than 2,000 years of piracy. I chose seven periods in time from the eighth century BC to our own early history and in extent from Europe and the Mediterranean to the Americas and Asia. I examine piracy from Odysseus, who acted like a pirate and believed that he was not, to the Romans, who suppressed piracy throughout the whole of the Mediterranean, to the Vikings, the pirates who won, to the Buccaneers, outcasts impelled into piracy and then co-opted by warring states, to the Chinese pirates rising from a distinct social underclass, and to the Barbary pirates, motivated both by the desire for plunder and by ideology, and against whom we fought our first war as the United States of America. Each of these groups of pirates became powerful enough to attack settlements on land and to threaten governments.

Although the specific circumstances of their increase in power differ, the general conditions are the same: lack of international law or enforcement of international law, lack of a controlling authority, or, if a (potential) controlling authority exists, lack of engagement or will, the chaos attendant on wars, and a group of social and/or economic outcasts. The response to piracy also varied and was not always successful.

—— PART I ——
GREEK PIRACY

If you wish to sail to the isle of Rhodes
Just ask a seer, "How should I sail?"
And the seer will tell you this,
"Select a good ship and avoid the stormy months,
And you will come, safe and sound, to the isle of Rhodes
... Unless a pirate captures you on the sea."

1

Odysseus: Hero and Pirate

Pirates (according to the father of history, Herodotus) caused the great war between the Persians and the Greeks:

The Persians claimed that Phoenician pirates were the first to provoke the Greeks. The Phoenicians—their cities lay on the eastern shore of the Mediterranean—loaded their long ships with goods from Egypt and Assyria and sailed to many places . . . and one of those places was Argos—by far the richest city of all the cities in the land now called Greece. At Argos the Phoenicians disembarked and displayed their wares along the harborside for several days, but when, on the fifth or the sixth day after their arrival, they had sold almost everything, and they had prepared their ship to leave, they noticed that a crowd of women had come to the harbor and that one of the women was the king's daughter. (Her name was Io and she was the daughter of King Inachus.) The women approached the prow of the ship, to examine the Phoenician wares and to bargain, and the Phoenicians, then and there, decided to grab them and carry them off. Many of the women escaped, but the Phoenicians seized Io and her maids, threw them into the ship, and sailed away to Egypt.

This kidnapping of princess Io by the Phoenicians was the first and primary cause of the enmity between the two peoples, Persian and Greek, because it set in motion a chain of events: some Greeks—they were probably Cretans [the most notorious pirates]—in retaliation for this kidnapping sailed to the Phoenician city of Tyre and kidnapped princess Europê. Now that should have been the end of that, one crime balanced by another, but other Greeks committed a second outrage: they sailed in a long ship to the Black Sea, ravaged a kingdom there and stole the golden fleece (which had been their objective from the beginning), and kidnapped princess Medea. Medea's father, the king, sent envoys to Greece to recover his daughter and to seek compensation for the kidnapping. The Greeks told the envoys that no one had paid compensation for the kidnapping of princess Io and, therefore, they would not pay compensation for princess Medea and, furthermore, would not return her.

A generation later (the story goes), Priam's son Paris, a Trojan, who knew of these events, conceived the desire to kidnap a wife from Greece—and he believed that he would never be called to account, because the kidnappers of princess Medea had not been. So he kidnapped Helen. The Greeks sent envoys to demand Helen's return and compensation. The Trojans replied that when the Greeks kidnapped Medea they did not offer compensation and they did not give her back to those who asked for her and so the Greeks should not expect to be compensated.

Up to this point the issue between Europe and Asia was only one of women who had been kidnapped, but the Greeks (the Persians say) put themselves completely in the wrong for what they did next, because the Greeks were the first to turn to war and to cross from Europe into Asia with an army. True, men in general accept as a principle of conduct that kidnapping women is not proper behavior, but, even so, to make a big deal out of a kidnapping is the height of folly; sensible men don't bother themselves about it, because they know that a woman who does not want to be carried off will not be carried off.

"We," the Persians say, "did not make a big deal out of the Asian women who had been kidnapped, but you Greeks, for the sake of a Greek woman, sailed to Asia with a huge expedition and destroyed the kingdom of Priam."

ॐ ॐ ॐ

Piracy is as old as ships and man's acquisitive nature. Pirates of all eras, and the earliest pirates, too, were driven by one primary motive—to acquire wealth—and one form of wealth was the human being, captured, enslaved, and sold. Sometimes pirates were just pirates and nothing more. Sometimes they were explorers or traders in long ships, as ready to trade with the strong and vigilant as they were to plunder the weak or incautious. Sometimes the plunderers were warriors on their way to the theater of war, or, warriors in the theater of war, who plundered their enemies or the neighbors of their enemies, or warriors on their way home from the theater of war.

The myths of Greece give piracy a prominent—sometimes a decisive—role in the events of early Greece (1200–700 BC). If only we could talk with a Greek from the eighth century and ask him about piracy—what was the distinction between a band of pirates and a band of warriors, how did pirates operate, who were their victims, and what was their position in society? And, indeed, we do know such a man, Homer, one of the greatest writers of all time, and he does answer our questions, but he answers them with stories, the stories of "Odysseus the Hero" and "Odysseus the Pirate."

After the sack of Troy the vagaries of the wind carried Odysseus to Ismarus and to people called the Cicones. Some of the Cicones lived by the coast and had the bad luck to be on Odysseus' way home. They did not have an immediate place of refuge and they were taken by surprise by the Greek raid.

"We killed the men, and we carried off their wives and so much plunder that every man got a share big enough to make him happy."

Too happy.

When Odysseus urged his men to take to the sea, the "blind fools" did not listen to him, they drank huge quantities of wine and they feasted on the shore of the sea, while the survivors were rushing about the countryside and rallying the rest of the Cicones.

The inland Cicones marshaled their forces, attacked the raiders, killed some, and drove off the rest, but then the action was over—the surviving raiders escaped to sea and were free to raid elsewhere. No nation existed, strong enough to pursue raiders by sea and destroy them in their homeland so they could not raid someone else.

The lesson for the raiders, of course, was *raid and run*.

After the fight with the Cicones, Odysseus happened upon a beautiful island with freshwater springs, wild goats that had never been hunted, a good harbor with a beach on which to draw up his ships, and no human inhabitants; his men wanted to stay there and recover from their tribulations, but he had seen that the mainland was inhabited and he told his men,

"I want to investigate these men, who they are, are they violent men and ferocious, or men who know justice and are kind to strangers and reverent to the gods."

He took one ship and one crew. When they landed they could see a big cave at the very edge of the sea and a vast pen constructed of gigantic slabs of stone and tall pines and oaks and in the pen were flocks of sheep and goats.

"As we were to learn, a giant man lived here; a man who had little to do with his fellow men, a godless man, who chose to live off by himself and to tend his flocks away from his neighbors. And what a monster he proved to be!—for he did not look at all like a man who eats bread, but rather he looked like a forested peak in the high mountains, one that towers above the others.

"I chose the dozen best of my shipmates to accompany me and I ordered the rest to remain by the ship and guard it." I filled a large wine skin with sweet, black wine and I carried that and some provisions in a bag, for though my courage did not fail me, I had a feeling that we were going to meet a savage man who knew neither the laws of man or God.

"We quickly reached the cave and we found no one inside, but the Cyclops (for so he was called) was following his daily routine with his rich flocks. We went into the cave and investigated everything. We found baskets stuffed with cheese, buckets filled with whey, and pens bursting with lambs and kids—they had been segregated by age.

"My shipmates begged me, first to take the cheese to the ship, then to return as quickly as we could, drive off the lambs and kids from the enclosures, and set sail on the salty sea, but I was not persuaded for I thought it might be much more profitable to meet this creature. Perhaps, I thought, he would give me gifts

of hospitality when he arrived . . . but his arrival proved to be sad news for some
of my shipmates.

"We kindled a fire, butchered an animal, selected some cheeses, said a prayer,
and then we ate; afterwards we sat down and waited for him to come back from
the pasture. When he came, he was carrying a mass of dry wood to use when he
fixed dinner. He threw this down with a horrible crash. We were afraid and we
huddled in the recesses of the cave. He drove his fat flocks of ewes into the wide
part of the cave and then he placed a huge boulder in the doorway, a boulder so
large that two dozen heavy four-wheeled carts could not have budged it from the
ground. That was the rock that he placed in the doorway.

"He sat down and milked the ewes and the bleating goats, one after another,
and he set the young ones, each to its mother. Then he saw us and asked,

'Strangers! Who are you? Where are you from? Are you crossing the watery
ways of the sea as merchants or are you just cruising here and there as pirates who
risk their own lives to do harm to strangers?'

"So he spoke, and our hearts hammered in our chests in fear at his harsh voice
and immense size, but I responded to him in these words:

'We are Greeks, coming from Troy but blown off our course by contrary winds
on the vast reaches of the sea. We wished to go home by another way, but we came
here, for Zeus has made a plan to prevent our returning home. Yes, honored sir,
respect the gods, for we are suppliants and Zeus is the protector of suppliants and
strangers. He is the god of guests and watches over the rights of travellers.'

"That is what I said and he answered me immediately with a cruel heart.

'You are a fool, stranger, or you have come from far, far away, that you bid me
to fear the gods or respect them. The Cyclopes take no account of aegis-bearing
Zeus or of the blessed gods, since we are stronger than they are. I will not keep
my hands off of you for fear of Zeus, not unless my heart commands me.'

"In his cruelty he seized two of my shipmates in his hands and he smashed them
on the rock like puppies, and their brains poured out on the ground and dampened
the earth, and he tore their bodies apart and feasted on them. He devoured them,
and he left nothing, not flesh or entrails or even the bones filled with marrow and
we stretched out our arms to Zeus and cried aloud, to see such horrible deeds.

"When the Cyclops had stuffed his great belly with human flesh and had drunk
pure milk, he threw himself down full length among his flocks and I, impelled by
the courage of my heart, wanted to approach him, draw the sharp sword sheathed
by my thigh, and, with my left hand feeling for his liver, stab him through his
chest, but second thoughts restrained me, for we would also be destroyed, every
man of us, since we by ourselves would not be able to roll aside the boulder—the
one he had placed there in the high doorway—and so, groaning and lamenting,
we waited for the sacred dawn.

"When dawn had stretched out her rosy fingers across the sky, the Cyclops built
up the fire and milked the handsome ewes. And after breakfast he moved aside the
great door slab, drove his rich flocks from the cave, and just as easily as I put the

cap on my quiver he put the door slab back again. And then whistling a tune, the Cyclops drove his rich flocks off to pasture in the mountains.

"Meanwhile I was left with a darkness in my soul and a thirst for revenge, if Athena would answer my prayers. And on thinking it over this appeared to be the best plan."

৵ ৵ ৵

Odysseus found a length of green olive wood, as large as the mast of a ship, but to the giant just the right size to use as a club, when it had dried. He had his men cut out a section of it, sharpen one end, and turn it in the fire to harden it. They hid it in a manure pile and chose four men by lot to help Odysseus.

৵ ৵ ৵

"In the evening the Cyclops herded the wooly flocks, all of them, into the cave and he left none outside the deep cave, and again he set the great door slab in place and he hurried to complete his chores. And again he seized two of my shipmates and devoured them for his dinner. And then I approached the Cyclops with a cup of the black wine in my hands and I said,

'Cyclops, drink this wine, now that you have finished your meal of human flesh, so you can see what kind of a drink our ship brought here. I brought it for you, as a gift from guest to host, so that you might pity us and send us on our way home, but you are nothing but a monster. Insane creature, why would anyone from the cities of men ever visit you again after you have trampled down what is right and lawful?'

"That is what I said and he took the cup and drank. He liked the sweet draught so terribly much that he asked for a second.

'Be generous and give me more and tell me your name right away so that I can give you a friendship gift, one you will rejoice to have, for the fertile land of the Cyclopes bears grapes for wine and Zeus gives us rain enough, but this wine of yours is nectar and ambrosia combined.'

"That is what he said and I poured more of the dark wine for him. Three times I served him and three times he drank it without thinking and when the wine had loosened the Cyclops' wits, I addressed him with soothing words,

'Cyclops, did you ask me my name? It is a famous one and I will tell you what it is and then you may give me the guest's gift you agreed to. My mother and my father and all my comrades have called me . . . Nobody.'

"So I spoke, and he answered me from his cruel heart,

'Nobody, here is my gift to you. I will eat all your companions first and I will save you for last.'

"He finished speaking, lay back, and passed out. His heavy head drooped and sleep seized him completely and in his sleep he belched heavy wine fumes and he vomited wine and fragments of human flesh. I thrust the pole into the embers of the fire to heat it up and I spoke to all my shipmates, to give them courage, so that no one would become afraid and let me down. Then when the length of olive wood glowed fiercely with heat—it was green remember—we took it from the fire, and my shipmates got a good grip on it while a divine spirit breathed courage into us and we took the length of olive wood and we plunged the sharp end into his eye: I spun it like a drill, and the hot blood boiled around the hot spike, and his eyebrows and lashes burned off and the globe of his eye sizzled from the fire, just as the hot metal of an ax sizzles when a blacksmith plunges it into cold water—he does it to temper the metal—and so the eye sizzled just like that ... around the shaft of olive wood.

"The terrifying screams of the Cyclops reverberated throughout the cave. We were afraid and we scrambled out of his way. He grasped the shaft with his hands and tore it out and threw it from him. Blood streamed out and he screamed aloud to the Cyclopes who lived around him in shadowy caves on the hillsides. And in response to his screams they came, one from here, one from there, all of them, and they stood around his cave and asked him what was wrong.

'Why are you raising such a ruckus, Polyphemus, in the quiet and peaceful night, and waking us all up? Is someone driving off your flocks and you don't want him to, or is someone trying to kill you, by open force or ambush?'

"And the mighty Polyphemus called out from his cave,

'My friends, Nobody is trying to kill me, by open force and not by ambush.'

"And they replied with this ready response,

'Well then, if no one is doing violence to you, I suppose it is a disease and disease is apportioned by great Zeus. You should pray to your father, Lord Poseidon.'

"So they spoke and then they went away and I laughed to myself that that name, *Nobody*, had fooled them and protected me."

ॐ   ॐ   ॐ

Odysseus and his men—the survivors—escape to sea (after they have loaded the flocks of the Cyclops on board their ship) and Odysseus cannot refrain, against the entreaties of his men, from taunting the monster, and the monster who really is the son of Poseidon calls upon his father to avenge him. Poseidon hears his son and prevents any of Odysseus' shipmates from returning home and keeps Odysseus away from home for ten years. In the world of Odysseus a hero is not punished for piracy or violence or a raid on the Cicones or for a moral wrong, but because he has injured the son of a god and the god is angry. The gods of Greece do not enforce any ethical code—they react in a personal way to personal benefactions and injuries. A hero never knows—he can lead a life of violence, raiding and robbing, kidnapping, killing, with no divine interest in him and then he blinds a cannibalistic one-eyed monster and the monster has connections and the hero pays.

The story of the Cyclops is a wonderful story, the tallest of tall tales, not to be taken too seriously, perhaps, even if it does reveal a way of thinking—Odysseus expects to be welcomed as an honored guest and to be given gifts—notwithstanding his crew's impulse to rustle the flocks and carry off the cheeses—because Odysseus refrained from plundering the cave. The Cyclops was not impressed with this reasoning and if he could tell the tale, we would have a different version—how a hapless shepherd, tending his flocks and living peacefully by himself, wanting only to be left alone, was beset by pirates, but through his strength of arm he captured them and served them as they would have served him. Alas, they deceived him, they got him drunk, and, in his drink-besotted sleep, they blinded him and then escaped. In the future—too late!—he might take a vow to dispatch any suspected pirates as soon as he got his hands on them and he might resolve to live a little closer to his fellow Cyclopes and to cultivate a better relationship with them.

For the Cyclopes it was all too likely that someday in the future, now that Greeks knew of their land, that some Greeks would return and found a colony on the island off the coast of *Cyclopsland*; they would hunt the wild goats, tend crops, and fish, and perhaps they would engage in trade: Greek wine for the Cyclopes' animals and cheese, and perhaps the two peoples might get along as neighbors, but should the crops fail and fishing and trade fall short, the Greeks might well raid the Cyclopes and seize their animals and cheese, as a way more profitable than trading (and safe, too, because the Cyclopes had no boats from which to retaliate).

For Odysseus and the Greeks, little separated a hero and a pirate.

After terrible trials and tribulations Odysseus returned to his homeland, the island of Ithaca, where he assumed the disguise of an old beggar man and found a welcome in the hut of Eumaeus, the swineherd. (Eumaeus, himself, as a boy, had been kidnapped by pirates.) After the supposititious beggar was made comfortable, Eumaeus said to him,

"But come now, old one, and tell me—since I know that you cannot have walked here on foot—how did you come to Ithaca?"

And the devious Odysseus told him the tale of the Cretan Pirate:

かか かか かか

"I am proud to be a native of the plains of Crete; my father was well known, but he had many other sons raised in his court, legitimate sons from a lawful wife, while the mother who bore me was his concubine; nonetheless, my father treated me as well as he treated his legitimate sons, and, he, in turn, was honored like a god by the Cretans and envied, too, because of his wealth and his stature and his mighty sons; yet, for all his wealth and power, the spirits of death came for him, too, and carried him off to the realms of Hades, and his haughty sons cast lots, divided his estate, and apportioned me a miserable little piece of land and a house. Despite them and on my own merits—I am nobody's fool and I am not afraid of war—I took the daughter of a wealthy man in marriage.

"As far as any kind of work and family life and the raising of beloved children, I didn't like it, no, ever and always I preferred oared ships and wars and smooth javelins and arrows, wretched things, which fill others with dread. I loved what the gods had placed in my heart to love, as others love other employments. Before the sons of the Greeks disembarked at Troy I had already commanded nine expeditions of man and ship in battle, man against man, and a great plenty of booty had fallen to me. For my leadership I received whatever I chose first and I also received a great deal more as my share in the formal division of the spoils."

But he was drawn into the Trojan War and only after ten years of war did he return to his home.

"I had been home only a month—enjoying my children, my wedded wife, and my estates—when the spirit moved me to collect some ships and sail to Egypt with a noble crew.

"I outfitted nine ships as my summons swiftly brought together the required men to form nine crews. For six days I provided the sacrificial animals to honor the gods and I laid out a feast for my shipmates. On the seventh day we boarded the ships and sailed from wide Crete; such a strong north wind blew behind us, that it seemed as though we were being carried along by the current of a river. We lost not a single ship, and rested on the benches, whole and entire, while the wind and the steersmen brought us to Egypt. In five days we had reached the broad Egyptian river and there in that great river I brought the curved ships to and I bade my shipmates to remain by the ships and stand guard while I sent out our scouts to look around, but they were so confident in their strength that they lost their heads and immediately set to looting the fertile fields of the Egyptians; they killed the men and they drove off their wives and children.

"The attack roused the city; the king and the townspeople attacked us at dawn. They filled the whole plain with infantry and horses and flashing bronze. Danger threatened from every side. Then Zeus, who loves the thunder, turned my men into cowards; not one had the courage to face the enemy. The Egyptians killed many of us with the sharp bronze, and they captured some alive (these were destined to work as slaves), but Zeus had a special plan for me and he set his plan in my mind. Better then if I had died and met my fate in Egypt and saved myself from so many future troubles! Instead I cast down the well-made helmet from my head and the shield from my shoulder, I dropped the spear from my hand and I ran to the king in his chariot, I clasped his knees in supplication, I wept, and he pitied me, and he protected me, he took me up on his chariot and bade me sit and he took me home with him. The multitude wanted to kill me and they thrust at me with their spears—for they were enraged—but he defended me from them, for he would not anger Zeus the Protector who most of all avenges cruelty to suppliants."

He stayed in Egypt seven years and acquired great treasure among the men of Egypt, for they are generous people, but when his eighth year rolled around, he fell into a plot devised by a Phoenician—Phoenicians know all the ways of treachery—to lure him onboard a ship, seize his property, and carry him off and sell him as a slave. The plot failed because of a storm with a violent north wind.

"The north wind blew us directly across the sea past Crete and beyond Crete we had no other glimpse of land, but only the sea and the sky while Zeus gathered the dark clouds above the hollow ship and stained the sea with darkness, and then he thundered and he struck the ship with his lightning bolt; the ship was hit hard, it was choked with the reek of brimstone, and it foundered. The whole crew was knocked off the ship and tossed about on the black waves like sea crows; in truth, the god stole their homecoming. I was the only one whom Zeus pitied and he brought the mast, spun free from the wreckage of the blue-prowed ship, to my hands, so that I might escape the ultimate disaster. I clung to the mast and for nine days I was borne hither and yon by the contrary winds; on the tenth in the dark of the night a great breaker cast me upon the shore of the Thesprotians where the king of the Thesprotians—his name means *Faithful* and truly he was a hero—treated me to his hospitality.

"His beloved son came upon me, where I lay half-dead with exhaustion and distress; he supported me with his own arm and he took me home to his father's palace where he gave me a complete set of clothing.

King Faithful placed the "pirate" on board a ship headed to Long Island and instructed the crew to take him there, but . . .

"They hatched a criminal plot against me—so that I would plunge to the depths of wretchedness—for, when they had sailed away from the land, they stripped my new clothes from me and they threw filthy rags around me, the rags now before your very eyes, and they made me a slave. When they reached Ithaca—it was just at dusk—they bound me fast by the rower's benches and they hastened from the ship to make their supper along the seashore and then the gods pulled apart my ropes, a task easy for gods. I put the rags on the top of my head, slid down the smooth boarding ramp into the sea, chest high, and I tread water and swam. . . ."

⨎ ⨎ ⨎

And so the "pirate" escaped and came to the hut of Eumaeus, the gentleman swineherd.

"Odysseus the pirate" and "Odysseus the hero," their victims might say, are scarcely different, but "Odysseus the hero" distinguishes himself from "Odysseus the pirate"—the pirate had no interest in risking his life for honor (though he was loath to lose the name of honor), whatever risks he ran he ran for booty, and he would avoid combat if he could, while the hero, who certainly sought and acquired booty, nonetheless was driven first and foremost by the need to win honor. The "pirate" received an aristocratic education, but in truth his birth was not legitimate and the taint of illegitimacy may have predisposed him to a life of piracy rather than a life of honor, although in the end, as do all men, he did what he did because the gods had placed it in his heart.

In the world of Odysseus no city or state had the power to assert control over the seas; the best they could hope for was to defend themselves from both the heroes and the pirates.

— 2 —

Greeks and Barbarians

The Greek world was divided into small kingdoms and aristocratic states, in which no central authority existed even to prevent blood feuds between aristocratic families; no one state was strong enough to dominate the others, certainly no one was strong enough to suppress Mediterranean, or even Aegean, piracy. In a world without a superpower, or even a balance of power, piracy flourished and each separate state and each single individual living close to the sea, or sailing on the sea, was responsible for his own security. Thus the major Greek cities were built one or two miles inland around the natural citadels of which Greece abounds, close enough to the coast to use the sea but far enough away to gain some warning against the incursions of pirates. (That is not to say that these cities were all innocent bystanders—some would light beacon fires on shore to lure unsuspecting ships unto the rocks and the citizens would salvage what was left in the wreckage and, if there were survivors, enslave them.)

In time, the aristocrats learned to cooperate with each other and to accept that they were part of a larger entity, the polis ("city-state"). They cooperated because their cooperation made the polis a powerful instrument through which they could protect their own interests and dominate their neighbors. Their cooperation led to greater security at home, more settled conditions, and a growth in population, but the population growth strained the land resources of the polis, and the excess population had to find other ways to support themselves. In the eighth and seventh centuries in one of history's most massive coordinated undertakings, the Greeks dispatched hundreds of colonizing expeditions across the seas to found new polises and to settle in new lands, from the coasts of the Black Sea south to North Africa and west to Italy, Sicily, and the northern coast of the western Mediterranean, under the direction of the oracle at Delphi and (as they believed) the god Apollo. The expeditions as a whole consumed greater resources—with greater returns— than any of the wars Greeks fought among themselves and, perhaps, greater than any single war fought in the ancient world. Usually the Greeks did not have to fight to establish themselves, although they were prepared to do so; they came by sea, they did not have to force their way through settled territory, and they occupied land the indigenous population did not use.

Odysseus in his encounter with the Cyclops had discovered the perfect place to colonize, "an island, wooded, with innumerable wild goats, where there were no shepherds or farmers and the land had never known the plow. It would bear crops in season and it had fruitful, well-watered meadows by the grey sea, just right for growing vines. There was rich soil for plowing and every season men could reap a harvest. A good harbor made anchor stones and ropes to tie down the stern unnecessary. You could beach your ships and relax until the longings of the sea life and fair winds beckoned you out again. By the harbor was a spring with fresh, cool water."

Greeks sought just such a place: each polis—or sometimes a few cooperating polises—would dispatch its own expedition. Each expedition was an independent military operation under the sole command of one man—the founder—who was "to ring the town about with a wall and have the houses built, to make shrines for the gods, and divide up the farmland into lots."

As the Greeks penetrated into the western Mediterranean, they encountered Carthaginians (in North Africa, Sicily, Sardinia, and Spain) and Etruscans (in central Italy), and they raided their shipping, as those powers raided theirs. The Phocaean colony at Alalia (in Corsica) committed such blatant acts of piracy "that the Carthaginians and Etruscans each contributed sixty ships to a united fleet and fought the Phocaean fleet of sixty ships in a sea battle in the Sardinian sea. The Phocaeans won the victory, but it was no victory at all, because they only had twenty ships survive the battle and these ships, their rams bent, were useless, so the Phocaeans gathered their women and children and all their possessions and abandoned Alalia."

Another colonizing expedition in the beginning of the sixth century failed to establish a colony where it had been planned, but the colonists seized the Lipari Islands and exterminated the natives who did not flee. The new colonists suffered constant attack by Tyrrhenian pirates; but, as so often happens, the constant attacks and the continual need to defend themselves forced them to develop a particular expertise in sea warfare: first, they began to hold their own, then they were able to defeat their enemies, and, finally, they became the aggressors. Their newly acquired skill and the poverty of their resources channeled their energies into piracy and they created a sort of pirate utopia. The citizens held all land in common—the land was apportioned by lot and then reapportioned after twenty years—and they apportioned themselves by lot, some to work the land and some to work the ships: the produce of the land and the booty from their piracy was distributed in equal shares to all citizens except that they set aside a tenth and sent the tithe of their plunder to Delphi to curry favor with the god Apollo (and to win over Greek public opinion). They cultivated good relations with Rome as it became more powerful. The pirates of the Lipari Islands thrived.

Another pirate state (with no pretensions to being a utopia) was established on the Aegean island of Samos by the tyrant Polycrates. After he seized power, he built a fleet of one hundred penteconters (fifty-oared galleys), raised a force of a thousand bowmen, made an alliance with the Pharaoh of Egypt, and sent out expeditions to plunder the Aegean. He attacked friend and foe alike. (He said that a friend who had been plundered would be happier to get back what had been taken than he would if he had never lost anything in the first place—such is the nature of gratitude.) An expedition was mounted against him; he defeated it and set the prisoners to forced labor on the fortifications around the harbor and elsewhere on the island. He did not even make a pretense of declaring war nor was he a legitimate ruler—he was a "pirate tyrant."

He sent a fleet to the island of Siphnos, a small place with rich silver and gold mines—the mines were so productive that the little island was able to build a treasury at Delphi as grandiose as the treasuries of the greatest states of Greece, but the Siphnians were not naive; they knew full well that they had something worth stealing and they asked the oracle at Delphi how long their good fortune would continue. The oracle replied that when the forehead of their marketplace shone white, then they should beware of the scarlet messenger. The Siphnians did not understand the oracle until too late—they had no sooner decorated their marketplace with white marble (the "white forehead") than the Samian fleet arrived—the ships were decorated with red paint—and the captain demanded a "loan" of a sizable sum (10 talents). When the Siphnians refused the "loan," the Samians attacked them, plundered the island, and sailed away only after being paid an additional ransom of 100 talents.

Particularly noxious and frightening were the pirates' coastal raids. Pirates could turn a profit, no matter how poor an area might be, so long as there were people to kidnap, either to hold for ransom or to sell into slavery. So voracious was the pirates' appetite for gain that even the gods were not exempt from their depredations. In the *Hymn to Dionysus*, a hymn composed perhaps as early as the seventh century, the god Dionysus appeared "on a promontory along the shore of the cropless sea and he looked like a very young man in the prime of life. His beautiful hair blew in the seawind and he wore on his shoulders a wine-colored robe."

Now it chanced that a ship of pirates—who little knew that their doom was near—passed on the wine-like sea. They saw the god and concluded that he was the son of a king. They nodded to each other, and then rushed out of the ship, seized him, bound him hand and foot, and carried him onboard; the bindings fell away from his limbs and his eyes mocked them. The steersman understood what they had done and he called to his comrades, "Have you lost your minds? Do you not know that this is a god whom you have seized? Put him ashore immediately before you anger him and he brings a storm upon us."

The captain laughed at him. "Fool, look to the ship and the sails and let the real men deal with this fellow. A god has brought him to us and I guess he will wind up in Egypt or Cyprus or the lands of the far north or someplace else, unless he tells us who he is, how much property he has, and gives us the names of friends who will pay a ransom for him."

No sooner had they launched the ship, hoisted the sails, and got under weigh, than the ship was filled with the odor of sweet wine, wine spilled across the deck, vines spread down from the tops of the sails, grapes burst forth in clusters, and ivy twined around the mast. At last the crew was struck with dread and the captain ordered the steersman to steer the ship to land. Too late! The god transformed himself into a lion, seized the captain in his jaws, and drove the pirates overboard—as soon as they touched the sea they were transformed into dolphins. The god spared only the steersman.

No one was safe. Pirates seized isolated individuals and they attacked gatherings of people at public celebrations outside cities or religious festivals at distant shrines. Pirates particularly liked to raid the coasts of the western Peloponnesus, because the major cities were inland and the authorities (just like the Cicones) needed some time to collect their forces and come to the aid of the coastal dwellers. Cities erected chains of watchtowers along their coasts and inland, both to spread the warning, if a strange sail was detected, and to serve as refuge and strongpoint.

Every settlement and farmstead kept watchdogs, and the barking of dogs meant just one thing—intruders. Men responded with immediate and vigorous action against those whom they assumed to be pirates. Inevitably there were some cases of mistaken identity. On the island of Rhodes lived a young king who had left his homeland on Crete because of an oracle that he would be responsible for the death of his father, the king of Crete. To avoid the fated pollution he and some companions had sailed off to the island of Rhodes and there he established his own kingdom. He, too, had constructed a system of watchtowers and issued the same instructions that so many other kings had—to take immediate action against pirates. Time passed. The father missed his son and in his old age decided to sail to Rhodes, to see him one last time and to name him his heir to the throne of Crete. He sailed to Rhodes to convey the inheritance, but when he landed with his retinue the herders' dogs began to bark, and the herders believed that the father and his Cretans were pirates—Cretans were infamous pirates—and they attacked them. The father shouted that their king was his son, but the barking of the dogs drowned out his voice, and the herdsmen killed him.

Piracy was not curtailed until the Persians conquered the Phoenicians and used the Phoenician fleet to assist in the conquest of the Ionian Greeks in their cities on the western coast of Asia Minor and then to incorporate the Greek fleets into a general Persian navy and control the eastern seas and bring an end to the careers of "pirate tyrants" like Polycrates of Samos. Then, as the Persians could congratulate themselves that they had brought stability to the eastern Mediterranean and the Aegean, they were stunned by a revolt of the Ionians. The Persian response was immediate—they gathered the vast resources of the Persian Empire for an assault upon the scattered Greek cities of Asia Minor—and most Greeks expected the assault would overwhelm the Ionians. The Ionians sought help from Sparta and

Athens. The Spartans refused them, but the Ionians found some enthusiasm for their cause in Athens and Eretria (on the island of Euboea).

The Athenians and the Eretrians sent an expedition, ostensibly to bring aid to the Ionians, but, in fact, rather as a large piratical raid on a rich target with the war as pretext. The allies crossed the Aegean to the coast of Asia Minor, moved inland, and sacked the wealthy city of Sardis. Their expectations of booty, however, were dashed when an Athenian soldier torched a house; the fire leaped from house to house and engulfed the whole town. In their disappointment the allies withdrew to their ships and across the Aegean, the Athenians to Athens, the Eretrians to Eretria, and they did not participate again in the war. On balance, their assistance did more harm than good—they infuriated the Lydian people (whose capital was Sardis) and turned them against the Ionians and they got themselves embroiled in a war with the Persian king, Darius. Darius was furious at their interference and he was determined to seek retribution.

The Persians converged on the Ionians by land and sea, and the world expected that their victory would be swift, but the Persian navy was defeated by the Ionians at sea (498 BC) and their army was annihilated by the Carians (Ionian allies) on land (497 BC). These two disasters paralyzed the Persians and three years passed before they were prepared to launch the next attack. The three years should have been a time for the four great Ionian naval powers, Chios, Lesbos, Samos, and Miletus, to consolidate their position and prepare to defend themselves, but instead they bickered among themselves over the supreme command, they couldn't agree on a coherent strategy, and they failed to win useful allies. Nonetheless, they did have the resources—a fleet of 300 ships—to defeat the Persians, but in the sea battle of 494 BC, as the Chians distinguished themselves by their bravery, the Samians deserted the fleet, the Lesbians followed them, and the Ionian cause was lost. The Persians reduced Ionia city by city, transported the population of Miletus into the interior of the Persian Empire, and conducted an intense manhunt for rebels everywhere (except, of course, in Samos).

The Persians sent an expedition across the Aegean Sea to punish the Athenians and the Eretrians. The Persians defeated the Eretrians, sacked their city, and transported the population into the heart of the Persian Empire, but they were defeated by the Athenians at the battle of Marathon (490 BC). The Ionian revolt and the campaign of Marathon were the first acts of war in the great war between the Greeks and the Persians. As far as the Athenians were concerned, the hero of the hour was the Athenian Miltiades who had convinced the Athenians that they could defeat the Persians: he had conceived the strategy by which the Athenians had won the battle of Marathon.

Miltiades traded upon his prestige in Athens to convince the Athenian people to entrust the Athenian fleet to him for a secret expedition which, without furnishing any details, he guaranteed would enrich the Athenians. His raid was scarcely more than a piratical enterprise entered into between himself and the Athenian assembly and shows how little difference there was between piracy and warfare at this time in Greek history. Miltiades used the fleet to attack an island city, but he failed

Greece and the Aegean Sea

to carry it and had to withdraw; he had been injured, the injury festered, and—a dying man—he came back to Athens, where he was put on trial for "deceiving the Athenian people" (technically, that he had undertaken the expedition for private, not public, reasons). Although he was found guilty of the specified charge, in reality he was condemned because he had failed to deliver to the Athenians the promised plunder.

His political successor, Themistocles, convinced the Athenians to prepare for the return of the Persians (who intended to avenge their defeat at Marathon) by using a bonanza from their silver mine to build a fleet of two hundred triremes, the premiere warship of the time. The decision to build the triremes—which had a crew of 170 oarsmen and about 20 supernumeraries—transformed Athens into a naval power. After the Athenians defeated the Persians in the momentous sea battle at Salamis (in 480 BC), they became the premiere naval power of the Aegean. Once the Athenians, the Spartans, and their allies had cleared Greece of the invading Persians, the Athenians used the prestige of their victories to assume command of the allied fleet and transform the anti-Persian naval alliance into a league, the *Delian* league. Athenians determined the amount of money, ships, and crews each member owed and they forced those to join who, in their opinion, tried to reap the rewards of the league without running any of the risks, and they compelled those to remain who, once the Persians had been defeated, wanted to withdraw from the league. By these actions they transformed the Delian league into an Athenian empire.

— 3 —

Greek vs. Greek

The Athenians set the first payment of the members of the Delian League at 460 talents (or enough money to commission forty-two triremes and crew them for the eight-month sailing season). The three-tiered trireme was high, long, and narrow, a balance between speed and maneuverability, as light as it could be, held together by rope and just strong enough to deliver a blow and survive. (As the Athenian crews became expert in handling the trireme, they came to prefer an even lighter, more maneuverable ship.) The Athenian trireme could cruise thirty-five to forty-five miles a day, but it could not comfortably spend the night at sea; it had no deck to protect the crew from the weather, no hold in which to carry supplies, and no place to sleep its crew, so it had to beach each night and the crew had to scrounge firewood, food, and water. The trireme required constant refitting and repair. Typically the Athenians would keep about a third of their total fleet of 300 ships at sea, a third in reserve at home, and a third in dry dock, being prepared to go to sea again.

The Athenians organized the Delian League to fight Persia, to project their own power, and to promote their own economy, but as they forced each Greek naval power to join the league and as they drove enemy navies off the water, inevitably they suppressed piracy, because pirates no longer had safe havens or safe targets. Every polis by the sea was vulnerable to the Athenians and any which was suspected of sponsoring piracy or harboring pirates could be attacked and destroyed by the Athenians. The Athenians fortified and garrisoned key points around the Aegean from which they could interdict movement within the Aegean, protect such rich targets as the island of Euboea, and close off the approaches into the Aegean.

Under the leadership of Pericles the Athenians dominated the Aegean Sea. Pericles understood the power that command of the sea gave Athens, but he also recognized that Athens itself could be cut off from the sea by an enemy army—for instance, Sparta and its allies—and put under siege; therefore, he transformed Athens into an island on the mainland by constructing the "long walls," two walls which connected the city of Athens to its port (the Piraeus). His assurance that Athens could never be defeated (so long as the Athenians preserved their fleet and guarded their walls), his aggressive policy, and the consequent growth of Athenian power raised the apprehensions of the Spartans and convinced them that they had to fight the Athenians before the Athenians became too powerful to defeat. Thus the Spartans' fear of Athenian imperialism, and the Athenian imperialism itself caused the Peloponnesian War (431–404 BC).

At the outbreak of the war the Athenians immediately cancelled all civil projects that drew upon their annual income of 800 talents, they created a reserve of 6,000 talents, and they put 100 trireme hulls in storage. Pericles and the Athenians could consider the impending war with confidence if not with equanimity—they not only had the largest fleet in the Aegean, but they had also developed battle tactics so sophisticated and so demanding that only Athenians (and the crews trained by them) could perform them. The Athenians would row, bow on, as fast as they could at their enemies, and then at the last moment veer off just enough to glide down the side of the enemy ship. The Athenian oarsmen would ship their oars, and the enemy, caught by surprise, would not. The enemy oarsmen would be battered, their oars broken, and their ship helpless. Or the Athenians would dash through the enemy line and turn, before the enemy could, and ram them in the rear. Or they would circle the enemy, until they could catch an enemy ship with its side to them, and then they would ram it and roll it over.

The Athenians were conscious that the democratic navy was a new source of power. (Democracy, one Athenian wrote, while despised by all right-thinking men—because it gives control to the people—nonetheless is justified because the people are the oarsmen of the fleet and the fleet has brought Athens its power.) The Athenians had a hoplite force which, while not as good as the Spartan hoplite force, still was better than any force Athens' subjects could muster and so was sufficient to control them. Moreover, their subjects were divided by the sea and could not combine against the Athenians (the way the allies of the Spartans could combine against Sparta). A naval power could carry its own provisions in supply ships and it could travel without hindrance wherever the sea reached. A naval power could ravage the land of a stronger power: it could find a weakly defended place to land, catch the enemy completely by surprise, plunder and burn, and if the enemy forces approached, reembark and sail away. They could undertake distant expeditions as easily as local expeditions. They could hit the enemy; the enemy could not hit back, and, inevitably, they would wear the enemy down. (The one factor which the Athenian leaders had not considered was the cost: the war was far more expensive than they had expected—one siege, for instance, cost them 2,000 talents, that is, two-and-a-half years' income.)

The immediate cause of the Peloponnesian War was the request of Corcyra—an island way station between Greece and Italy—that the Athenians help them against the Corinthians (allies of Sparta). The Athenians agreed, event piled upon event, and the consequence was war. Corcyra itself was wracked by a civil war which developed between the pro-Athenian and the pro-Spartan factions; one faction drove the other faction into exile, and the exiles (about 500 men) seized a fort on the mainland and from there they conducted raids on the island and on the shipping; their raids were so effective that they caused a severe famine. (In the end, the two factions devastated Corcyra and all but destroyed each other.)

The enemies of Athens also commissioned "privateers" to attack Athenian shipping in the Aegean, but, as the risks were real and the profits tenuous, few accepted commissions, before the Athenians exceeded the limits of their power and were defeated in Sicily. Then, as Athenian control of the Aegean slipped, pirates took advantage of their weakness to raid indiscriminately (although most professed adherence to Sparta—since the Athenian side shipped more cargo). One of the pirates, Theopompos of Miletus, had had his operations curtailed by the Athenians, when they were at the height of their power, and now he joined the Spartan admiral as an ally in the final campaign against the Athenians.

The Athenians had grasped the potentialities of sea power, but the underlying principle of Pericles' strategy, always to ensure the security of their fleet, escaped them; their failure to understand that concept underlay two disasters, the first in Sicily and the second in the Hellespont, where the Athenians fought, and lost, their last battle; only one captain had foreseen the dangers of their situation and taken precautions: Conon the Athenian—when he saw the overwhelming Spartan fleet approaching the unprepared Athenians, he sailed his detachment of ships off into the Aegean. Conon supported himself and his small fleet by piracy; his activities brought him to the attention of the Persian king whose need for a competent naval commander overrode his distaste for a pirate and he offered Conon an appointment as his admiral in chief.

A certain sort of quasi-legal piracy was encouraged by the peculiar Greek situation. Greek cities had no police forces, no public prosecutors: citizens were expected to defend their own homes (and were granted almost absolute power within the walls of their houses) and they were expected to prosecute their own cases (or to speak in their own defense), and, with the dissolution of the Athenian empire and the end of Athens' assumption of supreme authority, the citizens of one state had no higher court in which to appeal against the citizens of another state. The plaintiffs' only resort, if they had a grievance against a citizen of another state, was the authorization by their own state to take reprisals. These reprisals, as they were sanctioned by state and by custom, were not considered acts of war but rather a kind of legal piracy to recover the value of what had been lost. So the Spartans (in a time of peace) had issued a proclamation of support for those who took reprisals against the Athenians after the Athenians had injured the interests of some Spartans during the course of a campaign against the island of Melos. Other actions were taken by exiles who banded together and raided their own states in reprisal for their confiscated property and also to put pressure on the current government to reinstate them or to reimburse them.

States separately attempted to suppress piracy by setting penalties to punish those within the state who helped pirates, and collectively states concluded reciprocal agreements to protect each other's citizens. A city—call it Alpha—would conclude an agreement with a city—call it Beta—that no citizen of Alpha could kidnap a citizen of Beta, resident in Alpha, nor seize his property, and vice versa, except if "a pirate be caught in the act of piracy at sea he may be seized and any foreign goods on his ship may be confiscated without penalty." Such agreements were particular and limited and, of course, whatever protection they might afford to the citizens of the two contracting cities, they did not protect them from third parties nor protect the third parties from them. Much of the antipiratical legislation of the Greek world was little more than wishful thinking, because there was no power strong enough to enforce the agreement.

The Peloponnesian War had raised the level of violence across the Greek world while also impoverishing Greeks everywhere. *An army marches on its stomach* was no less true in the ancient world than in the modern; generals had been quite ready to use their forces to plunder or to extort money to pay their soldiers and sailors during the war; after the war, when the Athenians could not pay the indemnities demanded of them, the Spartans encouraged their allies to raid Athenian shipping and the home territory of Athens itself, and in the fourth century Athenian admirals, driven by the necessity to raise money to pay their troops, often acted more like pirates than like generals sent out on a military mission. Some generals altogether forgot that their mission was not the acquisition of plunder, and not only generals, but others, too, kept their eyes open for opportunities. Piracy became common in the Aegean in the fourth century, although the line between pirate and privateer, as always in the ancient world, was narrow.

Some Athenian ambassadors on a visit to king Mausolus (of Mausoleum fame) seized an Egyptian ship with 9 talents worth of goods on board. The ambassadors were brought before an Athenian court to defend their capture; the court ruled that the seizure was valid because the Egyptians were in a state of revolt from Persia and the Athenians were allies of the Persians, so the envoys, as the legal representatives of the people of Athens and, thus, by definition not pirates, had the legal right to seize the Egyptian ship, but, the court continued, because the envoys *were* officials of the Athenian people, they should be considered to have acted as *agents* of the Athenian people, and, therefore, the booty belonged to Athens: the ambassadors had to cough it up. Athenian rapaciousness affected so much of the Greek world that Athenians could not travel abroad without risking their lives and persons; they might be seized and sold into slavery by someone seeking compensation for his previous losses to Athenians.

One of the great unspoken fears of the ancient world was to be seized and sold into slavery. No one was immune from such a chance. A child, taken and sold, was a common plot in comedy and drama. An ancient romantic novel set in the fourth century evolves from the kidnapping and enslavement of the heroine, the beautiful Callirhoe, the most beautiful maiden in Sicily; a malicious prank and her husband's jealous nature shocked her into a coma and she was taken for dead, sealed in a coffin with her jewelry and her dowry, and in a public funeral interred in a tomb on the shore of the sea.

The wealthy burial proved too much temptation for a rogue named Theron; he saw the riches and decided to rob the tomb. He owned a ship and he was "an evil man, who committed crimes at sea and had a pirate crew," although he claimed that the ship and crew were used only to provide a ferry service. He gathered a crew of sixteen rogues from brothels and bars; he had rehearsed a speech to persuade them to commit the crime, but as soon as they heard the word "loot," they grabbed sledgehammers and crowbars and presented themselves at the tomb; there, however, they heard eerie wailing. *Ghosts*, they feared, and would have run, but Theron drew his sword, entered the tomb, and saw the shape of the girl and understood—Callirhoe had been sealed in her tomb alive and now had revived. He led her out, loaded the treasure on board his ship, and considered what to do with the girl.

One pirate urged that they return her and claim that they were fishing and heard her calls, but another asked, "Will anyone believe that a gang of temple robbers like us have suddenly become honorable men? Let us take the loot and leave no witnesses."

Theron in turn proposed that they sell the girl.

"After all, we have chosen a risky life and we must be prepared to run risks."

And so they sailed with her from Sicily to Greece and around the Peloponnesus up toward Athens—but they avoided Athens itself because the Athenians were the most inquisitive of human beings and would ask endless questions, *who they were, where they had come from, what cargo they had, how they had acquired the cargo*—and they sailed away from Athens across the Aegean to Ionia, home of a people who "have money to spend and ask no questions."

They found a secluded spot to beach their ship; Theron instructed his crew to build a shelter for the girl, feed her, and care for her so that she could recover from the voyage and make a better impression on a customer, and then Theron went off and found a buyer, the manager of the estates of a wealthy man, a recent widower; he proposed that the manager purchase this girl, "the maid of a woman who was jealous of her beauty and so sold her to me. Because she is a slave, you will not have to worry about her or that your master will remarry and introduce a new mistress over you."

The manager was persuaded and Theron offered to bring the girl to the manager for his inspection, preferably to an outlying part of the estate, because he had beached his ship in a remote area where he could avoid the customs and excise officials. It was done—the manager looked at her, he was overwhelmed with her beauty, and he handed over the full price that Theron had asked. (At best Theron had hoped to get his hands on some earnest money and then flee—because he could not produce registration papers to show that the girl was a slave and legally acquired; if it were known that Theron had kidnapped a free person, he would have been arrested as a pirate, which, of course, he was.) Theron promised to come to the city and hand over the registration papers the next day. The next day came,

Theron did not, and the manager had to confess to his master that he had been duped. Still, they concluded that the pirate had probably sold them a slave he did not own, which was not so big a problem, until the master saw Callirhoe. He knew that she was too beautiful and too noble to be a slave.

Meanwhile Theron and his crew headed for Crete because it was a good place to unload merchandize. They never got there. A violent storm kept them at sea; the crew drank all their water—except a secret stash Theron had hidden just for himself—and one by one they died of thirst. The pirate vessel tossed hither and yon on the waves, until a Syracusan warship found it and on it "dead men and gold." Amid the celebration of their good fortune, Callirhoe's husband, who had been below decks crying his eyes out, came on deck to see what the hubbub was about and he recognized his wife's clothes. Theron was found alive. He claimed to be an innocent passenger knowing nothing of cargo or crew, and when he was returned to Syracuse and put on trial, he repeated his story and concluded his defense, "I never did anything wrong in my whole life."

He won the pity of the spectators, and he was on the point of being acquitted, when a fisherman said that he recognized Theron as a character who had hung around the harbor (and so was not an innocent foreigner). The authorities "used whips on the unholy man and they burned him and flayed him and still he held out" and almost defeated the torturers but his strength gave out at last and he confessed the truth. Theron was condemned to death and taken, accompanied by a crowd, to the place of execution, the tomb he had robbed; there he was crucified so he could look out to sea and reflect upon the misdeeds that had brought him to the cross.

Meanwhile the husband continued his search, was taken prisoner, mistaken for a pirate, sold into slavery, put to hard labor on a chain gang, implicated in an escape attempt and a murder, condemned to crucifixion, rescued, and finally reunited with Callirhoe.

Whether in fiction or in fact, no one was safe. Even Plato, the great philosopher, found himself on the auction block. He had accepted an invitation to tutor the heir of Dionysius, the tyrant of Syracuse, but he found the heir to be dull and indifferent to learning, and Plato felt nothing but contempt for the dissolute and violent tyrant. The tyrant felt equal contempt for the rigid, unworldly, and patronizing philosopher, but he feared that Plato, who had announced his intention to return to Athens, would spread an unfavorable account of the tyrant, so he arranged for pirates to seize Plato's ship and sell Plato into slavery. Plato was saved only because, when he came up for sale, he was seen by a friend and the friend purchased and freed him. Plato could well have spent the rest of his life as a slave.

—— 4 ——

Greek vs. Macedonian

As the Athenians recovered their naval strength (aided by Conon, the Athenian naval commander turned pirate and then hired by the Persian king as admiral in chief), they were menaced by an enemy more powerful than the Spartans or the Thebans had been, by a new and unexpected enemy, the king of the Macedonians, Philip II. One by one they lost their possessions in the north, they lost allies, and they lost trade. They accused Philip of double-dealing, of plotting against them (while he pretended to be their friend), and of conducting operations that had as their ultimate purpose the defeat of Athens, while they, in their turn, were accused by Philip of slander, of supporting and encouraging his enemies, and of "waging peace as though it were war."

Thus the Athenians struggled against Philip, sometimes in open warfare, sometimes covertly. They tried to protect their own shipping and their allies' shipping, while encouraging attacks upon the shipping of Philip and his allies. When their double game redounded unto themselves—when they could not defeat Philip II on land and could not maintain a local dominance over the coast of Macedonia—they tried to seize the moral high ground by implying that their campaigns really were directed against pirates and Philip's involvement with pirates. They gave the force of law to their campaign with a decree that required their allies and themselves, too, not to give harbor to pirates; they attacked isolated centers of piracy, such as the island of Melos, and they forced the Melians to pay an indemnity, but so long as they appeared to be encouraging piratical raids on Philip and so long as pirates could find safe haven with Philip, the Athenians were under constant threat. They had to react to separate incidents and their success was limited. In short, both sides traded accusations of piracy and both sides committed acts of piracy because they needed money—lots of money.

Philip, particularly, was known for his profligacy in the pursuit of policy and of the loyalty of his men and officers—whatever Philip's officers captured, these all went to the profit of the officers and men. When Philip [an acquaintance wrote] gained control of a large sum of money, "no one could say that he spent it, no, he threw it away; he was the worst money manager in the world, and everyone in his circle was just like him. Not a single one of his officers understood how to live right or to manage a household properly and Philip was to blame, because he was insatiable and extravagant, without regard to whether he was getting or giving, and on campaign he did not keep records of income and outgo."

Moreover, his officers had flocked to him from all over Greece, Thessaly, Macedonia, and foreign lands, and he selected them, not for breeding and manners, but, it seemed, for their lack of character—they were lechers, perverts, criminals. If anyone arrived who was not such a man, the daily life and habits of the Macedonians, the wars, the campaigns, the reckless extravagance transformed him into a profligate. They lived the licentious life of a pirate. They were ready for anything.

Philip used his wealth as an instrument of policy. His gold coins were known as *Philippians* and these Philippians paid his troops, hired mercenaries, bought allies, and seduced traitors. Philip lavished his wealth on the most influential men in various cities. He won them to his side, and then advised them to cultivate other citizens, both honest and dishonest, since he could "use the first and misuse the second." Philip commented that he would much rather increase his own kingdom through gold than through war, but after the work of bribery was done and a city fell to him, Philip no longer paid the slightest attention to the traitors. Indeed, when Philip was asked whom he most loved and whom he most hated, he said, "I most love those who are going to betray their city to me, and I most hate those who have done it." In short, his Philippians corrupted the whole of Greece and raised the Macedonian kingdom to the pinnacle of power.

Philip turned to piracy as one way to raise the money he needed. He captured and enslaved Athenian citizens in isolation on the islands of the Aegean, he seized ships, he raided the Athenian homeland at Marathon, and he captured the sacred trireme of Athens. When he had exhausted his resources in a lengthy and costly siege in the north of Greece, he seized an Athenian grain fleet of 170 ships (for which he received 700 talents) and when the Athenians accused him of piracy, Philip replied that the fleet was a legitimate target because it had been carrying grain to his enemies and, moreover,

It was not the Athenian people who instructed the commander of the fleet to do this, but certain leaders and others who for the moment are private citizens, and they intended in any way they could to disrupt the present friendship between the Athenian people and me and to bring about war—far rather would they accomplish this than bring relief to my enemies. They understand that war would fetch them money, but I do not think that this war would be profitable for you or for me.

Philip was by no means alone, neither in the necessities he faced nor in his methods. In the War of the Allies—the former "allies" of Athens now fighting

Athens—the allies plundered Athenian possessions until they had amassed enough money to pay the crews of 100 ships and prosecute the war.

With two major powers contending with each other, committing acts of piracy themselves, and encouraging pirates to attack each other, some complex situations arose. The Athenians used Halonnesus (a tiny, infertile island off the northeast coast of Euboea) as an outpost. They lost the island to a pirate named Sostratus and, perhaps, they were not so aggressive in retaking the island, and, perhaps, they even encouraged him to attack Macedonian shipping. Philip sent a small force to drive Sostratus out of Halonnesus and occupy the island. Greeks on a neighboring island (Peparathos, an Athenian ally) made a surprise attack on the island, captured the Macedonian garrison, and refused to release them despite Philip's attempts to negotiate. Finally Philip took the island back and "punished" the Peparethians. Then the Athenians demanded that he give the island *back* to Athens and he did offer to give them the island, but not to give it "back"—the word "back" would have been an acknowledgment that his seizure of the island had been an act of piracy—and the two sides bickered for months over the issue.

The Athenians were just as desperate as Philip to raise money. Even a small fleet operation was expensive—ten warships sent on an expedition required 40 talents to maintain, a little more than 90 talents to purchase the crew's rations, another 90 talents to pay the soldiers onboard, and 12 talents to pay 200 cavalry—in short, even a small fleet consumed a significant portion of Athens' annual income. Every Athenian general faced the dilemma of having to raise money in the field while not angering the allies on whom Athens depended. One Athenian commander, Chares, rented his force to a Persian satrap, Artabazus, who was in rebellion from the king. Artabazus won and repaid the favor by supporting Chares's whole force for the entire Athenian campaign.

The Athenians appeared to their allies to be rapacious and dangerous friends; to Philip they were pirates. An Athenian commander, Callias, raided (in a time of peace) and looted cities allied to Philip, seized ships on their way to Macedonia, invaded Philip's territory, enslaved two villages, and plundered the neighboring regions. When Philip sent a herald to negotiate a ransom for the prisoners Callias had taken, Callias seized the herald and tortured him until he agreed to a personal ransom of 9 talents.

In the end, Philip defeated the Athenians in the decisive battle of Chaeroneia and compelled them to sign a peace treaty. One of the provisions of the treaty read, "those participating in the peace may sail the sea, and nobody may hinder them or stop any of their ships; and if anyone should do this, he is to be the enemy of all participating in this peace." These were fine words, and from then on the Athenians no longer supported pirates as a matter of policy, but the treaty did not end piracy in the Aegean, because Philip had one powerful opponent remaining, the Persian king, and pirates continued to attack Greek and Macedonian shipping from safe havens in Asia Minor.

When Philip's son Alexander ("the Great") invaded the Persian Empire, he had to contend both with the Persian navy and with pirates encouraged by the Persians.

The Macedonians captured the island of Chios, killed the soldiers of the Persian garrison in the fighting, and impounded the Chian fleet. Among the regular ships of the Chian navy, they found fifty *lembi* (the ship preferred by pirates—small and swift vessels, designed to dart out from concealment along the shore and lay alongside merchants). The Macedonians identified the crews of the *lembi*, assumed they were pirates, and executed them; then they captured another ten pirate ships which sailed into the harbor: they had come to confer with their paymaster, the Persian commander, Pharnabazus, and had not realized that the harbor of Chios had fallen. These crews were also executed.

Alexander put an end to piracy in the eastern Mediterranean by securing all the harbors from which pirates could operate (and isolating the Persian navy in the process), but when Alexander died, his successors fought each other for the control of the empire, or a piece of the empire, and actively encouraged pirates to attack each other. The successor generals—later they took the title *king*— hired mercenary navies organized by military entrepreneurs who owned ships and recruited the crews. These military entrepreneurs had no loyalty to any particular king—whoever paid them, or issued letters of marque to them, received their services. Regardless of their legal status their opponents always considered them to be pirates.

One of the successors, Demetrius "the Besieger," invited pirates to join him (for plunder) in his siege of Rhodes, but the pirates found precious little plunder, because the Rhodians were well able to defend themselves, and they soon abandoned the siege for easier targets. In the end, Demetrius' siege failed and he never captured Rhodes, but he did capture the city of Ephesus and he delegated a general to hold it. One day, during a religious festival, a pirate presented himself at the gates with some "prisoners" and asked to be admitted to the city so that he could participate in the festivities. When the guards admitted him, the "prisoners" drew concealed swords, struck down the guards, and held the gates open while the pirate's real paymaster (a rival king) brought his army up and seized the city. The victor thanked the pirate, gave him a generous reward, and ordered him to leave the area immediately. Pirates make dangerous associates.

Another of the successor kings was trying to expel a tyrant from the city of Cassandreia. After a ten-month siege had strained the resources of both sides, the king appeared to give up and withdraw; no sooner had he withdrawn than a pirate appeared with a cargo of food and wine for the tyrant. (Pirates also made good smugglers.) The tyrant welcomed him and engaged in a night of immoderate drinking and feasting; while he was enjoying himself, the pirate and his men seized a portion of the city wall between two watchtowers and held their positions as 2,000 of the king's troops rushed from concealment, threw up ladders, climbed the wall, and took possession of the city.

In the period of the successor-states, few cities were able to maintain their independence. Only those cities with strong natural defenses and the determination to fight for their freedom could resist the kings successfully. The Rhodians had found themselves embroiled in the wars of rival kings and had almost succumbed to the siege of Demetrius, but their strong fleet and their steady resistance had forced him to abandon the siege. After he had withdrawn, they gathered all the abandoned equipment and from it they built the colossus of Rhodes to be a monument to their victory and a reminder of the source of their power—the promotion and protection of trade.

Rhodes' most important trading partner and ally was the kingdom of the Ptolemies in Egypt, but the Rhodians traded throughout the eastern Mediterranean, along the Ionian coast, and into the Black Sea. Rhodians sailed the seas themselves and they encouraged foreign merchants to use the port of Rhodes as a secure way station through which to pass their merchandise, or as a market to barter goods, or to buy and sell (since the Rhodians had money to spend). Rhodes was one of the great emporiums of the eastern Mediterranean: there merchants bought and sold the most lucrative of all articles of trade in the ancient world—slaves.

Besides Rhodes, the largest slave markets were in Crete, on the island of Aegina near Athens, and on the island of Delos. In these markets, and in all well-run markets, magistrates were appointed to ensure—in theory—that the seller of slaves had legal ownership of the slaves, that any free persons kidnapped by pirates would be protected, and that, if the slaves-for-sale had been stolen, the property rights of the legitimate owners would be preserved. Cities tried to provide protection for their own citizens by appointing as their representative a citizen in the major slave-market towns, so that, for instance, the Delian representative of Athens would intercede in any case in which a freeborn Athenian came to the slave market in Delos; more often, however, if victims were saved, they were saved by the individual act of a good Samaritan or by the chance appearance of a friend, as Plato was purchased off the auction block by a friend. Some Athenian citizens, taken captive in a raid by the Aetolian Greeks—a league that conducted raids by land and sea to collect booty and to force other Greeks to join their league—were brought to Crete to be sold and were rescued by a Cretan who just happened to like Athenians and wanted to help them. Cities made reciprocal agreements with each other not to allow the sale of freeborn persons in their markets, but in practice the demand for slaves was so high and the market so lucrative that such agreements were seldom enforced, and the magistrates of the market seldom interfered.

And there were enough markets where no questions were asked—

Pirates had kidnapped a little child and her servant and taken them to Caria, and there they were displayed for sale in the market; the servant sat and held the little girl in his lap. An officer came up and asked, "How much?" and he agreed to the price and he bought them. Next to the servant was another slave up for sale and he said, "My friend, take heart. The man who bought you has a good reputation and he is rich, too."

Such markets were essential to the practice of piracy. Pirates had to have a place where they could dispose of their booty, no questions asked, just as they needed a secure base where they could refit their ships, replace lost crewmen, and enjoy the profits of their expeditions. So long as the pirates had secure bases and markets, piracy could not be eradicated; to deny pirates their bases and markets would have required the cooperation of all the maritime powers, but in a thriving slave economy piracy was one of the easiest ways to furnish the desired number of slaves, and the maritime powers, rather than attempting to eradicate piracy, encouraged pirates by buying their captives and urging them to attack their rivals, while, at the same time, they attempted to secure immunity themselves from pirate attacks.

Pirates for the most part did not cooperate with each other; a market where one gang of pirates was selling their booty might be attacked by another gang. Tyrrhenian pirates, in particular, were considered the enemies of all, citizen or pirate, and they were noted for their cruelty—their favorite joke was to bind a living captive face to face with a corpse—and they were as apt to raid a market (once even the free market of Delos) as a shrine or a ship. Even so, buyers asked few questions and disputes in a community arose more often from the division of booty and one's eligibility for a share than over the legitimacy of the spoils themselves.

Kidnapping for ransom was a big part of the pirate trade as well, since a single prominent and wealthy person could bring more ransom than a boatload of captives sold at market price, but a successful kidnapping required accomplices on land to identify targets for the pirates. In one case some Athenians identified other wealthy Athenians for a band of pirates to kidnap and hold for ransom. The scheme worked; the ransom was negotiated, paid, and the pirates got away, but the confederates were caught and punished.

The most notorious nest of pirates was Crete—when a Macedonian king became an enthusiastic convert to double-dealing, double-crosses, and rapaciousness, in short, to the ways of a pirate, he was said to have "Cretized." Crete had been known as a pirate haven from the days of Odysseus—who identified himself as a *Cretan* pirate—and Cretans were still known as pirates in Roman times.

> Who has ever heard of an honest man in Crete?
> They have always practiced piracy, theft, and deceit.

Political divisions within Crete, the constant wars, the necessity to practice arms, ambush and raid, the convoluted coastline—all encouraged piracy—and rival kings, far from cooperating to suppress Cretan piracy, competed there for allies and soldiers and ships. ("Allies" to them, "pirates" to their enemies.) The pirates formed alliances when it seemed in their interests to do so, but no alliance could hold them on one side when the other side offered more money.

The Rhodians tried to suppress the pirates of Crete (the First Cretan War, 206–203 BC) and so did the Romans. Neither was particularly successful. The Rhodians promoted themselves as the champions of free trade and their prosperity depended upon trade, but they also did very well from the slave trade. At different times they defended themselves and their trade from the Athenians and other Greek states, from the Macedonians, and from the successor kings. They forced the Byzantines, whose prosperity depended upon the free flow of goods between the Aegean and the Black Sea, to rescind a toll they had imposed on shipping through the

Hellespont. (The toll was intended to offset the expense of securing the passage against pirates and local raiders who were attacking fishing boats.)

As the market for slaves increased in the second century, the number of pirates increased. As in any sector of an economy, piracy, too, was driven by supply and demand and the demand for slaves was strong. A verse composed about the slave market at Delos ran—

> Arrive and unload,
> Depart with the gold.

—— PART II ——
THE ROMANS

Pirates are the most hated enemies of Rome, and not just of Rome, but of all mankind.

Cicero

BLACK SEA

BOSPORUS

Rome

Byzantium

PONTUS

MACEDONIA

Brundisium

ANATOLIA (ASIA MINOR)

PAMPHYLIA

SELEUCID

Messana

LYCIA

CILICIA

Rhegium

Athens

SICILY

Syracuse

DELOS

RHODES

CYPRUS

CRETE

MEDITERRANEAN

EMPIRE

Tyre

SEA

CYRENAICA

Alexandria

PTOLEMAIC

EMPIRE

ADRIATIC

ILLYRIA

Tiber
River

Rome
Ostia

Caieta

Lissus

Naples

Epidamnus

Brundisium

Misenum

Apollonia

Corcyra

EPIRUS

AETOLIA

The Eastern Mediterranean with an Inset Map of the Adriatic

— 5 —

The Romans Take Decisive Action

The eastern shore of the Adriatic Sea—the Illyrian shore—with its many natural harbors and protected coves was a paradise for pirates. Illyrian pirates lurked in the sheltered hiding places along the shore; they crammed one hundred pirates into their little galleys (known as *lembi*), fifty to row and fifty to fight, and, when they spied a merchant ship, out they would dash as fast as they could row and come alongside, board, and overwhelm their victims. Merchants sought help from the states along the shores of the Adriatic, but none of the Greek states had sufficient forces to suppress piracy, even if they had had the resolve to confront the Illyrians, and the Romans had no inclination to go to the expense and danger of a campaign for the sake of a few merchants and an occasional threat.

When, however, one of Illyria's petty kings united the whole of Illyria under his rule, he also brought the pirates under his control; he transformed them from independent entrepreneurs out for what they could get for themselves into an instrument of state policy. His queen, Queen Teuta, succeeded him and continued the same policy—to use the pirates sometimes to harass and attack Illyria's enemies, sometimes to combine and operate as a navy, and sometimes just to plunder and provide a share of the booty to the crown. The beauty of the situation was that the rulers could disavow the pirates if necessary.

By 230 BC Queen Teuta had consolidated the Illyrians into the most powerful kingdom in the Balkan peninsula and she was determined to subjugate the whole of the Adriatic's eastern coast. She mustered her army and navy and ordered them to conquer the coast; she lifted the few restrictions left on the pirates and permitted them to attack any ship or any land. At one city the pirates pretended that they were merchants, and particularly inept merchants, selling their cargo at a loss. When they had attracted a crowd of shoppers by their apparent ineptitude and the shoppers were completely engrossed in the bargaining, the Illyrians seized a large number of them, threw them in their ships, sailed away, and sold their victims into slavery. At another city the Illyrians pretended that they needed to fill their water jars (in which they had hidden short swords), but the citizens tumbled to the trick and drove them off.

The pirates ranged as far south as the southern Peloponnesus, while the army and navy defeated the forces of the kingdom of Epirus, and the Epirotes, to save themselves from the Illyrian forces and from the continual attacks of pirates, made peace with the Illyrians, became their allies, and left the Greeks to fend for themselves. The Illyrian armed forces continued to advance south and the Illyrian pirates (operating under the protection of the royal family) ranged up and down the Adriatic, and no one seemed ready, or able, to stop them.

The queen was supremely confident of the power of her united Illyria and the pirates were supremely confident in their queen, far too confident, because they made a disastrous mistake—they plundered some Italian ships. The Italian merchants appealed to the Roman Senate. The Roman Senate listened to their long list of complaints and decided to send two envoys to Queen Teuta to persuade her to control these pirates. The queen, as so many rulers had done in the past and would continue to do in the future, totally misestimated the Romans. She listened to their complaints and she told them that it was not her policy to do injury to the Romans or to Italy and that she could give them a guarantee that her armed forces would not attack Romans or Italians, but she said,

"It is an ancient custom of the land of the Illyrians and of its rulers that the queen does not interfere with the actions of her private citizens in taking plunder on the sea."

The younger of the envoys replied,

"Queen Teuta, the Romans have an excellent tradition, which is that the state concerns itself with punishing those who commit private wrongs and with helping those who suffer them. With the gods' help we shall do our utmost, and that very soon, to make you reform this ancient custom of your kings."

The queen was furious and she let her fury show. The young envoy's ship was boarded by pirates on his journey home and he was murdered. Perhaps Queen Teuta had ordered the pirates to avenge this insult to her dignity, or perhaps the pirates had simply thought to please her; in either case, she was guilty in the eyes of the Romans and the Senate determined to act.

Yet time passed, murder had been done, and nothing seemed to happen. Queen Teuta assumed that she had given the Romans a sharp lesson in what the Illyrians did to meddlers, and in the spring of 229 BC she ordered an expedition to seize the two most important way stations for the trade between Greece and Italy, the Greek cities of Epidamnus and Corcyra. An Illyrian surprise attack on Epidamnus failed and the Illyrians withdrew, regrouped, and attacked Corcyra. Corcyra appealed to the Greek leagues: of the three leagues with interests in the region, one had already joined the Illyrians, another demurred, and the third league did send a few ships, but in the ensuing sea battle, when the first Greek ships caught the Illyrian ships broadside and rammed them, the bronze rams stuck, and the Greeks only then discovered that the Illyrians had lashed their ships together, four by four, to form a large unsinkable platform; Illyrian soldiers stormed the Greek ships and took them. When the captains of the other Greek ships saw what had happened, they turned their ships, fled, and abandoned the citizens of Corcyra to their fate. The Corcyraeans came to terms with the Illyrians and accepted a garrison under the command of Demetrius of Pharos (later to be king of the Illyrians). The Illyrians then sailed north and returned to the attack they had earlier abandoned on the city of Epidamnus.

At this crucial moment, when no Greek power seemed able to stand up to the Illyrians and many Greeks feared that Queen Teuta would subjugate the whole western coast of Greece, when Corcyra seemed firmly under Illyrian control, and when Epidamnus was about to fall, a Roman fleet of 200 ships (under the command of one of the Roman consuls) appeared before Corcyra. Demetrius, the commander of the Illyrian garrison at Corcyra, recognized immediately that the game was up and he surrendered to the Romans and made himself useful as an adviser. The Roman naval commander enrolled the Corcyraeans as "friends of the Roman people"—this designation meant that in the future the Romans would come to their aid and protection—and then took the fleet to Apollonia, where the second consul and an army of 20,000 infantry and 2,000 cavalry joined the first consul and the entire Roman force advanced on Epidamnus to raise the Illyrian siege. As soon as the Illyrian soldiers heard that the Romans were coming, they broke and scattered across the countryside. The Romans enrolled Epidamnus as a "friend" and then the two consuls conducted coordinated campaigns. The Roman army advanced inland and accepted the surrender of three of the Illyrian tribes (thus fracturing the unity of the Illyrian state). The Roman fleet attacked and captured Illyrian coastal towns, surprised and captured pirate vessels, and liberated Greek cities. While the queen fled to a fort in the interior of the country, the Romans recruited local troops and campaigned vigorously for one year. At the end of the year they believed that they had the situation enough in hand to release one consul to return to Rome with most of the soldiers and all but forty ships. The Romans placed Demetrius on the throne of a reduced Illyria and in the spring of 228 BC the queen capitulated completely: she offered to pay the Romans an indemnity of whatever they asked, to accept the breakup of Illyria, to acknowledge Demetrius, and to be content with whatever the Romans were willing to grant her and, finally, she agreed that she would not sail south of Lissus (see map on p. 34) with more than two galleys and those galleys would not be armed.

With the war concluded the Romans sent envoys to the Greek leagues to explain their actions, to delineate for the Greeks which places and people were now under Roman protection, and to reassure them that the Romans had no ambitions in that part of the world.

6

The Pirates of Cilicia

Many ancient authors considered piracy a moral choice. Yes, people who had ships, who had coasts with many harbors, who were poor, had reasons to turn pirate, particularly if they had nearby markets for their plunder, but many people in similar conditions rejected the temptations of piracy, and so those people who did turn to piracy could legitimately be condemned for their choice. Among the worst were the Tyrrhenians, the Illyrians, the Cretans, and the Cilicians, and of them all the ones the Romans considered the worst were the Cilicians.

The beginning of piracy in Cilicia, or the creation of the Cilician pirate career path, is attributed to a man named Tryphon who in the beginning of the second century wanted to wrest control of Syria from the Seleucid Empire. He encouraged the Cilicians to attack Seleucid possessions, he provided them with ships, and he paid the crews. These pirates-in-the-making were also supported by the other enemies of the Seleucids (such as the Ptolemies in Egypt) as a cheap way of weakening a rival.

Tryphon himself was not successful—he was run to ground and put under siege. With all his grandiose plans in ruin and no way out of the siege he committed suicide, but he left a legacy in Cilicia: a political situation in turmoil and a taste for plunder. The Cilicians organized themselves into communities ruled by pirate kings and dedicated to the taking of plunder. These pirate kings led raids throughout the whole of the eastern Mediterranean and the Aegean and some of them became quite famous in their day. They made slaving their specialty, because they found a ready market for slaves, no questions asked, at the island-emporium of Delos.

When, in the mid-second century, the Romans investigated complaints about piracy in the eastern Mediterranean, they concluded that most of the blame should be attributed to the weakness of the Seleucids and the Rhodians, an analysis true enough as far as it went but highly disingenuous considering that the Romans were not only responsible for the weakness of each power—they had defeated the

Seleucids, deprived them of territory, and meddled in their foreign policy, and they had established Delos as a free port and thus impoverished the Rhodians (because of their perceived support of one of Rome's enemies)—but also because their own voracious appetite for slaves made them the principal customers of the pirates.

When the Romans defeated the Seleucids and reduced the power of the Rhodians and the Ptolemies, they did not understand the potential problem they faced in Cilicia. Cilicia was cut off from the rest of Asia Minor by gorges and mountain chains, a craggy broken land with many inlets, perfect for defense and perfect for piratical raids. This land, which, to all appearances, was poor in resources, "a dreary wasteland of rock"—except only for ship-building timber—nonetheless became a magnet for wealth.

In the earliest days the pirates would mingle with sailors in harbor towns and listen to their gossip and so learn what cargo they carried and where they were bound and then rendezvous with those ships and capture them. Citizens in trouble with the law or the tax authorities ran off and joined the pirates, or, if they had resources, found a ship and formed a company of pirates. Some cities openly cooperated with the pirates and provided them with port facilities, others bought annual exemptions from raids.

Non-pirates competed with pirates to provide the market with slaves, but the pirates had the advantage of low overhead: they needed only a ship, a crew, and victims. The pirates sought occasions on which people gathered or places that drew crowds. One of their favorite targets—besides unarmed ships passing through their own territory—was some shrine where they could expect to find unprotected people. A quick descent, a surprise attack, the herding of captives, sailing away out of reach, and off they would go to market. Only when neighbor protected neighbor could the pirates be foiled.

The people of the island of Astypalaea learned that pirates were attacking worshippers (who had come from all over Greece) at the shrine of Artemis in the territory of the Ephesians; they mustered their fleet and after a desperate action they captured the pirate ships and everyone onboard. They transported them all back to their home island of Astypalaea and there they separated out the pirates from the victims, executed the pirates on the spot, and helped all the victims get back to their homes.

All too often, however, no one helped at all or the help came too late, and only Rome—potentially—had the strength to suppress the pirates in their homeland. Rome's allies in the east repeatedly asked the Senate for help against the pirates. The Senate appointed Marcus Antonius (the grandfather of the famous Marc Antony) as governor of the province of Cilicia with the mission to suppress the pirates. Antonius collected forces from Rome's allies and money from anywhere he could get it, crossed the Isthmus of Corinth (and had his fleet dragged across with him), and was joined by small fleets from Byzantium and Rhodes.

From a base within reach of Cilicia he attacked the pirates by land and sea. The pirates resisted fiercely. One of his staff officers was killed in the action. He forced a landing and attacked the bases of the pirates on foot. He collected enough plunder and caused enough damage to the pirates that he was granted a triumph in Rome for his action, but, although Antonius had won personal success, he had not solved the problem of the Cilician pirates. Within two years the Roman Senate returned its attention to the pirates, defined Cilicia as a praetorian province, and directed "the first consul elected" to "send letters to all those people who share a friendship and alliance of arms with the Roman people."

The consul was to "order them to take whatever measures they must to ensure that Roman citizens and allied Latins from Italy, not only may conduct their business, whatever they must do, without danger through the states of the East and the islands, but also must be able to sail the seas in safety." Furthermore they directed the consul to warn Cilicia and all the kings "who rule in Egypt, Cyrenaica, and Syria, all of whom are friends and allies of the Roman people," that they "take a care that no pirate egress from their kingdom nor from their land nor from their borders and neither magistrate nor commanders of garrisons, whom they establish, should associate in word or deed with pirates."

At last it seemed that the Romans were ready to take decisive action and that the seas would be safe. The Roman Senate had issued the clearest possible statement that Rome had declared pirates in general, and Cilician pirates in particular, the enemies of the Roman people; the Senate had also warned the powers of the eastern Mediterranean not to encourage or aid pirates; and, further, it had ordered these states to satisfy the Romans that they were doing everything in their power to aid in the suppression of piracy.

Then the Romans turned from fighting pirates to fighting each other, Roman against Italian, and then when that war had been settled (and all free Italians given Roman citizenship), the Romans were diverted by a war with the king of Pontus, Mithridates. Mithridates had engineered a slaughter of Romans throughout Asia Minor and poured molten gold down the throats of the most rapacious to see if "at last he could quench their thirst for gold." The king declared that he was the champion of the oppressed people of the east. Some of the "oppressed" people who turned to the king were the Cilician pirates who had long been treated as allies and associates of Mithridates—once when his flagship was wrecked he took passage on a pirate ship—and now found their activities circumscribed by Roman action: the Romans had closed the port of Delos and begun operations against the pirates in Crete.

These allies of Mithridates sacked Delos and attacked the Romans at their Italian port, Brundisium. They carried off 1,000 talents of plunder from shrines in the Aegean. The pirates hardly needed direction from Mithridates—all the powers had their attention diverted, war was being waged everywhere, and every place was up for grabs, either as an enemy of Mithridates or as an enemy of Rome.

Sulla was appointed to command the first war against Mithridates, but he had no sooner arrived in Greece than his enemy Marius seized control of Rome and left Sulla to his own devices. Sulla's army still was more than a match for the army of Mithridates, but Sulla had no fleet. He detailed his legate Lucullus to raise a fleet. Between Mithridates and the pirates Lucullus had a rough time. He traversed the whole of the eastern Mediterranean in search of ships. He was harried by the forces of Mithridates and several times he was almost taken by pirates, once off the coast of Rome's ally, Egypt. Another ally, the Rhodians, refused to help because they were being harassed by a fleet sent by Mithridates. When at last Lucullus succeeded in raising a fleet, he lost it in a battle with pirates. In all, Lucullus spent two years collecting a fleet large enough to help Sulla. In those two years Sulla had defeated Mithridates' army twice in Greece and with the fleet, and the capability of invading the king's territory, he was able to force the king to agree to all his terms. Sulla returned to Rome and defeated the Marian forces. Subsequent Roman commanders, and Lucullus himself, fought Mithridates until, finally, Pompey the Great defeated him. (Mithridates, with nowhere to run and no refuge, committed suicide.) The defeat of Mithridates isolated the pirates in Cilicia, but did not decrease their depredations, so the Romans undertook a series of local campaigns against them.

Publius Servilius Isauricus campaigned for three years (77–75 BC) against the pirates of Pamphylia in eastern Lycia and against the Isaurians, from which he took his title. He defeated the pirates' fleet and he invaded their homeland. One pirate chieftain, cornered by the Romans, burned himself to death. Nor did Servilius limit his attacks to the pirates; he also attacked the pirates' allies who, while not actually pirates themselves, still furnished a harbor and reaped the profits from trade with pirates. This Roman statesman, as Cicero wrote, "captured more pirate captains alive than all others before him. Did anyone miss the joy of seeing the captured pirates? Wherever he went he displayed chained and captured enemies. And so a crowd gathered wherever they were, not just from the cities along the route but from neighboring communities as well. And why was the triumph he celebrated in Rome among the most welcome and pleasing of all celebrations? Because nothing is sweeter than victory and nothing is a better proof of victory than to see the once feared enemy paraded on their way to execution."

The Romans (and not only the Romans) tried to check piracy by the ferocity of their punishments. They beheaded pirates, crucified pirates, and threw some pirates to the beasts. (Pirates have never been popular among their victims—a Turkish pirate chief taken by Greeks was turned slowly on a spit for three hours and roasted to death.) Custom generally allows that pirates taken in the act may be summarily executed.

Servilius reduced the border cities but did not reach into the Cilician heartland. His successor was supposed to carry on the war but he was incompetent and all the while the Cilician pirates became more powerful. A Roman rebel in Spain and the escaped gladiator, Spartacus, negotiated with the Cilician pirates for help against Rome. Help did not come—the Roman rebel was murdered and Spartacus was defeated and slain in battle—but the Romans were being forced to acknowledge that piracy was not a local issue and that pirates were growing in number. The lure of piracy continually attracted new recruits, and more cities and states were being forced to consider their options, to aid and abet the pirates and thereby prosper, or to reject them and become subject to attack. Some Greek neighbors of the Cilicians sought advice from oracles; the advice in one case was, "Resist violently and be ready to fight." Those who struggled against the minority who chose the pirate way were praised for living decent lives, but they had to buy their decency with their blood.

7

The Scourge of the Mediterranean

The pirates, equipped by Mithridates, if not to fight on his side, at least to injure his enemies, had formed into fleets with regular captains and admirals. They drew upon the whole of the Near East and Asia Minor for their recruits, men who had no land to farm and so "farmed the sea." Some of them ventured out in the smallest and most fragile of boats and some in the most modern warships—the trireme (a galley with three banks of oars). They attacked ships and towns, whether undefended or walled. They conducted sieges. They captured and sacked four cities on the Aegean islands, and the temples on just a single island provided them with 1,000 talents of loot. They held captives for ransom or sold them into slavery.

Men who preferred "to commit a crime rather than be a victim" flocked to shaggy Cilicia from all parts of the eastern Mediterranean, joined the pirates, and looted their victims for what they called "soldiers' pay." Soon they numbered in the tens of thousands. They made raids everywhere from Syria to the Strait of Gibraltar. They fought Romans on the high seas, defeated a Roman praetor in Sicily, and raided Italy itself. They kidnapped Roman citizens on land and captured them at sea. One crew of Cilician pirates captured the young Julius Caesar. (Rome had gotten too hot for him and he had slipped away to the east to relax and stay out of sight.)

The pirates at first were not impressed with this young Roman, and they demanded a ransom of 20 talents (something like a couple of hundred thousand dollars). Caesar laughed at them and told them that they did not know whom they had captured. He was worth at least 50 talents and he promised to send his friends out to raise the money. He kept one friend with him for company and two servants and he made the best of his thirty-eight days among the pirates, "as blood-thirsty a crew as ever lived." He exercised and competed with them, recited poetry he had written, and when they were not enthusiastic about it he told them that they were ignorant barbarians; when he wanted to take a nap he would send a servant to order them to be quiet; in short, he acted as though he were their leader and not their captive, and he told them—and they laughed at the joke—that when he was ransomed, he was going to come back and crucify the lot of them.

When the ransom came and he was free, he commandeered a fleet, returned to the pirates' lair, and captured the whole gang. The local Roman official did not punish them quickly enough to satisfy Caesar and so Caesar on his own authority had the pirates crucified (as he had promised, but because of his merciful and compassionate nature, once he had fulfilled his vow of seeing them on a cross, he cut short their suffering by slitting their throats). Caesar deceived the pirates by telling them the truth, but—the Roman orator Cicero would say—he had violated no moral code by tracking the pirates down and executing them, nor in deceiving them, and even if he had promised to pay them ransom and then had not, he still would have committed no wrong: oaths sworn with pirates have no moral force because pirates are criminals and not protected by the laws of war.

Caesar acted as a private individual and his single action had no effect on piracy in general. The Mediterranean was in turmoil; there was revolution in Spain, wars in the east, and pirates everywhere. In this crisis the Roman Senate appointed Marcus Antonius, son of the former commander and father of the famous Marc Antony, to ensure that supplies would reach Roman forces in Spain (and he was successful) and to suppress piracy on Crete (because some Cretan pirates had supported Mithridates). To prepare for the war Antonius requisitioned money from the eastern provinces and used part of it to pay the costs of his campaign and the rest of it to enrich himself.

"He was so supremely confident of victory that he transported more chains than weapons in his ships and he paid the price for his arrogance: the enemy took many of his ships and hanged the prisoners from the yard arm and the Cretans rowed into their harbors celebrating a kind of triumph."

Marcus Antonius then negotiated a peace agreement so shameful that the Senate repudiated it and Antonius himself was disgraced, and yet he had conducted a campaign consistent with Roman policy and he was all too typical a commander, arrogant and avaricious. Generally, the Roman Senate responded to requests for aid by appointing commanders and commands (provinces) limited to specific targets for a limited period of time. The Romans did not maintain a standing navy and they depended upon their client states to furnish ships and crews to keep the seas safe and they expected them to assume the expense of any Roman operation. Roman commanders used their commands to enrich themselves.

By 75 BC the coasts of Italy were declared unsafe. Pirates captured two Roman praetors with their lictors. They sacked towns and temples. They kidnapped Roman ladies and held them for ransom. They raided Rome's port city Ostia and burned a consular fleet. The pirates feigned terror when their captives announced that they were Roman citizens—*oh, no, a Roman? We must see that you are delivered from off our ship as soon as possible*—and then the pirates would heave them overboard. Trade stopped. Shortages hit Rome.

When Verres, as rapacious a man as ever governed a province (Cicero writes), was governor of the province of Sicily, he acted more like a pirate than the pirates. He was not only rapacious—most Roman officials were rapacious—but his rapacity made him neglect his duty. Once, as a legate in the east he had been given charge of a ship built by the Milesians to combat piracy; he took charge of the ship and crew, sold the ship, and accepted money from the crew members to release them from their obligation to serve. The Milesians recorded that their ship was lost not through the action of a pirate but through the piracy of a legate.

The governor of a province was supposed to organize the resources of his province to protect it against attack, but a corrupt governor could take advantage of this necessity to enrich himself. So Verres in Sicily instructed the citizens of Messana—who were required by an annual treaty obligation to furnish a warship for service, even in the Atlantic if necessary—to build him a transport vessel to carry his plunder to Italy, and he ordered the citizens of Rhegium to furnish the timber. Verres profited trebly—he not only got his plunder, but also a ship, and he received payments to exempt Messana from service in the Roman fleet which it, and other coastal cities in Sicily, were required to perform.

According to the treaty, every year each city would furnish a ship, crew, and a commander (who would receive a year's allowance to run the ship) so that the Roman commander in chief would have no responsibility to pay or provision the ships—but Verres took the pay, accepted bribes to dismiss the crews, and then kept the pay and ration-money of the discharged sailors. Verres used Messana as a depository for his acquired plunder. "With this ship," Cicero wrote, "you were supposed to protect the province from plundering, not transport your plunder from the province."

"Verres acted so openly that the real pirates believed themselves free to operate off the coasts of Sicily. Verres' half-manned fleet did have one success against a pirate ship encountered near Syracuse; it captured—or, rather, I will not say *captured*, for the pirate ship was so heavily laden with plunder that it could hardly sail—but they towed it—and it proved to be a ship full of handsome and beautiful youths, full of silver, coined and not coined, and beautifully woven vestments. When word came to this wretch, although he was drunk and engaged with those women of his, he rose up immediately and sent off guards under his own legate to bring everything to him intact.

"The ship was brought into Syracuse. Unloading the ship took one whole night. Everyone was eager to witness the executions, but Verres acted more like a pirate examining his booty than a magistrate punishing piracy. Of his prisoners, he executed as pirates those who were old or ugly, and he kept those who were young, handsome, or skilled and divided them among his staff, his son, and his henchmen. He gave a musical sextet to a friend of his in Rome. And as for the pirate captain, no one has seen him to this day, although many believe the pirate bribed Verres to let him go."

Verres got his mistress's husband (the Syracusan Cleomenes) out of the way by putting him in charge of the Roman fleet and sending him on a cruise. Cleomenes set sail in a quadrireme (built according to treaty) and a fleet of six ships—so heavily undermanned (because of the exemptions) that they could only operate under sail and not under oar. Also they were short of rations because Verres had confiscated the ration-money. Verres himself appeared in bathrobe and slippers, his arm around Cleomenes' wife, to wave goodbye to the fleet.

The fleet had landed to allow the sailors to forage on shore—since their stores were depleted—and their commander Cleomenes set up camp and lived in a tent on the shore and remained constantly drunk in imitation of his friend and master. Then he got word that pirates had put in at a nearby harbor. Cleomenes called upon the garrison of the closest city for soldiers and oarsmen, but Verres had sold them exemptions, too. So, at this point, Cleomenes had the mast raised, the sails hoisted, the anchor cables cut, and he issued the order—flee!

Cleomenes had a formidable ship and more oarsmen and so he was able to escape from the pirates and leave his six ship captains in his wake. They had prepared to fight as best they could with reduced and starving crews, but when they saw their commander in chief flee, they followed. The pirates caught the two slowest ships—one captain was killed, the other captured and later ransomed. Cleomenes, seeing that the pirates were coming after him, ordered his ship to beach; he jumped overboard and ran inland. The four surviving captains beached their ships and ran after him. The pirate chief, Heracleo, landed and burned the ships.

"In the dead of night this dreadful news was brought to Syracuse, not by beacon fire but by the flames of the burning fleet itself, and the Syracusans rushed to the governor's headquarters where just a short time before he had returned, leading a train of chanting and singing women. He had fallen asleep with Cleomenes' wife—Cleomenes had slunk home and was hiding there—and no one was allowed to wake the sleeping governor, even though the whole city had gathered at the headquarters. The noise of the crowd finally penetrated to the bedchamber and Verres came forth. The crowd demanded to know where he had been and what he had been doing, and was on the verge of riot, when cooler heads prevailed upon them to arm themselves and prepare to defend themselves from the pirates.

"For one night only the pirates delayed at the scene of the fleet's destruction, and then with smoke still rising from our ships, they pointed their bows towards Syracuse. Perhaps they had heard that there was no more beautiful sight than the walls and harbor of Syracuse and they decided if they ever wanted to see them, they had better see them now while Verres was governor or they never would have the chance again.

"First they came to his summer camp, the place on the shore where he had spent so many days in dissipation, but they found that that place was deserted and that the governor had moved elsewhere and so immediately and without any trepidation they decided to enter the harbor itself. Yes, the harbor itself—if you are unfamiliar with Syracuse this means into the city itself because the city rings the harbor and the sea flows into the heart of the city—and so, Verres, while you were governor, Heracleo and his four tiny ships sailed right up to the market place . . . and they sailed in a triumphal procession so close that their oars splashed spray in the face of the governor and they waved the wild palm roots that they had found on board our ships, to show what Sicilian sailors were forced to eat because of you. The pirates' rations were nothing but the finest Sicilian wheat."

Verres realized that he could well be called to account for this disgraceful episode and so he had all his captains—except Cleomenes—executed, but he did not thereby avoid prosecution: he was brought to justice in Rome by Cicero and forced into exile. Verres, perhaps, was more corrupt than most Roman governors, but, for all that, he was neither atypical in his attitude that provincials existed to be exploited nor for his disinterest in prosecuting a war against pirates. Nonetheless, despite corruption and failure and incompetence, the people of the Mediterranean feared the Romans and were wary of provoking them.

The Cretans had humiliated Marcus Antonius Creticus and they were apprehensive that their victory would have dire consequences for them. They came, city by city, to Rome to appeal to the Senate to recognize them as friends and allies. The Senators were not unwilling to be persuaded by one means or another, but one of the magistrates vetoed the proceeding and offered his own terms—that the Cretans hand over to the Romans all their ships and 300 hostages including the "pirate leader"; the Cretans refused and the Roman Senate decreed Crete a consular province for 69 BC.

The Senate appointed Metellus to reduce Crete. Opposing him were the Cretan leaders Lasthenes and Panares who gathered a force of 24,000 young men particularly skilled at archery (a Cretan specialty). Metellus initiated operations in western Crete and one by one attacked, besieged, and reduced the major cities of Crete. If the city was a harbor, he choked off the harbor entrance, isolated the city, encircled it with a siege wall, constructed siege towers, cleared the walls, broke into the city, and massacred the populace. So ferocious was he toward his captives that many Cretans poisoned themselves rather than fall into his hands. He prosecuted the war throughout the island with fire and sword. Lasthenes and Panares were ineffectual.

In their desperation, the Cretans sent representatives to Pompey (fighting in Asia Minor) and offered to surrender to him; Pompey agreed to send a prefect to Crete to negotiate the pirates' surrender. This careless and arrogant act of interference in another's province so infuriated Metellus that he became even more ferocious in "exacting the rights of the victor over the defeated." Metellus spent three years in the conquest of Crete, proceeding systematically from the west end to the east end, until he had subdued the whole island and earned the title *Creticus*.

The Roman Senate appointed the brother of Metellus Creticus to reduce the Balearic Islands. The Balearic Islands at that time was inhabited by savage men who had loosed a kind of piratical frenzy on the sea. These savage men living on these woody islands would keep watch from the high rocks and, when they saw a ship passing by—considered by them a sort of sacrificial offering provided by the sea itself—they would rush down to their hidden rafts and launch a sudden and terrifying attack. Their only weapon was the sling, but they were exceedingly proficient with that weapon because they practiced from boyhood; boys had to earn their suppers by showing their mothers that they could hit a target with their slings.

When Metellus approached the islands with his war fleet, these savage and unworldly people thought that the Roman ships were just more offerings provided by the sea for them to plunder and they rushed to attack with raft and sling. The Romans were not discommoded by the slings; they responded with their javelins and "the whole flock of the enemy wailed," fled to the shore, beached their rafts, and ran into the closest thickets to hide. The Romans landed and hunted them down. Metellus won the title *Balearicus*.

8

The End of Mediterranean Piracy

The Romans knew how to fight the pirates of a single region, but no sooner had they defeated one nest of pirates than another appeared, and they could see no easy way to solve the whole problem, to fight men of no fixed nation and no fixed property, who could avoid battle and then return to claim their victims again. Cicero reminded the Roman people of the situation.

"Did anyone take to the sea who did not run the risk of death or slavery? The merchant had to choose either the risks of a dangerous voyage in storms during which the pirates could not operate or the risks in good weather of traversing pirate-infested waters. We were faced with a war that was ancient, widespread, and shameful. No one believed that a multitude of generals could win this war in a year or that one general could win it in many years. What province was free of pirates? What ship-borne cargo was safe? What ally could you defend? Did your fleet offer any protection? How many islands, do you think, are deserted? How many of your allies' cities abandoned or captured by pirates? And I do not need to talk of events in foreign countries.

"It has long been the custom of Romans to fight their wars far from home, and to fight on behalf of their allies, not to defend their own houses. I say to you that during these years you could not reach your allies by sea, since your army dared not sail the seas from Brundisium except in the depths of winter. How many envoys came to you from foreign nations, to ask help for their captives, when Roman legates themselves had to be ransomed? Could I say that the sea was safe for trade when a praetor's twelve axes were pirate booty? Should I talk of those illustrious cities, Cnidus, Colophon, or Samos, and many more captured by pirates, when you know that your own port city fell to pirates? A praetor on an inspection tour of Caieta, your most famous and prosperous port, was seized by pirates; in Misenum pirates captured the children of the men who previously had waged war against them. Or should I even mention the misfortune and devastation of Ostia when you were all eyewitnesses to the capture and destruction of a fleet under the command of the consul elected by you, the Roman people?"

At last the Romans recognized that the problem would require extraordinary measures and they turned to their most famous and accomplished general, Pompey the Great (Gnaeus Pompeius Magnus), and granted him a three-year command to exercise the greater *imperium*—that is, the right to command all other commanders and compel them to cooperate with him—over the whole of the Mediterranean Sea and all contiguous waters and all the coast up to twenty-five miles inland. The Senate sent letters to all kings, dynasts, peoples, and cities with the orders that they were to aid Pompey; it gave him the power to draft troops and to appoint subordinate commanders—he created a staff of twenty-five legates with the lesser *imperium*—and the Senate voted to give him as much money (6,000 talents) and as many ships as he requested.

Pompey used his resources and his authority to muster a force of 120,000 men, 4,000 cavalry, 270 ships, which he apportioned among his legates. He divided these legates among different areas of operations. Their mission was to engage the pirates in the different areas of operations and fix them there so that they could not go to the aid of any other pirates or seek refuge elsewhere, while Pompey, himself, in command of a central fleet was to move systematically from area to area, driving the pirates before him, corner them, and administer the coup de grace. Pompey's plan required the utmost organizational ability.

Once his arrangements were in place he cleared the western Mediterranean of pirates in forty days. He then proceeded east from Brundisium. In the east the pirates had already found their plan to cooperate and counterattack thrown into disarray by the magnitude of the forces marshaled against them, the rapidity with which the measures had been put in place, and by their fear of the awesome reputation of Pompey.

"What an incredible man! [Cicero wrote.] What heaven-sent courage and ability! In a short time he caused the sun to shine upon the republic again! You, who, just a brief moment before, saw an enemy fleet at the mouth of the Tiber, now do not even hear rumors of a pirate in the ocean outside our sea. And this was accomplished so quickly, that I think it is worth describing, even though you, yourselves, are witnesses to it. For what merchant or trader ever visited so many places so quickly or made so many voyages as Gnaeus Pompey and his fleet? He sailed to Sicily, although the sailing season had not yet begun, he visited Africa, and he brought his fleet to Sardinia, and he secured these three granaries of the republic with powerful garrisons and a fleet. He returned to Italy, he secured Spain and Gaul (across the Alps) with troops and ships, he dispatched ships into the Adriatic and to Greece and he recognized the vital importance of the two seas around Italy and he appointed for them the greatest fleets and the bravest soldiers and then he himself set out from Brundisium. . . .

"Pompey himself came to Cilicia with many different specialized troops and siege devices because he expected different tactical situations and sieges would be required in inaccessible strong points. But, in fact, he needed none of them, because his fame and his preparations stunned the pirates. They hoped, if they did not force him to fight, that he would be lenient. First the fortresses of Cragus and Anticragus surrendered and then the Cilicians of the mountains and their neighbors; they handed over a mass of weapons, some still being manufactured, and ships in dry dock and on the water, and bronze and iron fittings for them, and sailcloth, and lumber of different kinds, and mobs of captives, some held for ransom, some put to hard labor.

"Pompey burned the lumber, towed out the ships and freed the captives to return to their own homes. (Many of them returned home only to discover that they had been declared dead and a funeral had been held for them.)"

On the forty-ninth day from the day he left Brundisium he could declare that Cilicia was under the total control of the Roman people. In all, in about four months Pompey captured 71 ships, accepted the surrender of some 300 ships, took 120 cities, forts, and places of refuge, and was responsible for the death of about 10,000 pirates, but he did not declare his mission accomplished until he had addressed the root causes of piracy, that his prisoners had taken to piracy not from any inherent wickedness but from poverty and necessity; he found land for them and he settled them inland in Cilicia, Asia Minor, and even in Greece.

Pompey was successful because he had the vast resources of Rome at his call and because he had the ability, personal and legal, to organize a comprehensive campaign against all the pirates everywhere at once, to find them, isolate them, attack them, and destroy them—or accept their surrender—and withal he had the foresight to address the root causes of piracy so that ex-pirates would not be tempted to look back to the sea for their living.

Pompey's campaign cleared the Mediterranean of pirates, but during the civil wars between himself and Caesar, and then between Octavian and Antony, piracy flourished again. Antony executed a Spartan for piracy and the Spartan's son, Eurycles, took up the family trade and allied himself with Octavian. Octavian welcomed all allies, even pirates. At the battle of Actium the Spartan finally had his chance to revenge his father; he brought his ship close enough to Antony's to answer Antony's hail, "Who is that?" with his reply, "The son of the man you executed, seeking revenge." But once a pirate, always a pirate, and no matter his thirst for revenge, the Spartan let Antony escape when he saw that he could capture a more profitable transport ship. Octavian, nonetheless, rewarded the Spartan by installing him as the hegemon of Sparta.

When Octavian established the empire, he curtailed military adventurers, put the legions on a professional basis, and created a permanent navy. So long as the empire remained stable, the Roman navy held piracy in check. Only with the rise of the Germanic peoples, the Heruli, the Goths, and the Vandals, was the Roman navy overwhelmed. One tribe, the Heruli, although they were a national

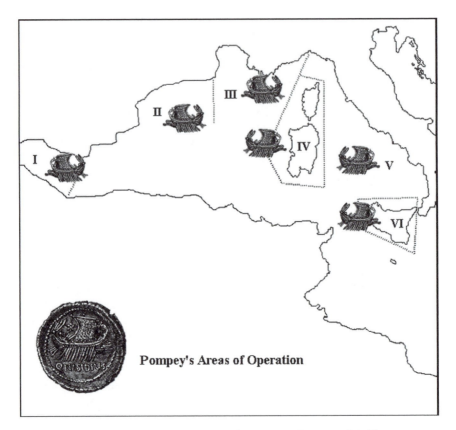

Pompey's Areas of Operation

Pompey's Legates and Their Areas of Operation, Western Mediterranean

I.	Nero	-	to close off the straits
II.	Torquatus	-	the Balearic Islands and the coast of Spain
III.	Pomponius	-	Gaul and Liguria
IV.	Atilius	-	Corsica and Sardinia
V.	Gellius	-	the west coast of Italy
VI.	Varus	-	Sicily

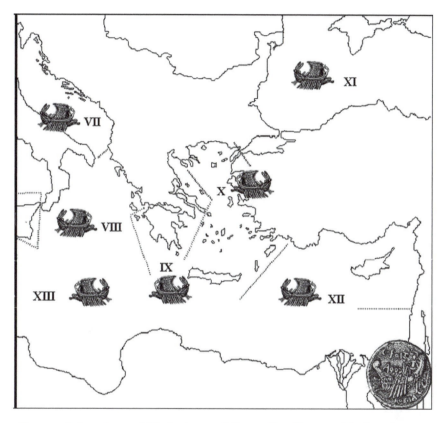

Pompey's Legates and Their Areas of Operation, Eastern Mediterranean

VII.	Lentulus	-	the upper Adriatic
VIII.	Varro	-	the Ionian Sea
IX.	Sisenna	-	the coast of Greece including Macedonia
X.	Lollius	-	the Aegean
XI.	Piso	-	the Propontis and the Black Sea
XII.	Metellus	-	the southern coast of Asia Minor and Phoenicia (but not Cilicia)
XIII.	Marcellinus	-	the north African coast

group attacking a nation, might legitimately be called pirates, in that they sought only plunder and not land, but the Goths and Vandals, while they sought plunder, primarily sought more land on which to form their kingdom.

After the fall of Rome the Mediterranean was wide open to pirates, but trade was so diminished that pirates had little prey and the seas were free of marauders until the time of the Vikings.

── PART III ──
THE VIKINGS

"I cannot understand why I have kept away from the sea for so long, for a well-manned ship is the best of all things. It is good to sit contented ashore, and no man need be ashamed to do so; but a voyage to a far land with booty awaiting a man and this smell in his nostrils, is as good a lot as could be desired, and a sure cure for age and sorrow. It is strange that we Northmen, who know this and are more skillful seamen than other men, sit at home as much as we do, when we have the whole world to plunder."

9

"From Merciless Invaders ..."

The monks of the monastery at Lindisfarne on the northeast coast of England were living a peaceful, ordered existence of regular prayer, chant, song, and study. They lived on the produce of their fields; they harmed no one and had no enemies; and they had no defense at all against the Vikings who descended upon them, murdered them, and looted their monastery. The helplessness of these pious Christians and their wealth lured other Vikings into attacking other monasteries, not specifically because the monasteries were Christian, although pagan Vikings had no scruples about attacking Christian holy places, but primarily because they were prosperous, isolated, and defenseless. As the Vikings struck again and again, Christians prayed for deliverance and searched scripture for an explanation of this affliction—"Out of the North an evil shall break forth upon all the inhabitants of the land."

The "Viking Age" is defined as the period that begins with the sack of the monastery at Lindisfarne in AD 793 and ends (in England, anyway) with the death of Harold at the battle of Hastings in 1066—when the Normans ("Northmen") won control of England. Put in another way, the Viking Age begins with scattered raids on isolated targets and ends with conquest and occupation, and yet the raids and invasions, motivated by the wealth and helplessness of their victims, would never have happened had the Vikings not had ships seaworthy enough to reach their victims.

The Viking ships developed from a technological breakthrough in Scandinavian boat building. The pre-Viking craft had looked rather like large canoes—and at first they were paddled like canoes and then they were redesigned to be propelled by oars and redesigned again for masts and sails; these redesigned ships, the ships the Vikings used, were small and could be easily maneuvered; they were fast and could cross open ocean, travel up rivers to London and Paris, and even be portaged over short distances; they could be beached on almost any level shore, and, if they had to take to the sea quickly, their two-prowed design allowed them to be launched and expeditiously gotten under weigh.

In modern times a Viking ship was excavated at Gokstad. The Gokstad ship (built in the middle of the ninth century) is seventy-seven feet in length, seventeen feet across at midships, and six-and-a-half feet deep at its deepest. The ship, constructed of oak, weighed seven tons, could freight ten tons, and yet drew only a little more than three feet of water. It had a pine mast and a sail of red and white strips of cloth, sewn double-thick. The ship was steered by a rudder-paddle and rowed by thirty-two narrow bladed spruce oars of various lengths: the different lengths allowed the oars to strike the water simultaneously from different rowing stations in the ship. The ship was designed more for sailing than for rowing—it had no rowing benches—but certainly, when necessary, it could be rowed: the oarsmen undoubtedly sat on their sea-chests. The ship carried—as deduced from the shield array—sixty-four men: they would have been uncomfortably crowded onboard a ship of this size, but the sixty-four could be divided into two shifts of thirty-two rowers, or, if more power or speed were required, all sixty-four could row, two men to an oar—and the larger crew was a more effective fighting force.

On April 30, 1893, a replica of the Gokstad ship left Bergen with a crew of twelve (and a thousand bottles of beer). The ship proved eminently seaworthy and quick, although the hull twisted and turned and kept its modern crew in a state of alarm until they became used to the working of the hull in the heavy seas. On May 27, 1893, after a voyage of twenty-eight days, the ship raised the North American continent.

Ships such as this one gave the Vikings every tactical advantage: the Vikings were always on the offensive and always held the initiative; they had clear, well-defined objectives; they achieved surprise; they could mass enough of a force, but a force no larger than necessary, to overwhelm their target; they had the security of a safe approach and a clear line of retreat; they followed and obeyed one leader on the raid; they had all waterways on which to maneuver; and they had the simplest of plans—fix on a target, attack it, take it, loot it, and leave it. Conversely, their enemies had every disadvantage: they were disorganized; they did not know where the Vikings would strike; they did not have sufficient forces to guard every target; and their forces often were intimidated by the Vikings.

While the sailing qualities of the new ship (which gave the Vikings the means to reach their targets overseas) were the most important factor behind the Viking raids, the urge to raid and plunder was also a factor. Even their gods, as they believed, went a-viking; in a tenth-century poem, *The Song of Rig*, the god Heimdall is advised by a crow,

> [Others] have better halls
> and better lands than you.
> You should go a-viking,
> deal wounds,
> let them feel your
> blade. . . .

And yet other factors did drive the Vikings away from their homes and onto the seas: the climate in Scandinavia was growing drier and colder and it was depressing agricultural production, while, at the same time, the birthrate was rising and producing more young men than the available land could support. These young men were drawn into the border wars of rival kings who were engaged in expanding their kingdoms at the expense of their neighbors. Some of the young men, and their chosen war leaders, were cut loose when the fighting was over; others found themselves on the losing side, and still others, though not directly involved in the wars, nonetheless were forced to leave their homes to seek their fortunes. All these aggressive young men, adrift in the times, took to raiding.

The loot of the Vikings, wherever it was taken, eventually trickled down to the Danish city of Hedeby, the preeminent trade center for all of Scandinavia. Every sort of craftsman and product was found there—glassware, wine, weapons, woven cloth, furs, coins minted in Hedeby, slaves—and merchants came there from all over western Europe to barter and buy the goods they required; afterward they returned to their homes with the goods they had acquired and also with unflattering stories of the barbarous Danes: unwanted children thrown into the sea, dead animals hung on poles outside the houses—an aromatic practice not unknown in modern times, although the hung animals of our day are not sacrificed to a pagan god—an unrelieved diet of fish and more fish, drunkenness, fighting, and cacophonous and atrocious singing.

Hedeby's Danes were conscious of their wealth if not of their barbarism and they looked to their defenses—south of Hedeby they built a wall, *the Danish Work*, across the whole peninsula; this wall did a good job of keeping raiders out of Denmark but it did nothing to keep raiders in. Danish Vikings—and Norwegians and Swedes—followed the successful attack on Lindisfarne in AD 793 with raids on other isolated monasteries; emboldened by those successes, they turned an ambitious eye toward the settled and prosperous states in Charlemagne's empire. They soon discovered that Charlemagne was well able to defend his empire: he threw up fortifications at threatened points, dispatched fleets and river patrols to protect waterways, and by vigorous countermeasures thwarted the Vikings. They bided their time, then, until Charlemagne had died, and then they tested his successor, his son Louis the Pious (AD 814). In 820 the Vikings attempted to enter the Seine and were repulsed, but the pious Louis did not have his father's ability, either to hold the great empire together or to defend it, and in 834 Danish Vikings broke into the northwest part of his empire, Frisia.

After the Vikings had plundered Frisia, they crossed Utrecht and attacked the Netherlander town of Dorestad. Dorestad, famous for its wealth, was a walled town ten times the size of Hedeby. The Danish Vikings devastated it, and the people they did not murder they carried off as slaves. After they withdrew, Dorestad was rebuilt and repopulated and it recovered its prosperity, but the Vikings returned and plundered it again. The city recovered again but the Vikings returned yet again—to plunder it or to extort money from the city—and this cycle continued

The Viking Raids

for twenty years until a natural disaster, the flooding of the Rhine in 863, put a permanent end to Dorestad and its suffering.

Dorestad was not the only city to suffer. Two years after (836) the first raid on it, Vikings made raids up the Thames into southern England and they made raids down along the coast of France to plunder the trade center and monastery on the island of Noirmoutier at the mouth of the Loire River in the Bay of Biscay.

A monk of Noirmoutier wrote:

"The number of ships increases, the endless flood of Vikings never ceases to grow bigger. Everywhere Christ's people are the victims of massacre, burning, and plunder. The Vikings over-run all that lies before them, and none can withstand them. They seize Bordeaux, Périgueux, Limoges, Angoulême, Toulouse; Angers, Tours, and Orleans are made deserts. Ships past counting voyage up the Seine, and throughout the entire region evil grows strong. Rouen is laid waste, looted and burnt: Paris, Beauvais, Meaux are taken, Melun's stronghold is razed to the ground, Chartres occupied, Evreux and Bayeux looted, and every town invested."

In the end the monks abandoned the island.

Louis the Pious died in 840. His empire split apart, resistance fragmented, and the Viking raids increased in frequency and in magnitude. A fleet of sixty-seven Viking ships returned to the Loire in 842. A local rebel had invited the Vikings (probably Norwegian Vikings) to help him seize the town of Nantes. The rebel advised the Vikings on the best time to attack and he provided them with pilots to show them the navigable channel of the Loire. The Vikings arrived at Nantes on a festival day (St. John's Day), June 24, 842, and they burst into the unsuspecting town, killed at will, and terrorized the townspeople. They loaded their ships with booty and with captives to sell as slaves, and then they sailed away, leaving the plundered town to the rebel. The raiders sailed back to Noirmoutier and decided to remain there for the winter, to dominate the Loire Valley, continue to raid France, and trade the goods they had acquired.

The Vikings plundered Rouen on the Seine River in 841 and Quentovic, south of Boulogne, in 842. In 845 a Danish fleet of 600 ships led by their king in person sacked Hamburg. Another fleet of 120 ships entered the Seine River and there encountered the French king, Charles the Bald, and his army. The king committed an elementary tactical error—he divided his army of Franks, one division on one bank and one division on the other, each completely incapable of supporting the other. The Vikings landed on the bank with the smaller of the two divisions, routed it, and captured over a hundred men whom they promptly hanged in view of the army on the other bank, before reembarking on their ships.

The surviving Franks, with their probable fate all too visible before their eyes, broke and ran. No one was left to contest the Vikings' passage to Paris and on Easter Sunday the Vikings sacked the city and held it while they negotiated a ransom with Charles the Bald of 7,000 pounds of silver and a guaranteed passage back down the Seine for their fleet and all their loot, including their prisoners. As disgraceful as the payment of ransom was, Charles the Bald, by making the

payment, did gain six years in which to recover from the blow and to organize the
defenses of his kingdom, for one truth was now certain—

> The wolf will soon return
> And the witch's horse will burn,
> His sharp claws in the ash,
> To taste the Frenchman's flesh.

France, and all of western Europe, including the British Isles, lay open to be
plundered, or to be coerced into paying the infamous Danegeld (so called in
England). To pay the attacker not to attack is logical and not always bad policy—
the Romans paid the Gauls to leave Rome and within a generation the Romans
were strong enough to defeat the Gauls in battle. Philip of Macedon paid off
the hostile powers encircling his kingdom and used the breathing space to create
the army which defeated the very powers that had accepted his money, but the
paymasters must profit from the purchased time to prepare to meet the challenge
posed by their enemies. Those who paid the Vikings prepared nothing and so their
money bought only a limited respite and then they had to buy another and another
until their treasury was exhausted and they no longer had the means to buy off the
Viking attack and its dire consequences.

Town after town fell to the Vikings; as terror spread before them, people lost
hope and fled from the towns to avoid both the Vikings and their own tax collectors
(raising money to pay off the Vikings)—every river that could float a ship seemed
to carry a Viking fleet—and governments in western Europe north of the Pyrenees
lost the ability to organize effective resistance. As resistance crumbled, the Vikings
organized more systematic plundering raids.

In 857 the Viking leader Bjorn Ironside led a fleet which took and sacked Paris—
still the richest city in northern Europe. Bjorn's raid left only four buildings
standing—by chance, four churches. Buoyed by the success of this expedition
Bjorn decided to continue his plundering expedition and to attack the greatest
city in the world—Rome. He led his fleet of sixty-two ships around Brittany
and the Bay of Biscay, all the while filling his ships with plunder—prisoners,
gold, silver—from the Seine River to Moorish Spain. Moorish Spain, however,
had already been the scene of some savage struggles between the Moors and the
Vikings, and, if the Moorish rulers were given time to organize, not always to
the Vikings' advantage. Bjorn found them to be too well prepared—and too little
intimidated—to allow indiscriminate plundering. At Seville 1,000 Vikings were
killed and 400 taken as prisoners.

Bjorn and his Vikings continued through the Strait of Gibraltar, plundered
Algeciras, raided North Africa for "blue men" to sell as slaves in the north, raided
the Balearics, Narbonne, and plundered their way up the Rhone for ninety-four
miles before being turned back. They continued their way east to the borders of
Italy and across the borders to Pisa, and on, until they saw a magnificent walled
city of gleaming white marble. *Rome*, they thought. They recognized that they

could not take so large a city, so well fortified and defended, by storm, and so the Vikings sent envoys to bring the word, *our chief is dying* and he had one last request, that he be baptized and admitted to the Christian faith. The bishop was suspicious, but he sent some priests to investigate and they reported back that they had found a subdued chief, ready to be baptized, and they had baptized him: so rejoice, a wolf has been converted into a lamb.

When, on the next day, the Viking envoys returned, heads bowed, and informed the city fathers that their chief had died, and they asked if he could be carried into the city and given Christian burial, the bishop gave permission. The bishop summoned his people to gather within the walls to witness the interment of the new lamb; with the collected populace weeping for the death of a Christian and rejoicing for the conversion of a heathen, the party of grieving Vikings, dressed in voluminous cloaks—their special mourning cloaks, they said—carried their chieftain into the city.

They laid him down gently by the grave and stepped back to give him room—to spring to his feet and plunge his sword into the bishop while the rest drew swords from beneath their cloaks, cut down the mourners, and seized and opened the gates for the rest of their comrades to pour into the city. They had seized Rome! But no, all too soon they discovered that the city they had taken was not Rome but Luna—Rome was still some two hundred miles away. The Vikings were furious. They massacred everyone not worth selling as a slave and burned the city to the ground.

Then the marauders continued on their way (they bypassed Rome) and hit easier targets around the Mediterranean before, finally, they turned toward home. At the Strait of Gibraltar they encountered a Moorish fleet that had been lying in wait for them—the Viking fleet itself had become a rich and tempting prize—and they had to fight a battle to force their way through; only twenty ships broke through, but those ships were laden with plunder and they cruised up the coast of France and found landfall—after a last raid or two—at the mouth of the Loire.

Legend and reality intertwined to lure other Scandinavians to try their luck at viking and ever more raiders took to the sea and terrorized their victims. In the Frankish lands, secular government broke down, and so did the governing authority of the church. Local areas looked after themselves. Towns raised fortifications and organized local defense; local lords recruited followers, built castles, and sought local dominance and independence. New bonds of loyalty were forged in the struggle and new tactics were developed. The Seine River was blocked with fortified bridges, which halted lesser raids, but in the year 885 a fleet of 700 Viking ships fought its way past the bridges and put Paris under siege. Paris held out long enough so that the new Frankish king, Charles the Fat, had time to deliberate whether he should defend Paris, to decide to do so, to collect a sizable army, to march, and to lay siege to the Vikings who were besieging Paris, but in the next year, much to the disgust of the Parisian defenders, he paid the Vikings 700 pounds of silver and supplied them with provisions to leave Paris and attack his enemies in Burgundy.

More Vikings arrived in France, seized land from local inhabitants, settled it, and defended it from other Vikings; the majority of the Vikings who settled in France were overwhelmed eventually or driven out or they were absorbed into the local populace and became largely indistinguishable from them in language and custom, except for the "Northmen" of "Normandy" who formed their own kingdom and defended it against all comers.

The Viking onslaught would have been even more ferocious, if the Vikings had not shown the same ferocity in their own homelands, and been absorbed in their own struggles, Swede against Swede and Dane against Dane; in the wars in which Denmark was united under King Gorm and his son Harald Bluetooth, the dissidents, discontents, and defeated left Denmark to seek new homes in the West.

> Ships' tents were struck and stowed away
> And past the town our dragon glides
> That girls might see our glancing sides
> Out from the Nid our brave Harald steers.
>
> Their oars our king's men handle well;
> One stroke is all the eye can tell.
>
> 'Tis in fight, not on the wave,
> That oars may break and fail the brave;
> At sea, beneath the ice-cold sky
> Safely our oars o'er ocean ply
> And when at Trondheim's holy stream
> Our seventy oars in distance gleam
> We seem, while rowing, from the sea
> A gull with iron wings to be.

—— 10 ——

The Rus

In the east, the story was somewhat different.

Even before the Viking era, as the whole of Sweden and eastern Scandinavia increasingly came under the control of the kings of central Sweden, the young men who lacked land and fortune and a secure place in the newly organized kingdoms looked farther to the east to trade, raid, conquer, and settle. They advanced along the shores of the Baltic, incorporated Gotland into a mutually beneficial trading partnership, advanced to the Gulf of Finland, subdued and taxed Latvia, suppressed a rebellion there, and continued to the Dvina River and the Dnieper River and along them to the Black Sea—or alternately down the Volga to the Caspian Sea—and thence to Constantinople.

They conquered and settled those places that advanced their control of the trade routes (and shut out competing Danes) from the Baltic to Constantinople, and, in the end, when they had gained control of the trade routes, and made these eastern regions so much their own that they called them "Greater Sweden" or "Cold Sweden," they concluded that the control of trade was more profitable than attacks upon the trade of others.

The Swedes did not win control of the river routes without opposition; the first wave of Swedish invaders (according to the Russian chronicle) was driven out of the river valleys by the local people—the Chuds, the Slavs, the Merians, the Vesh, and the Krivichians—but then these people fell into civil war, and so they sent to the Rus (the Swedes already settled in Cold Sweden) "rather than to the Swedes of Sweden, or the Northmen, or the Angles, or the Gotlanders," and they said, "We seek a prince to rule over us and judge us according to the law." Three brothers answered the call and occupied the land around Novgorod, which came to be known as Rusland and all who lived there as "Russians." ("Rus" derives from a Finnish word meaning "ship" or "oared ship" and thus the Russians were "men of the oared ships.")

The brothers, and their successors, reasserted control over the trade routes and built a line of forts to protect the routes; the forts became an instrument of assimilation between Swedes and the local Slavonian population as Slavonians were drawn to the forts to trade and to find protection; the ruling classes of the two people—the warrior/trader class of "Rus" and the Slavonians—intermarried and the two people gradually became one, the "Russians," as the word "Russian" came more and more to mean any inhabitant of the land that stretched from Lake Ladoga to Odessa.

Contemporary Arab accounts of Russia describe a land of warriors concerned about the clothes they wore and their personal appearance, avaricious men, devoted to carnal pleasure and to alcohol, distrustful—they carried their wealth on their belts—suspicious and ready to fight each other, drunk or sober, and just as ready to dismiss their quarrels and join together to fight outsiders. When a prince died, his body was placed in a temporary grave to preserve it while his funeral ship was built; his possessions were divided into three parts, one part for his family, one part for his funeral, and one part to buy enough mead to get everyone drunk. His concubines were asked, *who will die with him*, and the one who volunteered delivered herself to drink and to pleasure and to a guard who guaranteed that she would not repent her vow and escape. When the funeral ship was completed and placed on a bier of wood, the corpse was dug up and dressed and arranged on a couch by the "angel of death" (an old woman chosen for this duty). The dead prince was surrounded by food, treasure, his weapons, a dog cut in half, two horses and two cattle slashed to pieces with swords, and his concubine, stabbed and strangled by the "angel of death." Then the bier was set on fire and in an hour totally consumed.

Norwegians, Swedes, Danes, Vikings, and Russians, all were superstitious, hot-tempered, ready to fight, and prone to feuds. A saga tells the story of two friends whose wives quarreled and urged on their husbands' retainers to fight each other against their husbands' wishes. Murder followed murder and dark omens predicted more deaths. "I see," a friend of one of the husbands said, "a goat lying in the ditch in its own blood. What does it mean?"

And the husband, who could see the goat running along the street, replied to him, "You have seen the fetch that follows you. Now beware of yourself."

The fetch caught up to him, the companion was slain, some were slain in retribution, while others escaped to seek revenge. Those who were less ready to involve themselves in the round of murders, nonetheless, found their manhood questioned and themselves drawn into the feud. "Tell me," one of the more hesitant asked his brother (after the two of them alone had faced and slain eight men in combat), "am I less a man because I make more of taking life than others do?"

In the end the man who wished to be a peacemaker was burned to death in his own home.

The Russians' eagerness to fight and their courage and ability enabled them to dominate the northern peoples and the northern trade routes, but when they attempted to extend their control down the whole of the Dnieper, Volga, and Don

The Rus, Varangians, and Vikings

⊕ a "Rus" town
◦ a "Rus/Varangian" site
⊙ a non-Rus town

Finland

Baltic

Ladoga
Novgorod

Sea

Latvia ⊕⊕ ⊕

Dvina

Dniester ⊕ Kiev

Don

Bug

Dnieper   Donets

Volga

Danube   Odessa

Caucasus   Caspian

Bulgars   Kherson

Philipp   Black

opolis   Constantinople   Sea

Rusland

River routes, they ran into organized and fierce resistance from the Bulgars, the Khazars, the Byzantine Empire, and the Arab Caliphate; they offered the people of these river systems their first effective—and welcome—protection from the other major powers, but they found that they just did not have the manpower needed for the task and so they invited in bands of mercenaries from Sweden. These Swedes, the next wave to enter Cold Sweden, seemed different enough from the "Russians" to require a different designation and so they were known by a term which denoted *men bound by oath*, the first men bound by oath being the mercenary bands of Scandinavians, and the next, later, the "corporations" of merchants and warriors—the *Varangians*.

By at least the year AD 839 "Rus" traders had succeeded in reaching Constantinople and by the next century the Rus had succeeded in dominating trade from the eastern Baltic down to Kiev, their powerful city on the Dnieper River. A constant stream of goods passed up and down the rivers: silver and glass from the Caliphate, silk from China, and other wares from India and Constantinople, all of which were carried north to exchange for furs, honey, wax, and slaves, products of Scandinavia, even though Scandinavia's main resources were the iron, timber, and men that combined into warships and warriors armed with iron weapons. The Scandinavians traded and they raided: ever tempted by the riches of the Byzantine empire, usually dissuaded by the Byzantines' organized power.

In their great trading expeditions the Rus would sail from Novgorod to Kiev, the jumping-off point where they would prepare for the real journey to Constantinople; at Kiev they would transfer their goods to ships constructed locally for the next part of the journey, a journey in June down the Dnieper to the "Seven Cataracts" below Vytichev. The first three cataracts—named "No Sleep," "The Island," and "Cacophony"—required the crews to disembark and walk the ships through the rough water and rocks with an all too real threat of losing their footing and drowning or being crushed between ship and rock or, worst of all, losing the boat and all its cargo. At the fourth cataract, "The Pelican," the crews had to disembark, unload the boat, and portage six miles. Some carried the goods and dragged the boat, while others stood guard on the banks against attacks by the Pechenegs (one reason they negotiated the cataracts en masse). Cataracts five and six, "The Lake," and "Boiling Water," again required them to walk the boat through, and the seventh cataract, "Little Cataract" or "The Falls," required them to negotiate a narrow passage and falling water.

Until they cleared the falls and landed on the Island of St. Gregory, they were under constant threat of attack by the Pechenegs. Once safe on the island they gathered around a gigantic oak tree, sacred to them, and they gave thanks in their own particular way: they brought cages of roosters with them and now they cast lots to determine the fate of the roosters—to die, to be eaten, or to live. After they had performed these rites, they rested and then they departed from the island and coasted along the shore of the Black Sea to the mouth of the Danube while all that way the Pechenegs kept pace with them by land and waited for an opportunity to attack them; at the Danube the merchants entered the territory of the Bulgars, the Pechenegs turned back, and the traders were safe; they bartered and bargained with the Bulgars and then they continued on their way to the city of Constantinople.

The Byzantine emperor welcomed the trade, but he was worried enough about the Rus (and the Varangians) that he would not allow them to build any forts below the cataracts (forts which they could have used to defend their ships and themselves from the Pechenegs, but from which they also could have launched raids upon the Byzantines) and in Constantinople he had them confined to one district. In the beginning of the tenth century the emperor made a treaty with the Rus that he would pay Rus merchants a fee and travel money and six months board (to winter over in Constantinople) if they, in turn, would carry his goods north in the Spring. The imperial expectation was that the Rus would defend Constantinople while they were domiciled there and also defend the Byzantines' northern trade routes just by conveying and protecting their cargos. The Rus considered the fees tribute.

As early as the first half of the ninth century Norsemen (Russians and Varangians) had appeared in the Black Sea. Through the next hundred years the Norsemen continued to raid the Byzantine Empire—they made an abortive attack on Constantinople in 941—and they exhibited all the savagery of the Viking raids on western Europe. In one province of the empire, Bithynia, "of the people they captured, some they butchered, others they set up as targets and shot at, some they seized upon, and after binding their hands behind their backs, they drove iron nails through their heads. Many holy churches they gave to the flames while they burned monasteries and villages, and took no little booty on both sides of the sea." The Byzantines counterattacked, forced the Norsemen to take to their ships, and pursued them "in boats with Greek fire. They dropped Greek fire through pipes upon the enemy ships" and when the survivors—only ten ships escaped—returned home they told their friends and relatives that the Greeks had harnessed the fires of heaven.

When the Rus prince Igor (Ingvar) led a band of Varangian mercenaries on a raid in the Caucasus in 944, the emperor sent tribute to him and asked for peace. Igor asked his council to advise him and they replied, "What do we desire beyond gold, silver, and rich cloth without having to fight for them? Will we be victorious? Will he? Does he not have the sea for his ally?—for we are not marching by land, but through the depths of the sea. Death lies in wait for us all."

Igor took their advice and accepted the deal, but the consequence was that Igor found himself with a group of idle and restless Varangian mercenaries. They delivered an ultimatum to Igor (and a clearer statement of Viking—and piratical—philosophy could not be found), "The servants of Sveinald [his brother] are adorned with weapons and fine raiment, but we are naked. Go forth with us after tribute, o Prince, that both you and we may profit thereby." Igor was persuaded, but the attack went wrong, and he paid with his life.

During the tenth century the Byzantine emperors employed Varangians as mercenaries throughout the empire from Syria to Sicily. They found them so impressive that in 970 after the Byzantines had driven the Russians back from Philippopolis—but only after the city had been sacked—and then had defeated the Russians and compelled them to sign a treaty, one clause of the treaty required that the Rus furnish troops to the Byzantine emperor on a regular basis. These troops became the basis for the famed Varangian Guard created by the Byzantine emperor Basil II.

As it happened, Vladimir, king of Kiev, had called upon the Varangians to come help him in a civil war against his brother. After the Varangians had won the battle, they held on to Kiev and demanded a ransom before they would give it up. Vladimir rewarded some of them with land and convinced the rest to go south to Constaninople; he sent messengers ahead to advise the emperor not to let the Varangians into his city in one body or they would cause trouble—and he added that he would be just as happy never to see these Varangians again—but the emperor (Basil II) used the Varangians to put down the revolt of a pretender to the throne in 988. After that success he converted them into a private guard of 6,000 men to be the imperial bodyguard and an elite unit within the army.

— 11 —

Conversion and Containment

Christians believed that they were under attack by the Vikings because the Vikings were pagans and hated Christians. Therefore, Christians had a double interest in converting the Vikings, first, as their simple duty to convert the heathen and, second, as a tactic to ameliorate the Vikings' assaults upon Christians—or, at least, upon churches and monasteries. Christian missionaries put their lives at risk—and many lost their lives or were imprisoned and enslaved—to carry the word to Scandinavia. They found that the Scandinavians were not especially resistant to conversion, that is, the missionaries did not oppose an entrenched priesthood—the leaders *were* the "priests" and they were still the leaders if they converted—and they found an attitude that the old gods should and could take care of themselves and did not need human beings to do it for them (so that if they could not defend themselves from the Christian God, so much the worse for them). Finally, the missionaries presented a version of Christianity which did not require the Norsemen to change their way of life and suddenly become pacifists, as the following story from the sagas shows.

THANGBRAND IN ICELAND

King Olaf (says the saga) was in the process of converting the whole of Norway to Christianity and he sent Thangbrand, who was a highborn man and the captain of a ship, to bring the word, along with his trading goods, to Iceland. Thangbrand brought with him a companion named Gudleif who had come from Iceland and had a reputation as a strong man, fierce and bold—he had already killed many a warrior in single combat—and these two Christian emissaries entered Iceland prepared either to persuade the Icelanders to convert or to fight and kill them. They did encounter some leaders who refused to have any traffic with them, even to trade for their cargo, but they also found other Icelandic leaders who welcomed them, gave them an opportunity to display their goods, and deliver their message. The leaders who welcomed them did so despite the advice of some of their own followers, that it was a wicked thing to cast off the old ways, and they had to convince their followers to listen to those who came to preach this new faith, that this new faith might be a better thing. One leader, the host of Thangbrand and Gudleif, saw that on a morning Thangbrand rose early, pitched a tent, and sang mass. The leader questioned him,

"In whose memory do you keep this day?"

"In memory of Michael the archangel," Thangbrand said.

"What good does that angel do?" asked his host.

"Much," said Thangbrand. "He will weigh all the good that you have done, and he is so merciful, that whenever any one pleases him, he adds extra weight to the good deeds."

"I would like to have him for my friend."

"That you may well have," said Thangbrand, "only give yourself over to him by God's help this very day."

"I make this one condition," said his host, "that you pledge your word on his behalf that he will become my protector."

Thangbrand gave his word and his host and all his household were baptized.

When winter had passed, Thangbrand set out on horseback with his companion Gudleif to preach Christianity. Wherever he encountered men who denounced Christ, he drew a cross upon his shield and he challenged them, man to man, to single combat and, if they did not back down and accept Christ, he killed them. He rode from household to household and—despite sorcerers and witches, ambushes, and traps—he converted many a household. One day, as he was riding, the ground gave way beneath him and he felt himself and his horse falling. Thangbrand leaped from the saddle to safety, but his horse disappeared into the pit which had been dug by a sorcerer and his henchmen and the horse was never seen again. Thangbrand's companion, the manslayer Gudleif, searched for the sorcerer and found him on the heath; he pursued him across the heath until he had closed within range of a spear cast and he threw his spear, and by the strength of his arm he drove the spear completely through the body of the sorcerer.

Thus Thangbrand, by the power of his message and the power of his arm, continued to win converts, but only one household at a time, and the two companions decided to preach Christianity before a wider audience and win converts at a Thing (a meeting of the clans). To reach the Thing they had to fight their way through an ambush and at the Thing they had to defend themselves in a confrontation with the kinsman of the men they had killed. Christian and heathen might have come to blows, but Thangbrand had the support of the most influential leader there. Tempers cooled, he delivered his message, and he debated with a witch who told the crowd that Thor (the Norse god of Thunder) had challenged Christ to fight a single combat and Christ had been afraid to meet him.

Thangbrand replied, "I have heard tell that Thor would have been nothing but dust and ashes, if God had not willed that he should live."

By force and persuasion, and by the good fortune that seemed to follow him, Thangbrand was prevailing, but then his ship was wrecked and a witch spread the word that the shipwreck had been caused by Thor. Faced now with more stubborn opposition, because the shipwreck seemed to demonstrate that Thor was more powerful than Christ, Thangbrand decided to make a bold test of faith at a feast he was attending. This feast was expected to attract an unwelcome guest, a Berserker, who was immune to fire and sword, and Thangbrand challenged the sorcerers and witches to prove that their gods were stronger.

"We will sanctify two fires. You heathen men shall sanctify one and I the other, but a third shall be unsanctified; and if the Berserker is afraid of the one that I sanctify, but treads both the others, then you shall convert."

The head of the household agreed that that was a fair test and vowed to convert, himself and his whole household, if Thangbrand won the challenge. Thangbrand, his companion Gudleif, and the pagans kindled the three fires and all the men who had come to the feast took arms and stood back against the walls. No sooner had the fires caught and the men withdrawn from them to the benches around the wall than the Berserker burst into the room and strode through the heathen fire and the unsanctified fire, but he drew back from the Christian fire and went around it to strike a blow at the men on the benches. He swung his sword overhand and the blade caught in a crossbeam. Thangbrand stepped forward and struck the Berserker on his sword arm with a crucifix and the sword fell from the Berserker's hand; Thangbrand drew his own sword and plunged it into the Berserker's chest. Gudleif swung his sword and chopped the Berserker's arm off. The rest of the men then rushed the Berserker, struck him again and again, and killed him. The men at the feast concluded that Christ had prevailed and they converted to Christianity.

VLADIMIR IN RUSSIA

When Vladimir became king in Russia, he invited the powers who were his neighbors to send delegations to represent their religions to him. Vladimir received first (according to the story told by a Greek) a delegation from the Muslim Bulgars of the Volga; the delegates said to him, "You are a wise prince, but you are an infidel. Adopt our faith and revere Mohammad." Vladimir invited them to explain what would be required of him if he adopted their religion and they told him, "Prince, in this life you must be circumcised and abstain from pork and wine, but then in the next life in Paradise you will be able to enjoy every carnal pleasure— seventy virgins will be given to you and whichever you like the best, all the others will take on her appearance, and they will be your wives." Vladimir was tempted by the promise of the virgins, but he recoiled from the notion of circumcision and he would not give up pork and wine, "for," he said, "drinking is the greatest pleasure of the Rus."

The German Catholic emissaries who pressed the notion of rigorous fasting were no more welcome and the Jewish khazars gave offense not only when they enjoined him to be circumcised, to abstain from unclean flesh (pork and hare) and to observe the Sabbath, but also when they gave an unsatisfactory answer to the question, "Where is your homeland?"

"We have been scattered throughout the world," they told him, and he ordered them to depart from his realm because he did not want to suffer their fate.

The Greeks merely showed him a picture of judgment day, the righteous on their way to heaven, the damned on their way to eternal torment—and among the damned, of course, was Vladimir. Vladimir was not persuaded to convert by any of these emissaries so he sent envoys to report back to him on the practices of his neighbors and their various religions; the Muslims (the envoys reported) did not seem happy in their mosques and the stench was unbearable, the Romans lacked glory, but as for the Greeks "we did not know whether we were on earth or in heaven."

Whether Vladimir was motivated more by a search for the true religion than by ambition and power politics, no one can know, but when he besieged and took the Byzantine city of Kherson (a friendly informant explained to him how to cut off the hidden water supply), he accepted a deal offered to him by the Byzantine emperor: Vladimir would restore the city, convert to Christianity, and receive the sister of the emperor in marriage. Vladimir's union by marriage and by religion with the Byzantine imperial family and his native ability gave him the power to suppress all rivals and to unite his realm. He (and his son) maintained good relations with the Byzantines and with the kings of Sweden; he defended his borders, eliminated his internal opponents, enabled trade to pass unhindered between Swede and Byzantine, and he had no substantial foreign enemies.

The new, settled conditions in Russia left no place for Vikings.

IN IRELAND, ENGLAND, AND FRANCE

As in Russia, so in Ireland, England, and France the attackers became the defenders. They came to loot and they stayed to settle, farm, and trade; more came and occupied the land, and then found that they had to defend themselves from the next wave.

In Ireland "the sea spewed forth floods of foreigners over Erin, so that no haven, no landing-place, no stronghold, no fort, no castle might be found, but it was submerged by waves of Vikings and pirates." Norwegian Vikings in the first half of the ninth century overran Ulster, raided deep into Ireland, and desecrated temples and churches alike. When they discovered they could use one faction of the Irish against another, they set out to conquer the whole of Ireland and hold it and exploit it with a chain of fortresses and ports.

The Irish fought back. With the blessing of St. Patrick they invited the Danes, as the lesser of two evils, to help them fight the Norwegians. Together Irish and Dane defeated and annihilated the Norwegians, but the victory only called forth a large Norwegian expedition of revenge led by a "king." Irish, Danes, and Norwegians fought inconclusive wars across Ireland until the Danes accepted the Norwegian "king" as their own and the Danes and the Norwegians combined against the Irish. Gradually the survivors of the fighting learned to tolerate each other, while the disaffected left Ireland, first to raid and then to settle in northwest England.

In the 860s the Danes took advantage of a civil war between two English kings; they captured York and then defeated the two kings who had put aside their differences to defend themselves. By the 870s the Danish Vikings had occupied land and were farming it, and they were trading along the eastern and northern half of England; they intended to keep expanding and to conquer all of England, but unlike Viking expeditions in Ireland and France, the Danes who occupied England found themselves opposed by a truly great king, Alfred. The king of Denmark, whose expeditions were checked and driven back, was so impressed by the ability and character of Alfred that he made a pact with him and converted to Christianity. The Danes in England gradually followed his example and converted. The conversion made them no less covetous of their neighbor's land or of plunder, and no less ready to fight, but it did engender some respect in them for sacred Christian places.

Their conversion did not stop Alfred either. He organized his army, half to operate in the field, half to guard their homes, and, because he was not strong enough to fight the Danes in a set battle, he avoided set battles, but he dogged their invading forces, cut off raiding parties, and killed stragglers. He tried to contain the Danes with a chain of fortresses, he defended the rivers, and he built a small fleet. By such measures he regained control of London and was able to attack the Danes at sea, defeat them, and hang his captives as pirates. While Alfred's army was never a match for the Danes, army to army, Alfred so harried his enemies that in the end the Danes were content to remain within their own territory.

Alfred succeeded in containing the Danes; his successors, their borders secured by fortresses, continued to exert pressure on the Danes by building new fortresses in Danish territory; eventually they absorbed the Danes under English law and custom. The English and the Danes, together, cooperated to drive off Viking raiders (although the Danes were always ready to welcome new settlers).

Meanwhile in France in 911 the denuded and plundered region which came to be known as Normandy was ceded by Charles the Simple to Rollo, the leader of an army of Danes. Rollo had the nickname Walker, because he was so huge no horse would carry him. By treaty Rollo was to defend his land—and, as that included access to the Seine River, to stop Viking raids on Paris. Rollo paid nominal homage to Charles the Simple and accepted baptism. He divided the land among his subordinate leaders (who swore fealty to him) and he established strongholds throughout Normandy. He established laws to protect property—the Vikings were no more keen to lose their possessions than other men. He and his followers dominated and ruled the land, but, as a minority in a French-speaking majority, the "Norsemen" over the next two generations lost their Danish language to French and truly became "Normans" more than "Norsemen." Their subsequent invasion and conquest of England (and Sicily) devolved from Norman politics and ambition.

HARALD BLUETOOTH IN DENMARK

In 965 Harald Bluetooth "made the Danes Christians." Harald Bluetooth had a powerful adversary to the south in Christian Germany and he had powerful ambitions to rule all of Denmark and Norway and to control trade within and without the Baltic. Already many of his subjects and many more of the merchants who traversed Christian lands were Christian. At the very moment (the story goes) when it seemed most in his self-interest to convert to Christianity—to remove one reason for the German emperor to invade his realm—and he was debating the relative strength of Christ and the Norse gods, a Christian emissary drew upon his own hand a white-hot iron glove and it did not burn him. Harald was thus convinced (as well he might have been) of the power of the Christian God and he converted. Thereafter, so long as he did not disturb the Germans, they did not disturb him.

KING OLAF IN NORWAY

Olaf, the son of another Harald, had gone a-viking in his youth (at the age of twelve), had taken part in the fighting in England, and was one of many petty princes who could trace a "royal" lineage and claim the title of "king." In thirteen battles and innumerable raids he proved his courage and exhibited his ability to lead. (With freebooters, whether Viking, or, as we shall also see below, buccaneer and Barbary pirate, leaders tended to work their way up from the rowing bench or the gun deck, as it might be, and thus acquire an intimate knowledge of every aspect of ship and crew.)

Olaf served the kings of Normandy and in Normandy he was baptized. After eight years of freebooting, when he was about twenty years of age, he returned to Norway (in 1015). With 120 men he seized control of a point on the coast, established his authority there—he had a good strategic eye—and claimed kingship over all the Norwegians. He was fair, generous to his supporters, and merciless to his opponents—one by one he disposed of his rivals—and he used the support he won in the Things (the local councils) to establish the rule of law and to establish stability so that trade could flourish throughout his kingdom.

King Olaf, himself, was Christian, many of his subjects were Christians already—they had converted through the example and influence of Harald Bluetooth, the king of Denmark—and he was determined to extirpate all traces of pagan practice, to establish a national church, and to transform Norway into a Christian kingdom. He offered baptism, forgiveness for the errors arising from his subjects' ignorance, and membership in the church of Norway and the greater world of Christendom.

King Olaf had no patience for the stubborn and recalcitrant and when he heard that the people of the Trondhjem district had sacrificed animals and held a great feast in honor of the old gods, he ordered their leader Olver to report to him. Olver came and assured the king that the reports were false and that the feast was just a feast. Then in mid-winter the king received further reports of a feast and drinking in honor of the old gods and again King Olaf summoned Olver. Olver again assured the angry king that the people had not been honoring the old gods, but when at Easter King Olaf received yet one more report of pagan activity, he summoned his army, launched his ships, and paid a visit to Trondhjem. There he summoned his bailiff and the bailiff came with his wife and children and all his movable property and begged the king to protect him against the people of his district because they would soon know that he had informed the king that these people were honoring the old gods. The king inquired where the people were meeting, marched there in secret with 300 soldiers, surprised the revelers, drove off their cattle, and seized all their provisions. He captured the leaders and executed Olver and his closest associates; others he disfigured and released, some he fined, and some he kept as hostages. He let his soldiers pillage the district. Thus did King Olaf convert the people of Trondhjem.

Then when King Olaf heard that a prominent man named Dale-Gudbrand and his people refused Christianity, he marched his army into the territory of the heathen. Dale-Gudbrand led out his army and he intended to fight, but his army broke and ran. Olaf compelled Dale-Gudbrand to defend himself at a Thing. There on a rainy day Dale-Gudbrand asserted to the king that Thor was great and splendid and all of gold and if the Christians would pray away the rain they would see Thor for themselves; the next day the rain was gone, but the sky was still cloudy and Dale-Gudbrand said that if the Christians would bring out the sun they would see the magnificence of Thor.

"All can see Thor clearly unlike the God of the Christians, whom none can see."

On the third day as dawn lightened the sky in the east, the people carried in a golden statue of their god Thor. Olaf told his warrior Kolbein the Strong to strike the statue as hard as he could with his club when the people looked away.

"Look you," Dale-Gudbrand said as the people bowed before the statue. "You can see our god."

King Olaf pointed at the rising sun and said, "And there our God comes." All the people looked into the light, and, as they looked, Kolbein the Strong struck the statue of Thor with his club and the statue shattered and mice ran out and snakes slithered from the fragments and King Olaf shouted to the people, "See whom Thor protected—mice and snakes. Now choose! Become Christians or prepare to fight me."

Then Dale-Gudbrand stood up and said, "We have suffered much for our god Thor, but if he will not protect us, we will accept the God you believe in."

Dale-Gudbrand accepted baptism and a church was built on the spot.

With methods such as these King Olaf converted his kingdom, destroyed the sacred places of the pagans, executed pagans too stubborn to convert, and established a national church with a hierarchy of clergy. By force and by blandishments he made Norway a Christian kingdom and he freed it from Swedish domination by marrying a Swedish princess and by hanging the Swedish king's tax gatherers. In the end, however, he overreached himself with an unfortunate decision to enter into Danish politics; his meddling brought him to the attention of the powerful king of England, King Canute, and Olaf had to seek refuge in Russia.

Many kings, like Olaf, as they secured and expanded their dominions, found Christian concepts of central authority, control, discipline, and obedience appealing; more and more they saw pagans as disobedient, disruptive, and disloyal. Stability, good order, and Christianity seemed to march together. No room remained for the Vikings.

— PART IV —
THE WORLDWIDE STRUGGLE AGAINST PIRACY

Fifteen men on the dead man's chest-
Yo-ho-ho and a bottle of rum!
Drink and the devil had done for the rest-
Yo-ho-ho and a bottle of rum!

12

The Buccaneers

Once the Spanish had achieved domination in the New World, they were determined that no one would interfere with that domination: Spanish colonists were required by law to associate only with members of the Catholic faith and they were to eschew all other contact; they were to trade only with the mother country and no one else; and if, per chance, they desired or required supplies that they could not obtain through their own efforts or from the mother country, then they were to do without. The colonists paid lip service to the law and otherwise did what they believed that they had to do in order to survive and prosper. They bought, or bartered for, the necessities that the Spanish authorities could not provide to them in an illicit market provided by foreign merchants, and, thereby, they encouraged the foreigners, the majority of whom were British and French. As the merchants prospered and trade grew, and the Spanish authorities became more intransigent, their very intransigence seemed to guarantee the value of the prize they were protecting, and foreign governments rushed to establish colonies in the Spanish New World.

The Spanish attacked and destroyed the first colony established by the French in Florida, and, while they failed to prevent or destroy the English colony at St. Kitts, they intercepted several English ships and "cut off the hands, feet, noses, and ears of the crews and smeared them with honey and tied them to trees to be tortured by flies and other insects." The Spanish authorities justified their brutality as a legitimate punishment of pirates; the English authorities and the French asserted just as vehemently that their ships were manned with honest colonists and merchants—they publicly disavowed pirates. The French crown claimed that as it had no fortifications in the New World and therefore no juridical presence, it had no legal responsibility for the actions of Frenchmen there and the English crown affirmed that it had issued no commissions and that Englishmen who turned to piracy were acting as individuals; both governments granted the Spanish crown the right to deal with pirates as it saw fit without reprisal. Despite the avowals and expostulations, all the parties—Spanish, French, and English—were being disingenuous: the Spanish because they opposed not just pirates but also honest colonists and merchants, the British and French because, in truth, they were determined, by whatever means necessary, to carve out a portion of the New World for themselves and, in the furtherance of that purpose, they did encourage attacks upon Spanish shipping.

The first merchants settled in Hispaniola (Haiti and Santa Domingo), where they found plentiful game (domestic animals abandoned and gone wild).

In or about the middle of the seventeenth century [a former buccaneer writes] the Island of San Domingo, or Hispaniola as it was then called, was haunted and overrun by a singular community of savage, surly, fierce and filthy men. They were chiefly composed of French colonists, whose ranks had from time to time been enlarged by liberal contributions from the slums and alleys of more than one European city and town. These people went dressed in shirt and pantaloons of coarse linen cloth, which they steep in the blood of the animals they slaughtered. They wore round caps, boots of hog skin drawn over their feet, and belts of raw hide, in which they stuck their sabers and knives. They also armed themselves with firelocks which threw a couple of balls, each weighing two ounces. The places where they dried and salted their meat were called "boucans," and from this term they came to be styled *bucaniers* or *buccaneers*, as we spell it. They were hunters by trade and savages in their habits. They chased and slaughtered horned cattle and trafficked with the flesh, and their favorite food was raw marrow from the bones of the beasts which they shot. They ate and slept on the ground, their table was a stone, their bolster the trunk of a tree, and their roof the hot and sparkling heavens of the Antilles.

The original buccaneers numbered 500–600 men—French mostly—who hunted the wild cattle in Hispaniola. A band of half a dozen hunters, together with their indentured servants, would establish a camp where they would live for a year or two and from which they would set out early every morning to track the cattle. When they shot one, they butchered it and drank its "brandy"—the blood-hot marrow; these men lived exclusively on meat—and they continued to hunt, until every man in their group had killed a bull. Then they returned to camp and they or their servants stretched the hides out.

The life was hard in itself and dangerous because the Spanish authorities were determined to eliminate the buccaneers, in preference, by hunting them down and burning them at the stake. This brutal punishment, the Spanish hoped, would deter others from infringing on Spanish authority but the effect was quite opposite to the intention: the buccaneers were not deterred, but they learned to hate the Spanish and to fight to the death. Neither were the buccaneers so easy to find, nor, when found, easy to subdue. The soldiers who were charged with carrying out this mission exercised extreme caution and tried either to catch the buccaneers asleep or to surprise them from ambush. As the Spanish soldiers were required constantly to operate on the buccaneers' terrain, and yet did not have the woodcraft of the buccaneers, and, as they were expected to trade shots with the buccaneers, and yet did not have the buccaneers' proficiency with the musket—the hunters' one constant and continual amusement was target practice (they could drop an orange from a tree with a single shot that cut the stem and did not touch either branch or fruit)—few confrontations worked out well for the soldiers. Even if they surprised a solitary hunter and surrounded him, they could not expect the hunter to surrender (because of the horrible fate awaiting him if he did) and they could, and did, expect, as he leveled his musket at them, that one of them would die. Often enough the Spanish soldiers retreated when confronted by the buccaneer's leveled musket.

If the buccaneers were not captured or killed by the Spanish and otherwise had a successful hunt that filled their boat with hides, they would return to Hispaniola, sell their produce, squander the profits in a month's debauch, and return to the hunt with new supplies (musket, powder, shot, fresh clothing—bought by the few provident hunters before their debauch, by the rest on credit after). Not all men hunted the cattle; others supported themselves by hunting pigs or growing tobacco. No one had an easy life, except perhaps the men at the very top, but life was harshest for those at the bottom—the white indentured servants. These servants owed three years of service to their masters and many of the masters were determined to squeeze a lifetime of work from those three years—one master boasted that he had beaten to death more than a hundred servants and another, when he was advised by his servant that the Good Lord had ordained of every seven days that six are to labor and one to rest, replied with a stick to emphasize the words, "Get on, you bugger; my commands are these—six days shalt thou collect hides, and the seventh shalt thou bring them to the beach"—and yet men still offered their service in exchange for passage to the New World where they hoped to make a living and even gain a fortune.

The living was there to be made: the French and British planters and the Spanish colonists wanted the fresh meat, jerky, and hides provided by the buccaneers and the buccaneers, though their living conditions were harsh, nonetheless found them tolerable; they might never have abandoned the hunting life for the equally harsh, and rather more precarious, life of a pirate had the Spanish authorities only accepted the situation—that a relatively small group of ill-disciplined foreigners were operating outside their control—but the Spanish authorities in their insistence upon their own short-sighted trading and settlement policies treated honest merchants as pirates and settlers as criminals.

The Spanish were determined to uproot the buccaneers. They adopted a strategy of striking at the means of the buccaneers' livelihood—the wild cattle—to drive the hunters out of Hispaniola; in the process they gave the buccaneers more reasons to hate and despise the Spanish. The Spanish strategy did succeed in driving the buccaneers from Hispaniola; the survivors gathered on the little island of Tortuga (so named for its turtles), built their homes, founded a state based on egalitarian principles, and lived as best they could, mainly, at first, by turning to the sea and attacking the local ship traffic in hides and selling the hides from a market in Tortuga. Then one spectacular exploit showed them the path to fortune.

Florida

Havana

Cuba

Tortuga

Hispaniola

Jamaica

Santa
Domingo

St. Kitts

Port Royal

Mariegalante

Caribbean   Sea

Santa Catalina

Pacific Ocean

Cartagena

Gibraltar

Caracas

Porto
Bello

Maracaibo

Pigeon Island

Gibraltar

Panama City

The Caribbean with an Inset Map of Maracaibo

"Peter the Great" was a Frenchman from Dieppe. In 1602 he was the captain of a crew of twenty-eight men in a leaky boat out of supplies and ready to turn home when his lookouts spotted a lone Spanish ship. Peter's boat had not gone undetected, but when the Spanish lookouts of the lone ship, which happened to be the flagship of a Spanish treasure fleet, spotted Peter's boat and warned the captain, the captain—who already had been warned of the dangers of pirates—gave a contemptuous reply:

"I'm not afraid of a ship my size. Why should I fear a little boat like that?"

Peter followed the treasure ship until dusk and then he challenged his crew to board and seize the ship: "they are armed with pistols and cutlasses and so are we, and thus they have no better chance of victory than do we." While the pirates were swearing an oath to support each other to the death, their surgeon drilled a hole in the bottom of their boat to forestall a change of heart; the boat was foundering even as they came alongside and boarded the treasure ship. They caught the Spanish crew completely by surprise.

"Where had these pirates come from?"

"There is no boat!"

"Jesus!" the Spanish cried, "They are demons!"

The pirates killed the few Spanish sailors who put up any resistance, they occupied the gunroom, and caught the captain and his officers playing cards in his cabin. Of the prisoners "Peter the Great" put most ashore but kept enough to man the ship and sailed directly home to France. Before he entered port he obtained a privateer's commission (to cover his act) and then he sold the ship and lived the rest of his life comfortably away from the sea.

The success of Peter the Great inspired not only the hunters and planters to trade their harsh life ashore for a boat and a chance at riches, but brought many adventurers from Europe to Hispaniola; the attack of 1602 gave a new definition to the word *buccaneer*. The new breed of buccaneer ranged farther and their successes—two ships laden with silver were captured—encouraged more raids and financed a larger enterprise so that the buccaneers within a few years of the exploit of Peter the Great employed twenty-some boats. The buccaneers raided the ill-defended Spanish settlements and followed the treasure fleets, ready to attack any ship that became separated from the main fleet. The Spanish had to detail frigates to guard their trade.

The successful captains became famous, figures of romance, the French as famous as the English, but fame was often hard won as pseudonyms such as *Pegleg* attest. Still the possible rewards were great and a man only needed to have a boat to become a pirate captain: a crew would appear if a captain just announced that he intended to go buccaneering. Each volunteer crewmember brought his own armaments: gun, powder, shot, and cutlass and the volunteers and captain together would arrange for food—that is, meat—which they would purchase from a hunter (for a share of the plunder) or requisition from a Spanish farmer. (If the farmer was ungenerous, the pirates hanged him.) Then the crew salted the meat and prepared the boat. Crew and captain ate the same rations on the boat. (One crew, who caught their captain with special dishes, confiscated them and ate them while the captain had to be satisfied with the crew's rations.)

Once they had prepared the boat, they voted where to cruise and they worked out the finances: they calculated a fixed sum of money to be paid to the captain and to anyone who was severely injured—who lost a limb or had a wound that pierced his body—and then captain and crew calculated the shares, six or seven shares to the captain and his boat, one share or more depending on his specialty to each member of the crew, half a share to the ship's boys, and so on. Each member of the crew swore an oath on the *Bible* that he would not sequester any piece of plunder—the punishment for violating the oath was banishment without a share. Differences of opinion were settled by duel. If the duel was considered unfair—a shot in the back, for instance—the perpetrator would be tied to a tree and shot to death by a man he selected himself.

After a successful voyage with adequate plunder taken, the agreed payments were made first and then the rest of the loot was divided into equal shares and distributed as agreed; sometimes, if the pirates captured a ship better than their own, they would man the captured ship and burn their own, or, if they had a large enough crew, man both. As for the captured crew, if they had not enraged the pirates by too stout a defense of their ship, they were put ashore, although the pirates often solicited volunteers from their captives, or drafted the unwilling, to serve on board the pirate ship as indentured servants for a period of three years after which the servants were welcome to join the crew as equals. The buccaneers were desperate men living a desperate life, they risked their comfort, their health, and their lives for booty, they judged the most heinous crime among themselves to be theft—the punishment was death—and yet, if they thought the booty they had taken was insufficient, they might choose up sides and fight it out, survivors take it all.

Even when the pirates failed, still they believed that a fortune lay out there waiting for them and the knowledge that few succeeded and many failed could not dissuade them.

PIERRE FRANÇOIS

Pierre François and his crew of twenty-six men were frustrated with a long and unsuccessful beat in search of prey and so they decided to try a risky attack on the pearl fisheries that were guarded by a Spanish man-of-war. They rowed their little pirate boat up to the flagship of the pearl fleet (a ship with eight guns and a crew of sixty) and they demanded that the pearl ship surrender—the crew of the pearl ship had thought the pirates were part of their own fleet until they heard the ultimatum. The captain of the pearl ship refused to surrender and he fired one broadside into the pirate ship before they were able to close and board; then rather than fight the pirates hand-to-hand, the Spanish crew capitulated. Their captain believed that the man-of-war, which was on station to protect them, would soon come to their rescue and deal with the pirates, but François sank his own ship and raised the Spanish flag.

At first the ruse was successful. The captain of the man-of-war assumed that the pirates had been defeated and their ship sunk; he fired a "victory" salute and was satisfied with the situation until the pearl ship headed for the open sea. At last he tumbled to the ruse and ordered the man-of-war under his command to slip its cable and pursue. All the rest of the day and into the night he pursued, the pirates kept on all sail despite increasing winds, but hour by hour the man-of-war gained on them and forced the pirates to gamble that their mast would hold long enough to allow them to escape in the dark; the wind continued to increase, the Spaniards continued to close, and the mainmast shattered and came down. The man-of-war caught them, the two ships fought a fierce battle, and the pirates resisted so stoutly that finally the Spanish captain, who could not take a chance of sinking the pearl ship and its valuable cargo, allowed the pirates to surrender on terms—that they not be put to hard labor and that they be sent to Spain at the first opportunity. With regret the pirates gave up the shipload of pearls.

BARTHOLOMEW THE PORTUGUESE

Bartholomew the Portuguese, with thirty men and a little ship of four guns, attacked a Spanish ship of twenty guns and seventy passengers and crew. Bartholomew and his crew closed and tried to board, they were beaten off; they fired their guns again, and closed again, and boarded. Ten pirates were killed outright in the struggle and four severely wounded; thirty of the Spanish were killed defending their ship. The pirates found a cargo of 120,000 pounds of cacao and 70,000 pieces of eight, enough wealth to make each of them a rich man, but hardly had they celebrated their good fortune when they met a Spanish fleet of three sail; they were overpowered and had to surrender. When the Spanish sailed into port and word that they had prisoners leaked out, the local townspeople demanded that the buccaneers be handed over to them immediately except only Bartholomew himself, who, they asked, be kept safely imprisoned onboard the ship until they had had time to build a gallows. Bartholomew discovered what they were up to, cut his guard's throat, and jumped into the harbor.

They searched for him for days, starting him from his hiding places and chasing him across rivers and through jungle. He finally made his way to a natural harbor where, by chance, a pirate ship was anchored and he convinced the captain to lend him a boat and men, so that he could return and recapture the ship that he had captured once already. The pirates took the prize crew completely by surprise— they thought that the little boat was bringing them supplies—and Bartholomew cut the anchor cables and made off with the ship, absent its rich cargo; his luck was short lived: on his way to Jamaica he ran aground and the ship was destroyed. Bad luck continued to dog him, but did not diminish his zeal for the pursuit of Spanish wealth, until at last he died "in the greatest wretchedness in the world."

ROCK

The Dutch buccaneer Rock had been driven out of Brazil by the Portuguese; thereafter he had settled in Jamaica where he enlisted in a crew of buccaneers, impressed them with the force of his personality, and convinced some of them to leave their ship for a boat under his command. With this little boat he captured a Spanish ship laden with money, brought it into Jamaica, disposed of the cargo, and then, as so many buccaneers did, he and his crew squandered their wealth. Rock himself drank more than he could handle, he became belligerent, attacked the first person he met, and chopped off his arm. One pirate paid a prostitute 500 pieces of eight just to see her naked. Others bought a barrel of wine, opened it in the street, and gave every passerby the choice either to drink with them or to be killed. One bought a tub of butter and threw handfuls at passersby. All of them were encouraged in their indiscretions by the tavern keepers, of course, and they were given easy credit and indulged until their money ran out and the bills came due; then the tavern keepers were quick to demand a reckoning, and, no payment forthcoming, to have the debtor seized and sold into slavery to pay off his debt. Money flowed from the pirates to the merchants and soon the penniless pirates had to return to sea with all its risks of death by accident, combat, duel, and shipwreck.

Rock, like the other buccaneering captains, took to the seas to seek his fortune, but he hated the Spanish so much that he roasted his captives on a spit. He was prepared to run any risk rather than to surrender. He and his crew of thirty were once shipwrecked; they made it to shore, but the Spanish had seen them, and a force of a hundred Spanish cavalry pursued them and caught them. Rock swore to his men that he would never surrender, he convinced them they could hold out, and they fought with their muskets against the pursuing cavalry. Some they killed and some they wounded and knocked off their horses; the survivors abandoned the wounded men and their horses and fled. Rock ordered his men to kill the wounded and seize their horses, and the pirates rode away with the cavalry following at a respectful distance; as the pirates rode along, they observed a Spanish canoe being paddled ashore to cut timber for a boat at sea. The pirates attacked the Spaniards, killed them, seized their canoe, and then six pirates paddled it out to the unsuspecting boat and captured it. Rock and the rest of the pirates manned the boat, used it to capture a ship, and sailed the ship to Jamaica where they sold it, squandered the proceeds, and put to sea again.

Rock was wrecked again and captured too, and his captors intended to hang him on the spot, but Rock had prepared for this mischance: he kept in his pocket a note—he had written it himself—which appeared to be a compact entered into by the buccaneers to avenge him if he were hanged. His captors reluctantly refrained from putting the noose around his neck and instead extracted a vow from him that he would give up piracy and then they sent him off to Spain. The oath was as false as the note and Rock returned to the Caribbean to harass the Spanish again.

The careers of these three captains—François, Bartholomew, and Rock—and others like them, might have led thoughtful men to conclude that the slim chance of winning and keeping a fortune in the New World was not worth the enormous risks and the desperate life of a buccaneer, but, alas for the Spanish, there were plenty of men of an adventurous spirit who concluded rather that treasure was there for the plucking and all it required was courage and a little luck.

When the buccaneers found their easy pickings by sea curtailed because the Spanish were forming convoys and discouraging ships from sailing independently, they turned to the Spanish settlements themselves. The buccaneers were relentless. No ship could intercept all of them, no garrison could stop them, they would travel for days up rivers, attack while heavily outnumbered, defend themselves vigorously against any odds, loot churches, hold prominent citizens for ransom, and escape to an impregnable sanctuary where they would sell what they had taken, spend what they were paid, and go to sea again.

—— 13 ——

Tortuga and the Pirate Utopia

In 1640 a company of fifty French Calvinists led by a French Calvinist engineer departed from St. Kitts, attacked the Spanish on Tortuga, drove them off, and occupied the island. Their leader employed his engineering skills to design and build an impregnable fort—they cut steps into a rock cliff, higher and higher until the angle became too steep for steps and then they fixed an iron ladder to reach the top. On the top they build a fort, called the "Dove-cote," accessible only by the steps and the ladder, and they armed it with cannon. The fort soon proved itself: a Spanish fleet called at the port, the guns opened fire, sank several ships, and forced the rest to retreat.

Thus, from the scheme of a Calvinist engineer, a settlement was founded that was to prosper for almost a century. Here meat and hides, tobacco and sugar, brandy and rum, gunpowder and guns, cloth for sails and clothes, all could be purchased or bartered against the plunder of the sea. Here adventurers from France and Britain came and here, side by side with the original founders, these men, harsh and cruel as they might be to their victims at sea, developed an egalitarian society with strict rules enforced among members of the society. When a Frenchman or an Englishman had served out his time as an indentured servant, he would seek another man to be his partner and the two would strike a deal to work together, to share whatever they had and whatever they acquired, until death; at the death of one partner, all the possessions would pass to the survivor, excepting only that the survivor was to provide for his partner's wife. Once the agreement was made, one partner would go freebooting while the other partner farmed or hunted. Hunting was easy and game was abundant—cattle, horses, so many wild pigs that it seemed that hundreds could be killed day after day and never diminish the population, flocks of pigeons, crab, fruit, palm wine—enough to feed the whole island. As the settlement prospered, it attracted more pirates and more plunder, more hunters, farmers, and merchants, and it became more prosperous and powerful.

François Lolonois ("François of Olonne") came to the Caribbean as an indentured servant. When he had served his time, he joined the hunters and then went to sea with the pirates. His courage brought him to the notice of the governor of Tortuga and the governor assigned him a ship and ordered him to attack the Spanish. (France and Spain were then at war.) Lolonois hated the Spanish—he boasted that he had never spared a prisoner's life—and as he gave no quarter so he expected no quarter. He had already acquired a fearsome reputation when he and his crew were wrecked, cast on shore, and attacked by the Spanish. Most of his crew were killed and Lolonois was wounded; he knew what his fate would be if he were taken captive, so he smeared himself with his own blood, burrowed among the corpses, and feigned dead, while the rest of his crew were marched off as prisoners.

When the Spanish had withdrawn, Lolonois escaped into the jungle, made his way to a Spanish town, and there convinced some slaves to run away with him. They stole a boat and sailed to Tortuga. As he made his escape, the Spanish learned from their prisoners that Lolonois was "dead;" they lit bonfires and thanked God for their deliverance. While they were celebrating, Lolonois was acquiring another boat and recruiting another crew. He and twenty men returned to the Cuban coast and attacked the inshore shipping; the news of his depredations was brought to the governor by some fishermen who reported that the pirate Lolonois was back.

The governor knew that Lolonois was "dead," but he told the fishermen that he would sent a ship with ten guns and a crew of ninety men to settle the issue. The fishermen went back to the coast and warned Lolonois that a ten-gun ship was coming. They thought the news would scare him away but Lolonois saw the threat rather as an opportunity to acquire a fine ship. When the Spanish ship arrived and anchored in an estuary, the pirates disguised themselves as fishermen and paddled canoes up on both sides of the ship to reconnoiter. The Spanish hailed the "fishermen" and asked if they had seen the pirates.

The "fishermen" replied, "No, they have all run away."

The Spanish thus were confirmed in the conclusions they had already reached, that the news of their arrival would scare the pirates away, and they slept soundly in their misconception until they were wakened in the dense mists of dawn by the howls and war cries of pirates. The Spanish fired three broadsides in the direction of the voices, all in vain, because the pirates in their canoes had closed on the ship. Out of the mist they came, scrambled up the sides of the ship, and drove the panic-stricken crew below deck. Lolonois spoke to the terrified crew and promised them that they would be spared if they would come up, one at a time, to prove they had no weapons on them. As they came up, each man was seized and Lolonois, himself wielding the sword, cut their heads off—except that he spared one man to carry the governor a letter stating that Lolonois would grant no quarter to Spaniards and, as for the governor himself, Lolonois hoped someday to catch him and do to him what the governor had intended to do to the pirate. The governor was so furious that he issued an order to exterminate all buccaneers, but, before he could put his plan into action, his subjects who lived on the coast begged him to reconsider:

the buccaneers, they told him, could, and would, kill a hundred of them for every buccaneer he killed.

After Lolonois had gotten to know his new ship, he conceived a plan to assemble a fleet, recruit some 500 men, and raid the wealthy Spanish settlement of Maracaibo. He put out the word that he required men and ships for a large and profitable undertaking and, while they were mustering, he went to sea to collect supplies. At sea he met a Spanish ship of sixteen guns and fought it for three hours before he forced it to surrender (and added it to his prospective fleet). He intercepted a supply ship armed with eight guns and loaded with munitions and money to pay Spanish troops; he fired warning shots at the ship and it surrendered without a fight. Among his prisoners were some—one was a Frenchman—who were familiar with the seas around Maracaibo and who were willing to act as guides in exchange for their freedom and some of the plunder. He lured a former buccaneer out of retirement to command the land forces. This buccaneer, Michel the Basque, had accumulated so much plunder that he had decided to retire to a life on shore but when he heard news of the expedition he offered his services. Thus Lolonois put together a fleet of ten vessels, including his little ship of ten guns and the captured ship of sixteen, and the fleet sailed for Maracaibo.

Maracaibo lay on a strait at the head of a lake within a bay and was protected by a garrison on an island, Pigeon Island, in a fort that could bring fire upon any ship trying to enter the bay. About 4,000 people lived in Maracaibo and another 1,500 in Gibraltar, a large village on the far shore of the lake. The citizens of this region harvested timber, cultivated cacao and tobacco, and raised sheep. They were prosperous and had already suffered one pirate raid, so they had taken measures to prepare for another, they knew about Lolonois' raid because of the pirates' extensive and open preparations, and the citizens of the two towns and the garrison of the island fort were on the alert. The commander of the fort had figured out the pirates' expected line of advance if they landed on the island and he had laid an ambush for them, but when the pirates arrived, they dispatched a scouting party that discovered the ambush. The pirates surrounded the ambush site and killed almost all the Spanish troops; they advanced rapidly on the fort and in less than three hours they had taken it.

Meanwhile the few survivors of the ambush had fled directly to Maracaibo with the terrifying news that a huge force of pirates—four times their actual numbers—was on the way. The people did not wait for news from the fort—they had little confidence in the garrison there; they gathered what belongings they could and fled by boat, horse, and foot. Even as they were fleeing, the pirates were bringing their fleet into the bay, landing on the island, and razing the fort, but they did not know the people had fled, they believed that the city would be vigorously defended, and spent the rest of the day in preparation for the assault on Maracaibo. In the morning they approached the city cautiously and maneuvered their ships to provide supporting fire for the landing party. To their surprise, they found that the city was deserted.

They occupied the city, set guards, searched out food and drink, and then Lolonois allowed the pirates a night of celebration and rest to recoup from months at sea. In the morning the pirates searched the surrounding area for people and their treasure. (Plunder, after all, was their chief motive in taking Maracaibo.) The pirates caught some twenty people and Lolonois wasted no time in putting them on the rack and demanding that they tell him where their money was, but even on the rack no one would talk, so Lolonois seized one of the prisoners and in the sight of the others hacked off his limbs. The pirate's utter savagery persuaded the prisoners to talk, but they could only reveal where their own possessions were, because each person had chosen a secret hiding place for himself, and no one had shared that secret with anyone else.

After two weeks of futile search, the pirates decided to board their ships and attack Gibraltar where, they assumed, the people of Maracaibo had sought refuge. The citizens of Gibraltar had already sent an appeal for help to the governor, an experienced military man. He acted quickly, brought about 400 troops to Gibraltar, and drafted another 400 men there. He threw up fortifications and emplaced sixteen cannon along the approaches to the town. He had confidence in his troops and his own ability, and did not expect to have much trouble with irregular troops such as the pirates.

When the pirates arrived they saw that the direct approach to the town was blocked by a wall, guns, and massed troops; Lolonois warned his men that they were in for a real fight, but the risk would be worth it, because the more men arrayed against them, the more loot there must be to be protected. His men agreed.

"Forward then," he said. "I will lead and I will shoot the first man who shows cowardice."

At dawn 380 pirates landed. Lolonois called, "Follow me," and they advanced, not by the direct route as the governor had expected, but rather by a flanking route through a swamp. Nonetheless, the swamp was within range of the guns and the pirates had to endure a continuous fire until they reached dry land. As soon as they reached dry land, the governor launched a sortie against them, but the pirates easily disposed of the attacking force, advanced, and assaulted the fortifications. They encountered grapeshot, musket fire, and a vigorous defense that forced them back. Lolonois feigned defeat and turned a withdrawal into what seemed to be a panicky rout back to the swamp: the Spanish charged from their works to finish the job and drive the pirates into the swamp, but once the troops were too far from their fortifications to fall back, the pirates wheeled around and charged them, the Spaniards broke and fled for their fortifications, but the pirates came hot on their heels, too close for the guns to fire on them, and they surged over the wall. The Spaniards surrendered on condition only that their lives be spared.

The pirates herded all their prisoners together into a church and posted guards. They thought that they had defeated one part of the Spanish forces and they expected a counterattack, but, when they counted the dead, they discovered that they had killed more than 500 men, and taken another 150 men prisoner, and they realized that they had no more to fear from the Spanish. (They themselves had

had forty killed and thirty wounded—most of the wounded died from gangrene.) They disposed of the corpses by loading them on two boats and sinking them in the middle of the lake.

After a brief respite they began to collect the booty; they sent search parties out to scour the countryside and collected slaves from the nearby plantation. They fed their prisoners on donkey and mule meat while they ate sheep, pigs, beef, and poultry. Some of the prisoners refused to eat mule and starved to death. The pirates took all the money, some by force, some by way of payments for food. After a month they threatened to burn the town if they were not paid a ransom. At first the Spanish refused, but when the pirates set some buildings on fire, the Spanish agreed to pay. The pirates demanded ransom for their prisoners and they carried off their loot and the slaves (for whom no one would pay) to Maracaibo; there they looted the churches and demanded a ransom for that city and a pilot to guide them through the channel (a demand gladly acceded to by the Spaniards). While they waited for the ransom, they provisioned themselves for the return voyage, and when the ransom was paid, the pirates boarded their ships, returned to Tortuga, and divided up the spoils. For a moment they were wealthy, but within a short time they had spent everything and they turned to Lolonois to figure out a way to fill their pockets again.

The sack of Maracaibo and Gibraltar had made Lolonois famous among the buccaneers and, when he conceived a plan to make an expedition against the Spanish settlements in the interior of Nicaragua on Lake Nicaragua, he had no trouble attracting a force of 700 men. The nature of the terrain they would be traversing—the necessity of navigating rivers into the lake—required small craft, but the acquisition of small craft was not a problem: the pirates raided fishermen and took their canoes. Once supplied the pirate fleet reached the coast of Nicaragua without difficulty, but then Lolonois' luck changed. The fleet was blown off course into the Gulf of Honduras, supplies ran low, and he and his men had to beat back and forth along the coast and raid the coastal dwellers for food—they found only just enough to keep themselves fed and leave the coastal dwellers destitute. They seized one small town and demanded that their Spanish captives answer questions. If the Spaniards did not immediately satisfy Lolonois with their answers, he had the poor wretches stretched on the rack, and, if still they did not answer, he would slash them with his cutlass. Some of his victims agreed to lead the pirates to a treasure, just to escape the torture, but when they failed to uncover any, they were hacked to death.

Two prisoners agreed to lead Lolonois and 300 men along a trail to an inland town, but the Spanish had laid ambushes along the trail. The pirates fought their way through one ambush after another, took prisoners, interrogated them, and murdered those who would not cooperate. *Was there another path?* When one prisoner was defiant, Lolonois cut open his chest, pulled out the heart, took a bite of it, and thrust it in the face of another prisoner—*talk!* The prisoner, thus cowed, agreed that there was another path, but a difficult one. The pirates followed it and found it so rugged that it seemed worse than the path with the ambushes; they returned to the first path and Lolonois declared, "Those Spanish buggers will pay for this!"

After the pirates had fought through three ambushes and killed every Spanish soldier they encountered (to leave fewer to fight in the future), they came upon the town and immediately assaulted the breastworks. The Spanish troops leveled their muskets, the pirates dropped flat, the first volley went over their heads and they sprang to their feet and attacked with musket and grenade. They were forced back. They came on again, crawling, a few men at a time, and taking aimed shots. They were better shots than the Spaniards and their continuous aimed fire wounded and killed many of the garrison; toward evening the Spaniards asked for terms and the pirates agreed to grant them two hours to gather their possessions and clear out. The pirates lived up to the letter of the agreement, but, when the two hours had passed, the pirates stopped all Spaniards still within reach and robbed them. They pursued those who had already gotten away.

The pirates rested, looted the town, set it on fire, and then returned to the coast. There they learned from their mates that a ship from Spain was due to arrive. They decided to wait for it, the wait stretched into three months, and the Spanish ship turned out to have forty-two cannon and a crew of 130 men. Nonetheless, Lolonois attacked with his one ship of twenty-eight guns and a smaller vessel. After an exchange of gunfire that poured out clouds of smoke between the ships, Lolonois was forced to give way, but four canoes of pirates slipped through the smoke, came alongside the Spanish ship, the pirates boarded, and the crew surrendered. The pirates searched the captive ship and they discovered that for all long wait and dangerous battle, the ship had been mostly unloaded and contained little booty.

Many of the pirates were dissatisfied. The first-timers had expected, more or less, that pieces of eight would rain down on them from the skies and even veterans of other voyages found the result not commensurate with the effort. They blamed Lolonois and they turned to other captains in other ships until Lolonois was left alone with his own ship and his crew of 300 men. He, too, was ready to give up the expedition, but his ship ran aground and the crew had to settle on an island, salvage the ship, and use its timbers to build a longboat; the construction of the boat occupied them long enough (six months) that they sowed and reaped a crop of beans and corn. When the boat was completed the men drew lots to see who would set out with their captain to find a ship. Those who had won the lot put to sea, but they were observed by a Spanish ship and forced to flee, and then they were attacked by Indians. Lolonois was captured, roasted, and eaten. Meanwhile, those who had been left on the island remained there for four more months before a passing ship of buccaneers picked them up and finally returned the survivors to Tortuga.

The Spanish attacked the buccaneers on Tortuga again and again and from time to time succeeded in driving them off, but each time, as soon as the Spanish withdrew, the buccaneers returned, and the Spanish would have to collect troops and ships and invade the island all over again, until, finally, they wore the buccaneers

down and forced them to seek another refuge. (The buccaneers had already begun to squabble among themselves as they began to identify themselves more as
French or English, or Protestant or Catholic, than as buccaneer.) The Spanish had
recently lost the island of Jamaica to the English and the new colonists at Port
Royal believed that it was only a matter of time before the Spanish tried to retake
the island, so they welcomed the buccaneers and, in exchange for the protection
afforded by their men and ships, offered Port Royal as the principle headquarters
of the buccaneers.

Buccaneering had entered a new phase. The Spanish no longer had to deal
with scattered attacks of rapacious individuals but with a concerted attack on their
possessions aided and abetted by the governments of England and France, both of
which wanted to assert their claims to a portion of the new world. In these changed
circumstances some buccaneer captains became national heroes.

— 14 —

Henry Morgan

The most famous, and ultimately successful, of all the buccaneers was Henry Morgan.

Morgan was born into the British yeoman class, and could have lived a safe, secure, and prosperous life, but he was drawn by a sense of adventure, and, perhaps, the lure of treasure, to run away to sea and to work his passage to Jamaica. There, like so many others before him, he was sold into indentured servitude (although for the rest of his life, while he did not deny the worst atrocities committed in his name and sometimes by his authority, he always claimed that he had never been indentured). He certainly did not remain in servitude, but rather worked out his time, joined the buccaneers, and soon rose to prominence among them. He was a natural born leader, known for his courage, judgment, and good luck: he was as lucky with dice as he was with plunder. While other buccaneers squandered their loot in debauchery and gambling, he held on to what he had won, and added to it, until he had amassed enough money to buy a ship. Owning a ship made him a captain and he was able to form a company.

His skill and luck—he captured several prizes on his first voyage—attracted the attention of a successful English buccaneer, Edward Mansfield, and Mansfield invited Morgan to join a marauding expedition along the coast of Central America. Mansfield was an ambitious man and had grander plans than a single raid to gather loot: he had his eye on the island of St. Catalina (where the Spaniards had a fort); St. Catalina, while not important in itself, would furnish the buccaneers with a secure base off the coast of Nicaragua and Costa Rica from which they could dominate the whole area and raid at will. Mansfield landed on the island, attacked the fort, and forced the garrison to surrender. Then he strengthened the fortifications, constructed some new gun emplacements, and detailed a hundred men to hold the fort and the island.

Mansfield intended that in the future a permanent garrison would occupy this island and support itself by growing crops—the island had ample fertile land—but for now his garrison only needed to maintain itself while he convinced the British authorities to lend material support to his scheme; he found, however, that the authorities were wary. The governor of Jamaica refused his request—he feared that any public support would displease his sovereign, arouse the Spanish against him, and weaken his own forces—and yet, just the same, he approved of a scheme whereby the British could secure a base from which to expand their influence in the Caribbean and thereby weaken the Spanish, and also furnish an opportunity for personal enrichment. Therefore he instructed a ship to go and scout the situation and even lend aid to the buccaneers, if necessary, but he kept the news of his intentions from the pirate, so that he could disavow a scheme that was all too apt to come to a bad end.

Mansfield, then, since he believed that his scheme had been rejected in Jamaica, set out to enlist other support, but while on the voyage, he died. Before anyone else could take his place and arrange reinforcements, the Spanish landed on St. Catalina Island. The Spanish were all too aware of the threat posed by a permanent fort so close to their possessions and they had moved quickly to raise a force and transport it to the island. They landed their forces, advanced upon the fort, and called upon the garrison to surrender immediately or be put to the sword. The pirates replied with gunfire and the two sides exchanged volleys while the Spanish advanced. Finally, when the pirates could see no escape or hope of rescue, but while they were still capable of resistance, they negotiated terms—assurances of their personal safety and compensation for their possessions—and they surrendered. Sometime after they had surrendered, the English ship sent by the governor of Jamaica arrived and, not suspecting that the island had fallen, sailed in and was taken by the Spaniards.

Morgan, meanwhile, gathered a fleet off Cuba with the intention of attacking and plundering some Spanish settlement. Almost 700 men gathered and held a conference. Some proposed that they attack Havana itself, but others, who had been prisoners there, argued that it was too well defended and that the buccaneers would need 1,500 men to succeed. Finally they decided to attack Puerto del Principe (on Cuba), a market for the trade of hides. While they were making their preparations, a Spanish prisoner escaped and carried word to the town that the pirates were coming. The Spanish commander organized a force of 800 men to defend the market and to lay ambushes for the pirates, but while he was placing the ambushes along the main route, the pirates advanced by a different route and took the Spaniards by surprise.

The commander drew up his troops in a field and sent a force of horsemen to circle the pirates and to pursue them as they broke and ran (as he expected they would when they saw the size of the force opposed to them). Instead the pirates advanced with drums beating. The battle continued for four hours, during which the pirates' accurate and continuous fire killed the commander and many of his soldiers; the Spanish formation broke and ran. Most of the survivors fled into the forest, but a few ran to the town and tried to organize resistance to protect the town from looting.

The buccaneers quickly put an end to the scattered resistance by threatening to burn the whole town down. The Spanish surrendered and the pirates herded them into the church and then set about looting the countryside. With the town as their headquarters, the country open to them, plenty of beef to eat, and enough drink, they had just the life they enjoyed. The prisoners languished in the church, ate scraps, lived without water or sanitary facilities, while some, and then others, were taken out and tortured to reveal where they had hidden their possessions. Those who did not break were hanged. Those who had too little to satisfy the buccaneers also were hanged.

When at last Morgan thought that he had squeezed everything possible from the citizens and the country, he demanded that each person pay a ransom for himself and his family or be transported to Jamaica and sold and, further, that all the prisoners collectively come up with a ransom to prevent the town being fired. Four prisoners were sent to the governor to negotiate the payment, but they returned in tears and begged Morgan to wait for two weeks while the money was collected. At the same time some buccaneers intercepted letters meant for the leading citizens: the letters informed them that the governor would be arriving with a relieving force in two weeks and that they should string out the negotiations. Morgan, therefore, without revealing that he knew their plan, loaded all the plunder onboard ship and demanded that the Spaniards furnish five hundred cattle, drive them to the ships, and butcher and salt them. He expected that the Spaniards would comply with his demand because they hoped to use his demand to delay him there until the governor and his troops could arrive.

While the cattle were being slaughtered, an English pirate helped himself to some marrow bones that a French pirate believed were his. The two argued and agreed to settle the issue with a duel. They found a quiet place and began loading their muskets. The Englishman loaded first and fired first and shot the Frenchman through the back while he was still loading. No one would have objected if both had loaded and been facing each other, but the French demanded that Morgan punish the Englishman as a murderer and Morgan agreed to hang the man when they returned to Jamaica. This decision did not satisfy the French and they left the fleet after the spoils had been divided.

Morgan then persuaded his English buccaneers to follow him in an attack on Porto Bello on the coast of Panama. The men objected that the place was too strongly defended and that they were too few. "The fewer we are the more for each of us," Morgan replied with the argument that almost always could convince pirates to fight against the odds. The town was defended by two forts and a large garrison, but Morgan brought his men up by stealth, surprised the sentry, and took the outer redoubt. The soldiers in the redoubt managed to fire one volley that alerted the town. The panicked citizens threw their richest possessions down their wells and rushed to the major fort. The governor was determined that the town would not fall to the pirates. Morgan attacked the main fort with the majority of his command and was forced back. Assault after assault failed and Morgan was on the point of withdrawing when he saw buccaneers from the other fort running toward him calling out, "Victory! Victory!" The other fort had fallen.

Morgan gave his troops a breathing space while he devised a scheme to take the main fort: he forced the monks and nuns of the city to carry siege ladders in front of the pirates and so shield them from fire from the fort. He expected that the governor would hold his fire, but the governor made no distinction between the pirates and the people compelled to help them. The pirates whipped the monks on, the monks called out to the governor to spare them, the Spanish directed a fierce fire on them, but, nonetheless, the ladders were thrown up and the buccaneers swarmed up the ladders there to meet resistance stout enough to drive them back off the wall. During the confusion of the assault, however, some pirates managed to set the gate on fire and the pirates again threw up the ladders and climbed them. The Spanish soldiers finally reached the end of their endurance and they fell back.

The governor refused to surrender and fired both on the pirates and on his own men in a futile attempt to force them back into the fight. The pirates called upon him to surrender and he replied, "I would rather die a brave man than be hanged for cowardice." The pirates admired his courage and they tried to take him alive, but in the end they had to shoot him. The pirates herded all their prisoners into the town and separated the men and women, put them under guard, and then got drunk and debauched the women. The next day the pirates tortured some of the prisoners to persuade them to point out which of the other prisoners were wealthy and worth torturing. They dragged out the marked men and tortured them until they revealed the location of their wealth. Once they gave up their wealth, the torture stopped, but, if they refused to talk, the torture continued until they died, or, if they had no wealth but the pirates thought they did, they were tortured to death just the same.

As the looting continued, Morgan learned that the president of Panama was collecting a force to drive the pirates out. Morgan was unconcerned. He had ships in which to escape and he believed that his men were superior to the Spanish in fighting ability and morale. When the Spanish force came, the pirates ambushed them and killed many, but the Spanish continued to advance and the pirates were forced back; they retreated into the fort and there the president ordered them to surrender and threatened to kill them all if they did not. Morgan's counterthreat was to fire the town and kill all the townspeople if the president did not withdraw. The president found Morgan's threat more credible than his own, so he withdrew and left the townspeople to their fate. Many already were dying—some from torture, but more from disease spreading through the town; the disease arose partly from the insalubrious nature of the place, partly from the confinement and sparse diet, and partly from the rotting corpses. The townspeople finally paid 100,000 pieces of eight to ransom themselves and their town.

The president could not believe that such a small force (perhaps 400 men) had taken such a strong position and he was convinced that the pirates had employed a secret weapon. He sent Morgan a request to see one of these weapons; Morgan sent him a French musket with a four-and-a-half foot barrel and a note that the governor could keep the musket until, perhaps in a couple of years, Morgan would come in person to retrieve it. The president sent back a ring as a gift and a note that advised Morgan not to try to visit him because his reception would be quite different than it had been here. When the buccaneers departed, they had an enormous amount of booty to divide, just as Morgan had predicted.

After his men had spent all their money, Morgan announced a rendezvous off Hispaniola for a new expedition. Morgan's fame attracted a large number of buccaneers; the governor of Jamaica sent a thirty-six-gun ship to join the expedition. A French captain also arrived in a ship of twenty-four guns, but as he had stopped an English ship and helped himself to provisions, he did not trust himself among the English on Morgan's ship, although he did trust Morgan personally and he consented to visit him on the governor's ship, whereupon Morgan had the captain and then his crew taken prisoner, because of the provisions they had taken from the English ship and also because the captain had a commission from the Spanish to attack English shipping. The French captain explained that he had obtained the commission as a ruse, so that he could trade with the Spanish, but that he had never intended to carry out the terms of the commission. As they argued back and forth on the governor's ship, sparks from the salutes fired from the ship's guns rendered the issue moot: the sparks set off the store of gunpowder and blew the front of the governor's ship apart and killed almost the entire crew. Morgan and the officers, who were getting drunk in the stern, were shielded by the bulk of the ship and escaped with minor injuries.

Morgan put the blame on the French and transformed an accident into an act of sabotage that justified him in commandeering the French ship. (The fleet stayed in place long enough to recover the bodies of the sailors—to strip their clothing and cut the gold rings from their fingers before throwing the bodies back for the sharks.) Morgan made his rendezvous and waited for other ships to arrive. He sent small parties on shore to get water and provisions. Pirates were willing to raid settlements to get supplies, and, in fact, they preferred that method, but only if they wouldn't have to fight, because they saw little profit in risking their lives just for rations, and so, in this case, the ration parties hunted, shot, and slaughtered cattle to provide beef for the voyage.

As they hunted, the Spanish planned an ambush—to lure the buccaneers to them by staging a cattle drive. The buccaneers took the bait and the trap was sprung, some of the buccaneers were killed, but the rest formed a square and defended themselves; the Spanish advanced on them, the buccaneers retreated to the woods and under the cover of the trees delivered such an accurate fire that the main Spanish force withdrew, but left a detachment behind to harass the pirates. The pirates, however, were furious, because some Spanish soldiers had mutilated the corpse of a pirate; they attacked the detachment, killed many of the soldiers, and drove the remainder off. The savagery, the courage, and the marksmanship of the buccaneers overawed the Spanish and induced in them a certain reluctance to face the pirates except with overwhelming odds (and even with overwhelming odds the Spanish forces didn't always win).

Morgan and his 500 men met to decide on their objective. They had thought about plundering the coast of Caracas, but 500 men seemed too few, and they discovered a French captive among them who had raided Maracaibo with Lolonois, and thought he could guide the fleet into the harbor and lake. They timed their voyage so as to surprise the newly constructed Spanish fort at dawn, but the Spanish were ready, fired their cannons, and held the pirates at bay for most of the day. At last the buccaneers closed with the fort, broke in, and discovered that the garrison had fled. They searched the fort and came upon the powder room; there they found that some of the casks were smashed and a burning fuse was one inch from the powder. They pulled the fuse out. Morgan confiscated the powder, spiked the sixteen cannon, burned the gun carriages, and threw the guns down from the parapet. The fleet then marshaled and those ships that could cross the bar were packed with pirates from the other ships; at noon the fleet arrived off Maracaibo. Morgan drew up his ships to provide covering fire for the landing, but the landing was unopposed—the people had fled with everything they could carry.

For three weeks raiding parties went out and returned with prisoners who were tortured until they revealed their riches or until they died. When the pirates thought they had gotten as much loot as they could, they decided to try Gibraltar. They expected heavy resistance and, indeed, their ships were fired upon—this seemed to be good news because it meant that the Spaniards had something worth defending—but when they landed they discovered that all had fled and taken even the gunpowder with them.

The pirates did capture one poor man. They asked him where everyone had gone. He told them, "I didn't ask them."

They asked, "Where is the gold and silver from the churches?"

He took them to the church and when it wasn't there he said, "It was here the last time I came."

Not sure whether he was cunning or simple, they beat him until he cried, "I will show you my house and money."

Now they were sure that they had caught a rich man playing the fool and when he showed them a miserable shack and declared that he was the brother of the governor, they tortured him in earnest. He promised to show them his sugar mill, his estate, and his slaves, but he had none, and when he confessed that he was a pauper, the pirates tortured him to death.

Their next captive offered to show them the people's hiding places; he failed and they hanged him. Their next captive was a slave; they offered him freedom and money and he was able to lead them to the hiding places. They had him murder some of the prisoners so that he would have to throw in with the pirates and the pirates raided the countryside for a week until they had too much loot to carry, even with mules, and over 200 captives. One by one they tortured the prisoners to reveal their own wealth or betray the wealth of others. After five weeks the buccaneers had taken a mass of plunder, a ship and four boats, and hundreds of prisoners, and they had almost captured the governor himself. They ransomed the prisoners; they extorted the promise of a ransom payment for the town of Gibraltar, and returned to Maracaibo. There they learned that the Spaniards had come in force—three men-of-war with a combined weight of ninety-two guns—and they had manned the fort again. Morgan's largest ship had fourteen guns; the pirates were outgunned and outnumbered.

The commanding general of the Spanish sent a letter to the "admiral of the buccaneers" to demand that he surrender all plunder and all prisoners in exchange for a free passage out. "Beware," he wrote, "I have with me valiant soldiers, yearning to be allowed to revenge the unrighteous acts you have committed against the Spanish nation in America."

Morgan read the letter to the assembled buccaneers and asked them what answer they wanted him to send. The buccaneers voted to fight to keep what they had. One pirate told Morgan that he knew how to construct a fire ship: he would disguise the fire ship as a man-of-war—caps on logs to look like the crew, hollow logs to look like cannon, the appropriate flags—and he and twelve men would destroy the Spanish flagship. They loaded the fire ship with tar, pitch, sulfur, and gunpowder. They also outfitted another ship to look like a fire ship. Meanwhile Morgan gave his men time to prepare by making a counteroffer: to depart without setting fire to Maracaibo, to forego the ransom, and to release the prisoners and half the slaves. The general refused.

Despite locking up all the citizens and slaves, news still leaked out to the general that the pirates were preparing a fire ship, but he contemptuously dismissed the possibility as beyond the capabilities of pirates. The pirates swore an oath on a Bible that they would stand by each other to the last drop of blood and then they set out—the fire ship leading, behind it Morgan's ship (to fight the largest man-of-war if the fire ship failed), and behind Morgan's ship the fake fire ship.

On the first day of May 1669 the two fleets joined battle. The fire ship grappled the Spanish flagship—and only then did the Spaniards recognize it for what it was. Frantically they tried to cut it loose and fend it off. It exploded and its burning sails set the flagship afire. The general abandoned the ship and with the survivors swam to the fort on the island. The second largest ship fled for the shelter of the island and ran aground. The third ship tried to flee and was captured. The buccaneers had won an extraordinary victory, but the fort still lay between them and the open sea. They landed and launched an assault. Their accurate musket fire cleared the walls, but when they tried to storm the fort, the defenders turned their cannon on the pirates and threw bombs at them and drove the buccaneers off with some sixty dead and wounded.

Morgan brought his prize—the Spanish man-of-war—back to Maracaibo, re-fitted it, and renewed his demand that Maracaibo and Gibraltar be ransomed. The Spanish residents agreed (though without the consent of the general) and Morgan resupplied his fleet with provisions—500 cattle. Once he had received the ransom for the town and for his prisoners, he tried to find a way past the fort. He hoped to use the prisoners as hostages, but, when some of the prisoners went to consult with the general, the general harangued them—they were cowards who had not defended the fort or themselves and had brought this fate down upon their own heads. He would not let the pirates pass.

For once the pirates were not ready to carry out their brutal threats—to hang the hostages from the yardarms. They had committed torture and murder regularly, but only to gain loot, not for any love of torture and murder, and they considered themselves good Christians, able to swear a binding oath on the Bible, and so Morgan sought another way to escape. Canoes full of buccaneers were rowed across to the island and then the oarsmen rowed empty canoes back to get another load of buccaneers, to all appearances massing the men for an assault on the fort, except that the assault was a ruse—the buccaneers, once they reached the island, lay flat in the canoes and returned to the mainland.

The Spanish in the fort were completely convinced that an attack in full force would be made on them from the landward side of the island and they shifted their cannon and the majority of their troops to that side. That night under a full moon the buccaneers slipped anchor and made their way through the channel. (Morgan had had the loot divided up before they left in case some made it and some did not.) Once safely through—the Spanish were so convinced that a large force of buccaneers was waiting to seize the fort that they hesitated to shift their guns—the pirates released their prisoners. The buccaneers still had to endure storms and bad weather, but in the end they returned safely to Jamaica.

Morgan had become the most famous buccaneer of them all . . . and his most famous exploit still lay in the future.

— 15 —

The Raid on Panama

"God permitted the unrighteousness of the buccaneers to flourish for the chastisement of the Spaniards."

All too soon the buccaneers had spent their loot and were ready for another expedition and Morgan was all too ready to lead another expedition, more grandiose and more profitable than any before—one he could retire on. Henry Morgan's fame was so great that he had only to announce his intention and name a place to rendezvous and there a fleet would gather—this time 2,000 men in thirty-seven ships, a flagship of twenty-two guns, others ranging from twenty down to four.

Morgan held a commission that gave him quasilegal cover for his depredations—as acts of reprisal—but left him on his own to support himself and his fleet, so, after the fleet had rendezvoused, a small detachment was sent to collect provisions and to gather grain. At sea the detachment had a stroke of luck—they captured a merchant ship loaded with grain—but on land they skirmished fruitlessly with the Spanish for two weeks, until the Spanish finally paid them (in grain) to leave. The detachment rejoined Morgan and with holds now crammed with salt beef and grain, the pirates set sail.

Morgan and his officers negotiated the shares—Morgan, of course, as admiral, received the largest share—1 percent of everything taken—captains, eight shares for their ship and one for themselves, and so on, to special shares for acts of courage or particularly bad wounds—the loss of a leg, for instance, was to be compensated with 600 pieces of eight or six slaves.

On the 20th of December 1670 the pirates sighted St. Catalina. Morgan's plan was to take this island, seek out prisoners who knew the route to Panama, and then proceed to Ft. Chagres, the jumping off point for Panama. The interlocking series of forts on St. Catalina had a garrison of 190 men and mounted some thirty cannon, well supplied with powder and shot. Had the forts been vigorously defended, they might have held out for a considerable time, but the governor was all too conscious that he was heavily outnumbered; furthermore, the Spanish had so exaggerated the ferocity and bestiality of the buccaneers in the stories they told their wives and children that they had managed to frighten themselves into incapacity.

When the governor was called upon to surrender he agreed on two conditions—that all prisoners be released on the mainland and that a mock fight be staged so that he could preserve his honor. Morgan acquiesced—but only if none of his own men were wounded or killed. The staged battle went forward, both sides fired into the air, and the pirates took possession of the forts of St. Catalina. Morgan destroyed all but two forts, manned those, interrogated the prisoners, and chose one of them, a rapist and murderer who needed little persuasion to join in a plundering expedition and who also happened to be familiar with Panama, to be their guide. The criminal convinced two more prisoners to join the pirates.

Morgan sent a small fleet with 400 men to take Ft. Chagres that guarded the approaches to Panama. He held the main fleet back in the vain hope that the Spanish would not figure out what his real objective was. Ft. Chagres was on a densely forested mountain slope and it was well armed with cannon. The fort's garrison had been reinforced until it almost equaled the attackers in numbers and it was well protected behind the palisade. As always the pirates had the advantage in morale and marksmanship, but the Spanish cannon were particularly effective when the pirates broke through the forest into the open. The buccaneers were driven back once and the Spaniards taunted them,

"Come on, you English dogs, you shall not get to Panama."

The pirates attacked again in twilight with no better results until one of them was struck in the shoulder with an arrow. He plucked the arrow out, wrapped the arrowhead with wadding, set it alight, and fired it from his musket into the fort. By chance it struck a thatch roof and set it ablaze. Other pirates followed his example and soon the buildings within the fort were on fire. The defenders were so engaged in the battle that they did not notice the fire until it set off a cask of gunpowder.

The blast stunned many of the Spaniards, others tried in vain to quench the blaze, while the pirates set the palisades on fire. The Spaniards fired on them and threw grenades down among them, but night fell and the pirates took up good firing positions outside the palisade and fired through the flames as they saw Spanish soldiers revealed inside. They kept up the fire all night and at dawn when the parapet collapsed they stormed the breach. The governor moved other cannon to the breach and fired directly into the attackers. A fierce battle raged, many of the pirates fell, and the governor kept his men in the fight until he was shot dead; only then was the fort taken. Over a hundred pirates had been killed and sixty wounded. The pirates took just fourteen Spaniards alive.

When Morgan arrived a few days later, he learned that his plan to attack Panama was no longer a secret and that the route had been prepared for him with ambushes and traps. Nonetheless, he organized the march to Panama, while his men repaired the fort. He had several flat-bottomed boats with two guns and he commandeered all the canoes he could find. He left 500 men to guard the fort, he left 150 on board the ships, and he set out with the remaining 1,200 men to raid Panama.

The success of Morgan's expedition was by no means guaranteed. The pirates had a difficult eight days' march through difficult jungle. The Spanish had Indian allies who knew the jungle intimately, hated the English, and were full participants in the defense of Panama. The Spanish could have fought a strategic retreat, taken their toll on the buccaneers, delayed them, and allowed hunger and stress to force them to retreat; instead, although they did strip the route of food, they abandoned their set ambushes as the pirates approached and fell back without engaging them.

The pirates had expected to find food along the way so they had packed little and they expected to be able to traverse most of the route by boat, and be protected by their guns, but by the second day they had to abandon their boats and proceed, some by canoe and some by foot and all without supplies. They pressed on for three days—with no food—and on the fourth day they ate leather. (They soaked it, beat it between two rocks, scraped off the hair, roasted it over hot coals, cut it into small pieces, and swallowed it without chewing.) On the fifth day they found a small cache of food and Morgan doled it out to the weakest of the buccaneers. On the sixth day they were reduced to eating berries, leaves, and grass until they stumbled upon a barn filled with corn that they devoured immediately. When they ran into a band of Indians, they charged them without hesitation—they were determined to seize whatever food the Indians might have, and seize the Indians, too, and if they carried no food, to kill them, cook them, and eat them, but they couldn't catch them.

On the seventh day they had to dismiss the canoes and everyone had to march. On the eighth day they ran into real resistance from the Indians, first an exchange of arrows and ball, then a skirmish hand-to-hand in which they killed a few Indians and lost eight buccaneers. On the ninth day at last they came within sight of the coast and a plain filled with cattle. The buccaneers charged down into the plain and shot every beast they could and soon had fires roaring and the beef roasting. Morgan allowed them a brief respite to roast the beef before he set them on the march again, eating as they marched. At the end of the day they came in sight of Panama City. A Spanish guard shouted to them,

"Tomorrow, dogs, we shall see."

On the tenth day the buccaneers prepared to attack the Spanish. The Spanish commander expected them to come along the main road, but the buccaneers hacked their own path through the jungle. This detour threw the battle onto ground the Spanish hadn't scouted. The buccaneers reached a rise in the ground and could see that they were outnumbered—4 infantry battalions, 2 squadrons of cavalry, and 2,000 cattle that the Spanish commander intended to stampede into the buccaneers to break their ranks. (The buccaneers shot some of the cattle; the rest turned tail and chased their herdsmen off the field of battle.)

The Spanish general ordered the cavalry to charge and they charged right into a swamp. Two hundred French buccaneer sharpshooters drew aim on the cavalry; some fired while others reloaded so that they could keep up a continuous fire. The cavalry couldn't close with the buccaneers because of the swamp and the Spanish infantry was stopped. Finally the cavalry broke and the infantry fired their muskets once, threw them to the ground, and ran. The pirates had routed a force almost double their size and killed 600 Spanish soldiers.

The Spanish barricaded the streets and set cannon loaded with grapeshot at the barricades. More of the pirates were killed here than on the battlefield, but they broke through the barriers, routed the defenders, and took possession of Panama. The pirates separated into small groups and individuals to search the city for loot and the scattered defenders killed some twenty of them. Morgan's men were outnumbered, they could not identify the defenders within the cover of the city, and they risked being picked off one at a time. Morgan retaliated by setting the city on fire, the fire spread, and in the end it consumed 2,000 middle-class houses, 3,000 ordinary homes, 200 warehouses, 7 monasteries, a convent, hospital, and a cathedral. The fire drove the defenders from their cover and it destroyed the remaining defensive works, but it also destroyed everything of value in Panama City except for scattered caches of silver that the pirates found amid the ruins.

The Spanish troops watched the pirates but did not attack them, while the pirates rounded up some 200 prisoners and inflicted the usual round of tortures on them. Morgan delegated one of his captains to capture the boats in the harbor and use them to seize all shipping. Instead the captain drank, feasted, and fornicated (some of the Spanish women proved willing to join in the debauch in exchange for good treatment—they had been surprised to discover that the buccaneers looked much like Spanish men and not like beasts) and he let the greatest treasure escape. Morgan only learned, too late, when his men captured a watering party that there was a galleon within reach, loaded with royal silver and all the valuables of Panama. Despite their (belated) efforts they failed to capture the galleon. Morgan was furious at this dereliction of the prime directive of pirate duty—plunder first, pleasure second—and his subsequent actions may originate from this incident.

Morgan sent runners to Ft. Chagres. He had anticipated that the garrison would soon run out of supplies and have to withdraw, but his runners reported back to him that the garrison had captured a supply ship loaded with food and was set to remain as long as necessary. Meanwhile Morgan's men in Panama City captured a supply ship of their own and so he remained for three weeks, while large bands of pirates scoured the land for loot and prisoners, and other pirates maintained a substantial guard at Panama City. The pirates tortured and robbed their prisoners and extorted ransom.

After the pirates had spent three weeks in Panama, Morgan announced that they were going to leave: he sent some of his men to find mules to transport the loot to the river where boats could bring it to the sea. (He had heard that the president of Panama was collecting forces to retake Panama and prevent their withdrawal. Only later did he learn that the troops had deserted rather than face the buccaneers.) Some of Morgan's men laid plans to seize a ship, load it with as much loot as they could—more than their fair share—and sail away to freeboot in the Pacific. Morgan heard of the plot, disabled all the ships, and so foiled the plot, but he became suspicious of his band of buccaneers.

His scouts reported that the way to Ft. Chagres was clear of ambushes. The pirates put the prisoners under guard and forced them to march with them. At night the women moaned and the children cried. The women appealed to Morgan to alleviate their suffering and release them. He replied—it could have been the pirates' credo—that he had not come to listen to moans but to get money. As the ransom money arrived, the prisoners were released. One beautiful woman of a prosperous family—she had not succumbed either to Morgan's blandishments or to his threats—had been carried off by the pirates because her ransom had not been paid. In fact, the monks charged with conveying the ransom used it instead to free their brother monks. (The deception was finally revealed and she was sent home.)

When the pirates reached the coast, Morgan insisted that all pirates be searched for booty. He did not require the usual oaths—to hold nothing back—because he suspected that the oaths would not be binding in this case (when some pirates had already plotted to desert the others). He himself was the first to submit to the search and then everyone else was searched. Some men complained, but the search went forward, the loot was collected under the eye of Morgan, and he had it put under guard.

Morgan, meanwhile, prepared his own ship for departure, ensured that he had food enough for the voyage and that his crew was ready to sail. His preparations left little food for the others, but as far as he was concerned the expedition was over; he split the loot among the ships, demolished the fort, and departed. The crews of the other ships thought that their share of the loot was suspiciously meager and they set out in pursuit of Morgan, but he had made his preparations and he had a considerable head start; he easily outsailed them and returned to Jamaica.

In Jamaica Henry Morgan received a hero's welcome (though he had abandoned many of his men and apparently kept their loot for himself). His new wealth gave him considerable power, and he needed it, because the British and the Spanish had signed a peace treaty and the Spanish protested Morgan's actions to Charles II. In 1672 a frigate was sent to fetch Henry Morgan back to England to stand trial for piracy. Such was his fame, however, and his influence—the king knighted him— that he not only escaped conviction, but he was returned to Jamaica as assistant governor with instructions to suppress the buccaneers.

When peace was established between Spain and Britain, trade flourished, the merchants and the authorities in Jamaica disavowed the buccaneers, and the buccaneers were forced to seek other ports. Gradually they turned their attentions to the Spanish Pacific coast. Sir Henry Morgan lived the last sixteen years of his life a wealthy and respected man. He was not the only buccaneer to end life wealthy and respected. Other prominent men in England began their careers in the Caribbean.

A retired buccaneer, finding himself in England, decided to look up a former comrade. When he inquired if anyone had heard of a certain Lancelot Blackburne, he was informed that a man with that name was Archbishop of York. Opinions differed whether the pirate and the archbishop were the same, but the archbishop had spent some two years in the Caribbean and certainly he retained a sword (still to be seen) with a curse upon it—whosoever draws it shall bring bad luck down upon his head. Horace Walpole feigned (at least) to believe the story: "the jolly old archbishop of York, who had all the manners of a man of quality, though he had been a buccaneer and was a clergyman, retained nothing of his first profession except his seraglio."

The buccaneers were not necessarily blasphemers and heretics, even though they did sack the churches of their enemies; many of them professed their own faith and did not consider themselves impious. One French pirate in need of provisions raided the house of the local Catholic priest and brought the priest and his household to the ship, where, as the crew gathered provisions at the expense of the priest, the captain proposed that the priest hold mass. The captain saluted the mass with his cannon, fired at the *Sanctus*, the *Elevation*, the *Benediction*, and one last salute at the *Exaudiat*. When a less pious member of the crew seemed to mock the *Elevation*, the captain rebuked him, the pirate replied with a curse, and the captain drew his pistol and blew the pirate's brains out—just next to the priest.

"Do not be troubled, father," the captain said to the priest, "the rascal just needed to be taught a lesson."

When the mass was finished, the corpse was thrown overboard and the priest was given some presents to compensate him for the experience.

Buccaneering (if not piracy) ended in 1697. England and Spain had become allies in a war against France. When the French mustered a fleet to attack Cartagena (in Columbia), the governor (Ducasse) of Hispaniola convinced the 650 buccaneers to join in the attack. The "allies" bombarded Cartagena for two weeks, took it, and seized a huge amount of treasure. The buccaneers demanded the treasure as their payment for participating. The French admiral refused and departed for France. The buccaneers returned to Cartagena and sacked the town in earnest to pay themselves for their trouble, but on their way back to their hideout they met a combined fleet of English and Spanish ships and they lost four ships and the treasure. The buccaneers never recovered from this blow.

—— 16 ——

The Infamous Captain Kidd

William Kidd, as so many others, went to sea to escape the confining life of the shore, specifically in his case, the life of the son of a Calvinist minister in Scotland. Kidd experienced what so many others had experienced in the Caribbean but he garnered no fame and appeared in no records until he was in his mid-forties (1689). Then Kidd found himself caught up in the war between England and France, a war in which the two countries turned from the struggle against Spain to a struggle between themselves for the domination of the New World (and the old). French and English buccaneers who had previously worked amicably together onboard ship were embroiled in the war, crews split, and they fought among themselves for possession of the pirate ships (and the acquired booty). It was just in this way that Kidd seized his first ship by leading the non-French members of the crew against the French.

Kidd sailed the ship to the English port of Nevis, rechristened it the *Blessed William*, took on a crew of eighty buccaneers, and received a commission as a privateer to operate as part of a small squadron (three ships and two sloops) in an attack on a French port. The English commander saved money by promising privateers loot rather than paying them wages. The fleet attacked and plundered the island of Mariegalante and then sailed to St. Martins to rescue an English force trapped there; soon it found itself engaged in a battle with a superior French fleet. The English made two passes in line but failed to grapple and board, so they made another pass and another until the French had had enough and sailed away. Kidd had accumulated £2,000 in loot on this expedition, but his crew was dissatisfied with his leadership—they had signed on to plunder and they were willing to fight to acquire plunder, but they had not signed on to fight sea engagements broadside to broadside for some nebulous strategic gain. Kidd dismissed their grievances and the crew bided their time until he had gone onshore and then they sailed away with his ship and his £2,000.

Kidd, however, had caught the eye of the British authorities and he was given a new ship (the *Antigua*) with the mission to run down the pirates who had "stolen" the *Blessed William*. He pursued the *Blessed William* to New York, but he arrived there after his former ship had already put in, taken several prizes (under the authority of New York) and departed, and Kidd and the *Antigua* became embroiled in the fervent politics of New York. Kidd chose the winning side and, as his reward, he was granted a share of the prizes of the *Blessed William* and a bonus. Kidd married a woman of property, settled down in New York, and there he could have remained, living a quiet, middle-class life, but he felt the call of the sea and the lure of the profits to be made—legitimately or illegitimately.

New York was suffering a lack of its usual trade because of the French War, but trade with pirates was flourishing. Not only did New Yorkers welcome pirates (or rather their money and cargo) in New York itself—pirates seeking pardon could buy it in New York and, if subsequently they returned to piracy, then, as the governor said, "That is their mistake, not my crime"—but they also set up trade with the pirates in the new pirate base in Madagascar in the Indian Ocean. By the end of the seventeenth century pirates had shifted to Madagascar because by then the centralized powers had come to realize that they shared three particular and compelling reasons to close their ports to pirates: they no longer needed to employ them as an irregular navy, they wanted to protect regular trade more than they wanted the intermittent profits of piracy, and they were suspicious of the pirates' egalitarian, utopian ideas about community.

Pirates throughout history had formed their own societies because they were social outcasts; some of those societies were remarkable. The Greek pirates of the Liparian Islands, the Barbary pirates at Sallee, and the buccaneers at Tortuga, all created a kind of utopia in which some members of the community would tend to affairs on shore while others took to the sea. At set intervals they would switch roles. All would share in the plunder. The Caribbean pirates' egalitarian ideas were particularly distasteful to the authorities of their time and were considered dangerously revolutionary.

The pirates, driven from the Caribbean, occupied an island off the coast of Madagascar—Madagascar offered harbors, supplies, and a native population eager for guns, for military training, and for allies against each other—and there with Yankee ingenuity, entrepreneurship, and daring, they developed a port where they could sell their booty, arrange passage home (if they wished to retire), find drink and credit, and buy supplies for their next voyage. Ships carrying slaves, cargo, and retired pirates sailed on a circuit from New York to Madagascar and back to different American ports, to Europe, and back again to New York. They transformed their island into the largest haven for pirates in the world.

Meanwhile, Kidd had become a man of substance in New York: he was ready and able to do favors for the authorities and in turn he was a man valuable enough to be cultivated. He won the patronage of a powerful man (in New York) and followed his patron to London, where he hoped to receive a letter of marque, become a privateer, and make a fortune against the French, but the patron proved to be rather small potatoes in London and Kidd found himself temporarily adrift while his patron caballed with a faction proposing to dismiss the present governor of New York and to replace him with their own man. Kidd's patron got his partners' attention with a scheme by which Kidd would command a ship, proceed to New York, and intercept, capture, and loot a pirate. So inflamed were their imaginations by this scheme that they put the minimum profit expected at £100,000. Eventually even the king could not resist such fabulous wealth and he lent his support to the enterprise in exchange for 10 percent of the loot.

Kidd secured a thirty-four-gun ship, the *Adventure Galley*, and a crew of seventy men. They negotiated their contract: so many shares in toto, so many to Kidd (many because he had to satisfy his backers), so many to the officers and to the men. He had no difficulty attracting men—the lure of riches was enough in itself and privateering offered sailors a way to escape the discipline and flogging of the Royal Navy. Kidd had little respect for the Royal Navy, and as a man typical of the times, as ready to lord it over his inferiors as he was to toady to his betters, he made a foolish error and ignored the courtesies due from his ship to the royal yacht. In this case, he had mistaken his inferiors. He was ordered to stand to, he was boarded, he was stripped of his sailors, and his patrons had to intercede to have his crew returned. Once again at sea, however, his fortunes improved and he was able to take a prize even before reaching New York. In New York he increased his crew to 150 men. The new men joined his crew and gave their loyalty to Kidd only because they expected, as did Kidd (and his backers), to make their fortune at sea, and to make that fortune they would stick at nothing.

Kidd planned to make a shakedown cruise to Madeira and then proceed past the Cape Verde Islands through the "Doldrums" to Cape Town, South Africa, and on to the port of Tulear in Madagascar. On the way, and purely by chance, he fell in with a British squadron and was persuaded to sail with them. Kidd dined with the captains and spread himself in an unbecoming way; he dropped broad hints in ready ears (he thought) that he was prepared to seize any ship anywhere. The British commander was not impressed and he let slip his intention to requisition thirty men from Kidd. Before he could carry out his intention, the ships were becalmed, and that night Kidd set his crew to the sweeps and rowed out of sight of the fleet, and so for a second time he annoyed the Royal Navy and reaffirmed his bad reputation among those in the best position to hurt him. From ship to ship spread the tale (which they had good reason to believe) that Kidd was not a privateer but a pirate.

Before Kidd arrived in the Indian Ocean the most famous (or infamous) piratical exploit had been an attack by the pirate Avery on the fleet carrying pilgrims to Mecca. The pirates took and pillaged several ships. (As so often, the crews of the victimized ships, who were paid low wages and not likely to be victimized themselves, were less willing to risk their lives to protect their ship than the pirates were to capture a ship that then would be theirs, share and share alike.) The pirates divided the loot, returned to their base, and scattered to the ports of the world. The loot made them wealthy men, but those who had returned to England, and could be identified, were arrested and hanged. Avery, however, was never found.

Men such as Avery were supposed to be Kidd's target, but through accidents, scurvy, desertion, and tropical diseases, Kidd had lost many of the original crew and had had to recruit real pirates or would-be pirates. Whatever zeal the original crew might have had for attacking pirates had dribbled away, so Kidd instead of seeking Avery, or the others like him, decided to emulate him and attack the pilgrim fleet. He may have expected that he could vanish like Avery or he may have expected that his patrons would be enough mollified by the money to protect their agent, but his attack on the pilgrims met a determined resistance by an English captain and he sailed away. (Kidd comes off well neither as a person, nor a ship's captain, nor a pirate.)

Finally, Kidd took one prize, arguably legitimate, and then several others, which could in no way be justified by his commission—and thus in law he became a pirate—but he stuck to his story that he was searching for pirates even as the physical condition of his ship deteriorated and his crew became disaffected. As Kidd seemed willing only to commit piracy if the profits were certain and the struggle small and he preferred to avoid English ships (where the real profits lay) the disaffection grew. Kidd killed a crewman who argued with him. In all he took about half a dozen prizes, some by outright piracy, and then to escape the monsoons he turned back toward Madagascar with one of his prizes following. His ship was so unseaworthy that the crew was at the pumps twenty-four hours a day.

When Kidd arrived at the pirate refuge off Madagascar, his cover that he was to attack pirates, worked against him and he had to convince the pirates there that he "would have [his] soul fry in Hell-fire" before he would harm the pirates of Madagascar. Kidd was accepted at his word—he was a pirate—but he was not a very successful pirate: his voyage, while it had not been a total failure—his men had some money to spend—had not reaped the rewards Kidd himself needed to break even on his commission. The rewards were real. They had before them the examples of others who had made a fortune. (They also had examples of those who had labored for years and were destitute and broken, but they did not take instruction from these examples.)

The temptations that drew men to piracy were real—when an honest sailor (or officer), who made two to three New York pounds a month, captured pirates who had on their persons several hundred, or thousand, pounds, when the distinction between piracy and lawful raiding was blurred and non-Europeans were covered by no law, when pirates could hope to make a fortune and then return home (perhaps to New York), settle into society, and be accepted as an honest and respectable citizen, then the temptation to turn pirate was hard to resist. And, regardless of the rewards, many men preferred the more egalitarian life of a pirate community, the excitement of the chase, the pleasure of the debauch, and the dream of wealth.

The temptations lured many of Kidd's crew away from him, from his concerns about the appearance of legitimacy, and from his timidity, to join a pirate who made no claim to legitimacy; Kidd was left with a reduced crew to ponder the justifications he would have to give for his actions—he had never willingly engaged in any piratical act, always he had been coerced by the crew that now had deserted. Alas, Kidd cuts a sorry figure. He wanted respect, position, and wealth; his desire for respect stayed his hand from the bold acts of open piracy that could have acquired the wealth he wanted, while his desire for wealth led him to commit petty acts of piracy that would strip him of respectability.

While Kidd was making his preparations to return home in his only seaworthy ship (an Indian ship he had captured), unbeknownst to him, his actions in the Indian Ocean had created a maelstrom of protest. The East Indian Company traded with native powers who were convinced that all pirates were English and all English were pirates, and the Company had not only had their own losses to pirates, but losses also because they, being English, were thought to encourage piracy; the Company was determined to make an example of someone and the handiest target—it was his own fault—was Kidd.

Kidd was not the worst of the miscreants, but the worst, Avery, had escaped and six of his men, who had been captured, had been declared not guilty in their first trial (although they were convicted in a second trial on the same charges after the jurors had been threatened—"suffer pirates and the commerce of the world must cease"). The Company wanted to make an example of someone with a prominent name and they lobbied the authorities to bring Kidd to justice.

The authorities had used pirates to establish a presence in disputed territories and they had also profited materially from piracy, but now they were profiting more from honest trade. Their profits were diminished by piracy and they were determined to end piracy, although they preferred to pay as little to that purpose as they needed: first, they bribed the pirates with pardons and land grants, then they threatened them, they closed ports, they demanded action from distant jurisdictions (without giving those jurisdictions legal or material assistance), they pressured the British Crown to dismiss governors who countenanced pirates, and finally, reluctantly, they mustered the resources to support an effective navy.

While Kidd was at sea the British government worked out the legal apparatus for trying pirates. Seven naval officers or officials of the crown together could constitute a court to try pirates, or anyone who aided and abetted pirates, anywhere they were apprehended. They could pass a sentence of death and they could carry out the execution on the spot. Kidd had, as it were, sailed out in one era, with influential backers, relaxed attitudes toward piracy, and an inefficient legal system, and he returned in another, tougher era, in which the rules had been changed, and yet, in the end, if he had carried out his original mission—to attack pirates—he would not have been vulnerable to any legal proceedings. He was a failure in all regards: he had committed acts of piracy for small profit and he had no successes against pirates, no friends, and many active enemies.

As he made his slow way in his awkward ship, Kidd heard disquieting rumors about his reception—that his principle backers had second thoughts, that he would be taken as a pirate, and perhaps to his ultimate ruin—as he sold off his cargo—that he had with him a fortune of £500,000. He abandoned his Indian vessel, bought a sloop, and let his crew slip away out of the reach of the authorities a few at a time. When Kidd finally sneaked into New York harbor, he learned that his sponsor was fighting for his own political life; he had assumed a stance condemning piracy, first to please the government in London and, second, to discredit his enemies in New York.

Kidd's sponsor hoped for large profits, materially and politically, from his antipirate stance, but that stance forced his hand with Kidd, and Kidd had done himself no good, because he could only report failure, at most a profit of only £20,000. Even if the sponsor fully accepted Kidd's strained account—legal prizes, coercion of crew, desertions—his profit, a share of only £20,000, would be substantially smaller than if he declared Kidd a pirate and confiscated his ship and goods. The sponsor might have found a share of the rumored amount, £500,000, ample enough to quiet his reservations, but the truth sank Kidd. Kidd was arrested.

Kidd's sponsors deserted him to save their own necks (figuratively speaking, of course) and when Kidd had been returned to England to stand trial, they bluntly stated that sometimes "a Jonah must be thrown overboard to save the rest." The Kidd affair became part of politics—the "outs" used it as one stick with which to beat the "ins"—only after they had wrung what political advantage they could from the affair did they let it proceed to trial. In the meantime, the East India Company was so determined to secure a conviction that they had fetched the owner of the captured Indian ship from the orient to London and Kidd became notorious. Crowds sang

> I murdered William Moore
> And left him in his gore,
> Not many leagues from shore,
> As I sailed, as I sailed,
> Not many leagues from shore, as I sailed.

And they followed him when he was escorted from his cell to Parliament to give testimony; when he stopped at a tavern to take a drink—his guards had struck a deal with the tavern keeper—the crowds flowed in and made the owner's fortune.

Kidd's trial began on the 8th of May, 1701, and concluded on the 9th. He was denied the evidence he believed would clear him and he had no legal counsel to represent him. Kidd wrote a letter that set out his view of the proceedings, that his patron "thought it in his interest to make me a pirate, whereby he could claim a share of my cargo, and in order to it, stript me of the French passes, frightened and wheedled some of my men to misrepresent me, and by his letters to his friends here advised them to admit me a pirate, and to obtain a new grant of my cargo from the king."

Kidd was brought into court, he was bullied into entering a plea (without which the trial could not proceed) and the trial began. The first charge against Kidd was murder—he had swung a bucket, struck a crewman (William Moore) in the head, and the crewman had died. Witnesses told the story. Kidd claimed that the crewman was leading a mutiny. Witnesses disputed that. Kidd claimed that the crewman was sick and died of other causes. Witnesses denied that. Kidd claimed that he had thrown the bucket and the death was an accident. Witnesses affirmed that he had swung the bucket by its handle. The first jury was instructed—if Kidd struck, it was murder—and dismissed for deliberation; a second jury was seated to hear the case of piracy.

The trial had been under way for an hour when the first jury returned to deliver its verdict—guilty. Kidd now knew he would hang and he had still to conduct his defense against piracy. He claimed to have been a privateer, claimed to have taken ships carrying French passes (as he had) but could not produce the passes nor witnesses who could unequivocally state that such passes existed, claimed that he had wanted to return the only ship he had taken illegally but his crew would not let him. The court dismissed the defense, the jury found Kidd—and all but three of his men—guilty and a third jury was seated to hear the case of other acts of piracy. Court was adjourned for the night. The next morning Kidd was returned to court. He was found guilty, sentenced, and on May 23rd he was hanged.

His last words on the scaffold accused his patrons of perfidy, declared that the murder had been a moment of passion, and affirmed that he was not a pirate; then he was dropped. The rope broke. He was pulled back to his feet, returned to the platform, and dropped again—this time to his death.

The last period of concerted piracy in the Americas was occasioned by Queen Anne's War (1701–1714) during which all belligerents loosed privateers against each other. After the war ended and many sailors were put on shore, the privateers continued as pirates. One member of the crew of a privateer during the war had been Edward Teach. In 1717 Teach captured a ship (which he renamed *Queen Anne's Revenge*) and turned it into his headquarters and home. Teach transformed himself into a frightening figure, the notorious Blackbeard—he cultivated his bushy black hair and stuck burning slow fuses into the shaggy mat at the moment he attacked his victim. He preferred to attack English ships

Two entries from his journal of 1718 survive:

Rum all out. Our company somewhat sober—A damn'd Confusion amongst us! Rogues a plotting—great Talk of Separation—so I look'd sharp for a Prize. . . . Took one with a great deal of Liquor on Board, so kept the Company hot, damned hot, then all things went well again.

Blackbeard worked out an arrangement with the governor of North Carolina to buccaneer under a kind of legal immunity and to split the loot. The governor of Virginia, who was not privy to the agreement, hired two ships to pursue Blackbeard; the two ships cornered him and he fought, cursing those who seemed lukewarm in the defense of the ship, until he was killed. His head was brought back to Virginia on a pike and exhibited up and down the coast until an enterprising tavern owner bought it and converted the skull into the base of a punch bowl.

The British in particular, but other powers, too, made a concerted effort in the early 1700s to catch and hang pirates in the Americas. By the 1730s pirates in American waters were almost extinct.

── PART V ──
THE BARBARY PIRATES

Christians, be consoled. This world is full of vicissitudes. You shall be well used, I have been a slave myself, and will treat you much better than I was treated; take some bread and honey and a dish of coffee and God will redeem you from captivity as he has done me twice. . . .

—a corsair to his captives

— 17 —

Crescent and Cross in the Mediterranean

Between the fall of Rome and the beginning of the Crusades the Mediterranean was relatively free of piracy (except for the occasional Viking raid), because the Mediterranean was almost devoid of maritime trade and thus provided no targets to attract pirates. The Crusades lent impetus to the beginning of significant trade across the Mediterranean and the increased trade attracted pirates. The established powers were at first sufficiently powerful to protect their own shipping, but increased shipping strained their resources and pirates based along the North African coast ("the Barbary coast") seized the opportunity increasing trade provided. These pirates were motivated first and foremost by a desire to acquire the wealth passing in front of them, and, by enriching themselves, they could also strike a blow for Islam against Christianity.

Previously the Muslim states had never been much interested in the sea. They advanced where their armies could march and they employed only coastal craft—when the general who conquered Egypt was asked about the ocean, he said that it was "a huge beast which silly folk ride like worms on logs," but the individuals, who were attracted by the riches passing before them on the sea, acquired boats, learned to use them, and used them to attack merchant shipping. They formed a working relationship with the rulers of the Barbary states of North Africa (Algiers, Morocco, Tripoli, and Tunis). The rulers of the Barbary states became rich with the fruits of piracy—booty, slaves, and ransom (Cervantes, the author of *Don Quixote*, was for a time a prisoner of the pirates)—but in addition piratical raids on Christians furthered the cause of Islam, gave prestige to these rulers in the larger Muslim world, and were never condemned by Muslims, as attacks by the pirates on fellow Muslims would have been. The rulers of the Barbary states supported the pirates and their piracy for centuries.

In the beginning no single power was strong enough to check the raids, nor were Christians united enough to form a coalition to suppress the pirates, nor, even if they had been willing and able to form a coalition and fight a war, would they have had (in a sense) anyone to fight: no central authority in the Muslim world was strong enough (if defeated) to compel subordinate rulers to curtail piracy and the Barbary rulers, even if they had recognized some central power, still would not have obeyed an order to stop the pirates. The Barbary states were isolated between an inhospitable hinterland and the sea and only their access to the sea enabled them to prosper; their rulers had become dependent on the pirates not just for luxuries but for the daily necessities of life.

As Islamic and Christian powers confronted each other, Muslim pirates, with the encouragement and support of Muslim powers, attacked Christians, and Christian pirates, with the encouragement and support of Christian powers, attacked Muslims; between them they kept the Mediterranean in turmoil for 500 years.

In 1390 the Genoese organized an attack upon Tunisia to end its support of pirates. Henry IV (as he was to be) led the assault. English longbowmen covered the landing, drove the defenders to their fort, and Henry directed his men to close the siege. For two months by the force of his personality Henry sustained the siege and kept his men in the field, even though they were starved, even though they suffered the plague, until the two sides, both exhausted, reached a settlement in which the ruler of Tunisia agreed that his ships would refrain from attacks upon the allies' shipping.

In 1492 the forces of Islam were driven from the Iberian peninsula across the strait of Gibraltar to North Africa; the new population overwhelmed the resources of that country—and, since they did not accept their exile, they sought both a way to support themselves and a way to strike back at their enemy. They were well placed to do both—they knew Spanish, they had informants in Spain, and they were willing to learn navigation and ship craft, if these skills would only enable them to get revenge. They organized themselves, built fast ships, raided inner Africa for slaves to man the oars, recruited fighting men, and paid off the North African authorities with a regular tithe of their plunder to ensure themselves safe harbors and open markets.

In 1504 a Muslim pirate, the first of two "red-beard (Barbarossa)" brothers, attacked and captured a pair of papal war galleys. The captains of the two papal ships were so little concerned about their own security that they did not keep each other in view as they went on their way. The captain of the lead galley was unconcerned about a smaller ship approaching him until, too late, he saw that its deck was crowded with turbans. Unable to pull away or mount effective resistance, the papal galley was easily captured and the pirate captain (Arouj Barbarossa) with this single coup made his fortune, but he was not content with one coup—he stripped his captives, drove them into the hold, dressed his crew in the captured clothes, put his own ship in tow, and steered toward the second galley. The captain and crew of the second galley were so curious to find out how their brethren had taken a prize and so unsuspecting, that they allowed the pirates to board without resistance. Once the ships were secured, Arouj Barbarossa struck

The Western Mediterranean

the chains from the Pope's oarsmen—Muslim slaves—and replaced them with his Christian captives; under the lash they rowed him back to Tunis.

The two Barbarossa brothers were sons of a Greek potter of Mitylene; born Christian, they converted to Islam and became pirates. Arouj joined the Turkish pirate fleet; he rose through the ranks to command a ship, convinced the crew to follow him and break free of Constantinople's control, and to freeboot in the Mediterranean. His daring exploit against the papal vessels fired the imagination and ambition of men throughout the Muslim world and enabled him to secure a willing ally in the bey of Tunis. Tunis became the center of his operations. Recruits and ships showed up in Tunis to join Arouj and he assumed command of a fleet of pirates. His example also created many imitators. The threat from these pirates was so great that Ferdinand, king of Spain, the most powerful Christian monarch of the time and head of the greatest maritime power, assumed as his Christian duty the responsibility of suppressing the Barbary pirates.

In a series of attacks in 1509–1510, the Spaniards occupied and fortified an island that dominated the harbor of Algiers, forced the three principle Barbary powers to capitulate, and compelled Algiers to pay tribute, but when the main force of the Spaniards had withdrawn, the Muslim rulers repudiated their agreements and Arouj led a campaign to regain what they had lost. In the continued fighting Arouj was so desperately wounded that he lost an arm, but survived, and by the time Ferdinand died Arouj controlled 5,000 foot soldiers in addition to his fleet (commanded by his brother Kheyr-ed-din). Arouj was summoned to Algiers to help the local ruler recover the island occupied by the Spanish; Arouj, however, was more ambitious than the Algerian ruler had expected—he strangled the Algerian and took his place (while acknowledging the supreme command of the Sultan of Turkey).

Arouj proved to be a better pirate than ruler. His harshness drove the Algerians to invite the Spanish to help them rebel against him. The Spaniards seized this opportunity to rid themselves of their most prominent enemy; they made a surprise landing, outmaneuvered Arouj, and cornered him. Arouj might still have been able to escape, had he been willing to sacrifice his rearguard and abandon them, but he chose to stand with them and die. His death—so welcome to Christians at the time—motivated his brother, Kheyr-ed-din Barbarossa, to take revenge on a scale that Europeans could never have imagined, a revenge so great that it caused a shift in the balance of power in the Mediterranean.

Suleiman the Magnificent (the supreme ruler of the Muslim world) had defeated the Knights of Rhodes and taken the island, but he had been disappointed in his fleet and he was searching for the right man to assume command, transform it into an effective fighting force, and help him spread his rule throughout the Mediterranean. At this moment Kheyr-ed-din Barbarossa inherited his brother's forces and the right to his kingdom (that had rebelled). He appealed to Suleiman and pledged his fealty. Suleiman recognized his quality, appointed him governor of the kingdom yet to be won, and sent him 2,000 janissaries. Kheyr-ed-din regained his brother's kingdom, town by town. In 1519 he defeated a Spanish fleet of fifty men-of-war.

He extended his rule east and west from Algiers and attracted the most notorious pirates of that age—Dragut of Rhodes (who one day would succeed him), Sian, "the Jew of Smyrna," and Aydin, a renegade Christian.

Aydin raided the Spanish coast and freed 200 Muslim families held as slaves. Eight Spanish galleys pursued him, but the Spaniards had been promised a reward if they returned the slaves unharmed and they were so confident in their numbers that they thought they could intimidate Aydin and win back the slaves without a fight. Aydin and his crew were emboldened by the timidity of the Spanish, they turned on their pursuers, attacked them, and captured seven of the eight galleys.

Suleiman summoned Kheyr-ed-din Barbarossa to his capital and there he ordered him to create the Ottoman navy. Kheyr-ed-din spent the winter overseeing the construction of galleys and the training of their crews. In the spring he set out with the new fleet and attacked southern Italy. He sacked Reggio and Sperlonga and raided Cetraro. He took booty and captured 800 prisoners. He led a raid inland to seize the most beautiful woman in Italy (208 poets attested to her beauty) and bring her to the sultan to augment his harem, but failed by minutes to capture her; to assuage his disappointment, he sacked the town from which she had fled. While the whole world was being told of his exploits along the Italian coast and wondering where in Italy he would strike next, he returned to Africa and surprised and captured the Spanish dependency of Tunis.

Kheyr-ed-din was victorious everywhere; one task only remained to be done— to retake the island that blocked his harbor at Algiers. For sixteen days his artillery bombarded the fort on the island and on the seventeenth day an assault of 1,200 men took the fort. Its wounded commander was tortured to death. Kheyr-ed-din ordered the fort razed and a mole constructed to connect the island to the mainland. The mole was finished in two years with the labor of thousands of Christian slaves. (Many of the slaves came from an unfortunate convoy of transports bringing supplies and reinforcements—unaware that the fort had been taken.)

While Barbarossa was securing his domain, Charles V of Spain sent the Christian pirate, Andrea Doria, to attack Tunis. Andrea Doria seized the city and allowed his men and the freed Christians three days of relentless plunder and atrocity. For this deed Charles V was hailed as the savior of Christendom, but even while the king was being feted, Barbarossa sailed under Spanish colors into the port of Minorca—Port Mahon—seized the wharves, captured a Portuguese ship and everything on the wharves, and sailed away to Constantinople to bring his booty to the sultan personally; in return the sultan appointed Barbarossa High Admiral of the Ottoman fleet. Andrea Dorea and Barbarossa raided each other's domains and carried off enormous amounts of booty and slaves. Kheyr-ed-din ensured that an ample portion reached the sultan—after one raid in the Adriatic he dispatched 200 boys clad in scarlet, each with a gold and a silver bowl, 200 more with bolts of cloth, and 30 with purses filled with treasure.

In 1538 the fleets of Islam and the Cross met in the Adriatic Sea at Preveza. The fleets totaled close to 200 ships each. Andrea Dorea had more ships than Kheyr-ed-din, but he was curiously hesitant—some said because he did not want to fight for the profit of Venice. The Muslim routed the Christian fleet. In 1541 Charles attempted to retrieve the disaster with a great expedition against Algiers. Five hundred ships and an equivalent number of troops made success such a certainty—despite warnings by Andrea Dorea that they were sailing in the stormy season (October)—that Charles invited ladies to accompany him to witness the victory. Indeed storms did wreck the fleet, soak the miserable army, and turn a bright possibility into a nightmare—300 officers and 8,000 enlisted men were killed and so many captured that there was a glut of slaves on the market, and one Christian slave was "not worth an onion."

This disaster weakened Charles' grip on Europe and encouraged independence movements. In 1543 Francis I of France concluded a treaty with Suleiman for help against Charles; Suleiman sent Kheyr-ed-din to Marseilles to support his new ally. Along the way Kheyr-ed-din raided the coast of Italy and captured the governor of Reggio and his family—but the ninety-year-old pirate felt the stirrings of passion when he saw the governor's eighteen-year-old daughter and he took her as a wife and gave to her as a wedding present . . . her parents. After celebrating his nuptials he proceeded to Marseilles where he had the pleasure of witnessing the lowering of the flag of Our Lady and the raising of the Crescent. Ultimately his commission to injure the Spaniards was more satisfactory to him than to the French: he replenished his crews with raids upon the French coast, enjoyed the amenities of Marseilles, and conducted no operations against Spain. Finally he was dismissed with full pay and a large enough bonus to see him all the way to Constantinople.

Kheyr-ed-din died a few years later and was placed in a sepulcher built at his own direction. His corpse reappeared and had to be reinterred several times before a Greek magician advised that it be buried with a black dog. From that time to this he has remained at rest.

Kheyr-ed-din's death changed little in the Mediterranean except for the loss of central direction to the depredations of the pirates—a fine distinction that would have been noticed neither by the inhabitants of the coasts of Italy and Sicily nor by the owners and crews of merchant ships. His captains, all effective men, continued to prey upon the shipping of the Mediterranean. Dragut—one of the few pirate captains born a Muslim and a peasant—had run away to sea, won a reputation for his courage and his skill, rose to captain, and was recruited by Kheyr-ed-din to command a detachment of twelve ships. Dragut earned himself such a reputation that he had been specifically pursued by the nephew of Andrea Dorea and captured and chained in the uncle's galley. Four years he rowed as a slave and then, when Kheyr-ed-din was anchored in Marseilles, Valette, the grand master of the Knights of Malta, who himself had once been a galley slave on the very ship of Dragut, saw Dragut among the galley slaves and he called out to him, "Senor Dragut, fortunes of war!" and Dragut replied, "Fortune is changeable." Valette acted as a go-between and arranged a ransom for Dragut (both as a favor and for a small fortune).

Dragut became the commander-in-chief of the Turkish fleet and won the title "drawn sword of Islam." One by one he attacked those places in North Africa still in Spanish hands and planned for the day when he might drive the Knights of Malta from their island. The knights, begun as a hospital order, had fortified Rhodes, where up to their expulsion in 1522, they were the easternmost outpost of Christianity. For eight years the knights wandered in search of a home before they were granted Malta and Tripoli by the king of Spain—not out of any particular respect for their order but in the expectation that they would form a bulwark against Islamic piracy.

The knights were the Christian counterpart of the Barbary pirates—they were comfortable on the sea and in ships, they had the slenderest of resources, and they were encouraged by both piety and plunder to attack Muslim shipping. If their resources had equaled their skill, they might have dominated the western Mediterranean (for good or ill), but they had only seven large galleys (rowed by Muslim slaves).

Tripoli fell soon enough and the Muslims made several attempts on Malta, but Malta was so intimidating that when the first fleet delegated to take Malta arrived, its commander examined the fortifications and departed. In 1565 the sultan dispatched a fleet of 185 ships and 30,000 men to be joined by Dragut with his fleet. The knights' commander was Valette—who had been a slave rower himself and who had helped ransom Dragut. The Turks put the fortress complex under siege. They mined the walls, blew openings, and assaulted the breaches; the knights countermined, counterattacked, and the issue hung on whether help would come from Spain, would it arrive in time to save Malta or would it be too late? After six savage months had brought the knights to the verge of defeat—one determined assault might have carried the last wall—a rumor swept the Muslim army that the Spanish fleet was hours away. The army and the fleet broke and fled. Dragut, caught in a rearguard action, was killed. The knights were saved, not by the Spanish fleet, which had not yet sailed, but by rumor and panic.

Dragut's successor was an Italian (Ochiali) raised for the priesthood but captured by pirates and chained to the rowing bench. His decision to convert to Islam freed him from the rowing bench and his character and ability won him eventual promotion to command. Conspicuous service at the siege of Malta brought him to the notice of the Sultan of Turkey and he was made Beg of Algiers. He recaptured Tunis and he defeated a fleet of four of the knights' war galleys. (The knights' commander escaped and was tried, condemned, strangled in his cell, and thrown into the sea.) Ochiali then attacked Cyprus (the Venetian base for piracy in the eastern Mediterranean) and took the capital after a siege of forty-eight days. (The whole of Cyprus soon fell.) He continued a long raid from Cyprus to the Adriatic, but the fall of Cyprus had sent such a shock through Christendom that it inspired the Christian naval powers—despite their suspicion of, and distaste for, Venice— to unite in the creation of a war fleet of 206 galleys and 48,000 men under the command of Don John of Austria (son of Charles V). Spain's fleet was commanded by the nephew of Andrea Dorea and one of the officers was Miguel de Cervantes.

The Christian fleet was the superior in armament—the crews had firearms, the Turks bows and arrows. On October 7, 1570, the two fleets approached each other at Lepanto in the Gulf of Corinth. The Christian commanders sent a request to Don John for a conference to discuss tactics but Don John replied,

"The time of councils is past. Do not trouble yourself about anything but fighting."

At midday the two fleets rowed toward each other over a dead calm sea. Neither side lacked courage and the Turks were well practiced in the tactics that had served them so well for so long—ram and board—but the Christian firearms swept the boarders aside and the continual fighting, like a land battle at sea, wore down the Turks until evening when they tried to disengage. The Christian fleet immediately pressed on them and broke them.

— 18 —

War by Other Means

The battle of Lepanto broke Turkish naval power, and after that battle each pirate captain had to depend upon his own individual skill to succeed, but Muslim pirates still spread terror and destruction throughout the Mediterranean for centuries after Lepanto. One of the most successful—and not untypical—pirates was Murad. He had been born in a Christian family, but he was carried off at the age of twelve and wound up a slave in the hands of the pirate Kara Ali. Kara Ali was captivated by the boy and treated him as a son. Murad commanded a ship in the Turkish fleet at Malta in 1565, but he grew bored with the interminable siege and took his ship out of the action to go freebooting. His ambition exceeded his ability and he ran his ship aground. Although he escaped the wreckage, he found that his patron was far more furious at the loss of his ship than he was grateful for the salvation of his protégé—Ali disowned him. Murad commandeered a fifteen-oared ship and set out to prove himself to Ali. He returned from the coast of Spain with three prizes and 140 Christian slaves and regained Ali's favor.

In 1580 Murad achieved a coup that made him as famous in the Muslim world as Drake was in the English. Murad was coasting along Tuscany with two little ships when his lookout spotted a pair of papal galleys at anchor; one of them was the Pope's flagship. Murad was pondering how his little force might seize them when, as luck would have it, two more little pirate ships, following the same route, fell in with Murad. Murad took the ships in tow so that from a distance the papal crews would see what appeared to be only two ships, too insignificant a force to be a danger, and, anyway, the papal captains were disporting themselves on shore—the leaderless crews did not resist for long and Murad took both ships. As usual in these changes of fortune Murad freed the Muslim slaves on the rowing benches and replaced them with his Christian captives.

Murad's exploit inspired many would-be Murads, but his imitators found that the inhabitants of the Mediterranean had grown wary; one of his imitators cruised for two months and returned with a single blind Christian captive. The new Governor-Pasha was disgusted. *Where was his tenth of the spoils? Was he supposed to be satisfied with the arm or leg of a blind man?* He decided to take out a fleet himself to demonstrate to his incompetent captains how it should be done.

His first attack found his would-be victims ready and well able to defend themselves, but his second attack had better luck and he captured 700 Christians in Sardinia. He made a headquarters at the appropriately named Island of the Stomach-Ache and offered his captives back for a price. The Sardinians could not, or would not, meet his price, his activities attracted an opposing fleet, so he removed his captives away from Sardinia to the slave market and then tested the defenses of Spain. He took more prisoners and loot there and, with the whole coast of Spain aroused, he returned home to Algiers. He truly had shown his captains how it should be done.

Meanwhile Murad tried his luck in the Atlantic. He had only little boats ill-suited to a deep ocean and so no one expected that he could even survive out on the Atlantic; thus his attack on the Canary Islands was totally unexpected; among his many captives were prominent citizens who were ransomed for a heavy price (far more than they would bring in the slave market). Once he had received the money, he carried off the rest of his prisoners, the ones no one would ransom, to sell as slaves. The daring raid so outraged the Spanish that they stationed their fleet at the straits of Gibraltar to catch him on his return. Murad lay low in an Atlantic harbor and waited for a stormy night when he could slip through the straits and make his way home.

Four years later Murad was cruising off Malta where the crew of a French ship had told him he might intercept a Maltese treasure ship. His crew had little confidence in the advice of a Frenchman, but Murad consulted his book of prophecies and declared the omens favorable. The book proved true (and so did the Frenchman), but the treasure ship looked formidable enough that his crew expressed some reservations. Murad had to deliver a pep talk,

"Do you fear death? Fear not, for did you not leave your homes in search of wealth and fame and to serve our beautiful prophet Mohammed?"

Murad's first shot disabled the enemy artillery, he was able to come alongside and board, and after a half-hour fight he had captured the galley. The captives had to row their own ship into Algiers. On the way Murad attacked and eliminated a Christian pirate cruising off North Africa. The Pasha sent his own horse to fetch Murad to the palace to honor him for his great victory. Murad, and others like him, made fortunes from piracy, but their relentless attacks forced their enemies to learn to defend themselves; by the end of the century the pirates were finding few easy targets.

A renegade Christian, the Dutchman Simon de Danser, had one of the most extraordinary careers of the early seventeenth century; he lived a life of betrayal set upon betrayal and culminating in one last catastrophic act of bad faith. De Danser began as a sailor and he rose through the ranks to command a privateer in the war that separated Holland from Spain. De Danser, however, lost his ship not to enemy action but to the pleasures and temptations of the port of Marseilles—he spent his own money, sold his ship to reimburse himself, and then spent all those proceeds. Destitute and adrift in Marseilles he collected a crew of wharf rats, stole a small boat, used it to seize a larger ship, recruited Englishmen and Moors, struck a piratical alliance with an English pirate, and, finally, as a notorious pirate himself, found a base in Algiers. Here he endeared himself to the authorities not only by paying them a share of his plunder, but also by educating them in shipbuilding and navigation, and thus, in effect, opening the Atlantic and the deep Mediterranean to the Barbary pirates.

From 1606–1609, de Danser conducted piratical raids in the Mediterranean, amassed a huge fortune, built a palace in Algiers, and ingratiated himself with the Pasha and his staff, but he had not personally converted to Islam and he was all too aware that if he ceased to be a steady source of income for the Pasha, the Pasha might well decide to confiscate his wealth and rid himself of a superfluous Christian, and yet his choices were limited: freebooting was getting too dangerous and he was an outlaw in the Christian world—Spain and England had put a price on his head. Nonetheless he decided to see if he could strike some deal and find a refuge in a Christian country; after careful and secret negotiations he found one.

The king of France, Henry IV, for reasons of his own granted de Danser a pardon, but de Danser still had to figure out how to transfer his wealth to Paris. The Pasha would not just allow him to pack up and leave, so de Danser waited for his moment. When four pirate ships entered the harbor, he negotiated for the purchase of their booty. Most of the crew had already gone ashore when he boarded with his payment in hand and set free the Christian oarsmen, called upon them to seize and man the ships, escaped from the harbor, and sailed to Marseilles. (In Marseilles despite the king's pardon he escaped being lynched by his former victims only by recompensing them in full for their losses.)

De Danser arrived in Paris and received his pardon, as the king had promised, but with a condition—that he lead an expedition against Tunis. De Danser agreed and succeeded in burning the Pasha's ships, destroying his guns, and collecting a mass of booty. The Pasha was furious, to say the least, but he concealed his anger and he let six years pass in which the inflamed passions of this betrayal could appear to have died down and then he offered to return to the French king twenty-two captured French ships, ready to sail, if the king would send de Danser and enough captains to take charge of the ships.

The king ordered de Danser to go; although de Danser was apprehensive about the sort of reception he would receive, he concluded that he would be safe enough aboard ship. He sent two envoys ashore to test the temper of the Pasha. The Pasha received them graciously and the next day came out to the ship in person to visit de Danser. He was so friendly that de Danser agreed to return the visit. Still cautious, however, he took with him twelve Frenchmen to keep him company, but the Frenchmen were delayed in conversation by the Pasha's officers, so that de Danser passed through the gates first; as soon as he was through, the gates slammed shut behind him, and de Danser was seized and dragged before the Pasha. The

Pasha denounced him for his bad faith and betrayal and had him beheaded. The Frenchmen were escorted safely back to their ships and the twenty-two French ships were released as compensation to the king for the loss of de Danser.

De Danser's legacy, the deep-sea ships, powered by sail, free of the logistical requirements of crews of oarsmen, preyed upon ships of all Christian nations and almost closed the straits of Gibraltar because of their attacks on shipping there. In a period of fifty years, the Barbary pirates captured 466 British ships and sold the crews as slaves. Later, in one cruise, the pirates captured forty-nine British ships. British subjects in towns on the coasts of the British Isles lived in fear that the pirates would attack them. One pirate sailed up the Thames (although he was captured).

Another Dutchman, Jan Jansz, a privateer during the war against the Spanish, threw his allegiance in with the Barbary pirates, abandoned his Dutch wife and children, took a second wife (under Islamic law), and attacked the ships of Christian nations, even Dutch ships. Now that the Atlantic was open to the pirates, he sought a more convenient harbor and he found Sallee, a port on the Atlantic coast within the realm of the emperor of Morocco. There he—the "admiral of Sallee"—and his fellow pirates paid nominal allegiance to the emperor, while they established Sallee as an independent pirate "republic."

Jan Jansz, as admiral, had enough work to keep him on shore, but he could not give up the excitement of the life at sea. After one failed raid he put into a Dutch port (Holland and the emperor of Morocco were allies), rejected the appeals of his wife and children to give up the raider life and join them, and, instead, accepted many new recruits (even though the Dutch authorities tried to stop them), but on a second visit, after a battle that heavily damaged his ship and killed many of his crew, he was so coldly received that he had to "bury" his dead crewmen by surreptitiously sliding them under the ice. He recovered from this setback and in 1627 raided Iceland and plundered Reykjavik. Reykjavik was disappointingly bare and he had to be satisfied with 400 Icelanders to sell in the slave market.

While Christian nation fought Christian nation—and Christian pirates roamed the seas—the Barbary pirates were free to pursue their prey—and sometimes to act as the ally of one Christian nation against another Christian nation. From time to time different maritime nations bought protection for their own ships with a payment to the Barbary states. Different nations also sent punitive expeditions—which typically entered the harbors, bombarded the shore, did some damage, received promises of good behavior, responded with gifts to the rulers, and departed.

Neither gifts nor punishment had stopped the depredations and in 1655 Cromwell sent his admiral Blake to exterminate the pirates. At Tunis Blake entered the harbor and burned all the ships he found there; at Algiers he liberated all the British prisoners. The fame of the action was celebrated in a ditty—

> The barbarian pirates upon Tunis strand
> Felt the effects of his avenging hand.

More punishment proved necessary in the next two decades and in 1671, Sir Edward Spragg burned the Algerian fleet, an act that inspired the local population to stick their ruler's head on a pike. Five years later another expedition paid for the release of English slaves and then sent fire ships into the harbor of Tripoli and burned the ships there. Such expeditions checked the pirates for a time, but in the end could extinguish neither the pirates' aggressive spirit nor the necessity of their position—to wrest a living from the sea.

The pirates' willingness to attack any target despite the odds led to some great confrontations, great coups, and also great defeats. In 1681 the Algerian ship *Two Lions and a Crown* met the English man-of-war *Adventure*. (The captain of the pirate ship had been born in Copenhagen.) The two ships closed and fought for eight hours before they had to stand off to repair damage. The crews worked all night and renewed the battle twelve hours later. A well-placed shot by the pirate ship blew up three powder charges (held by a powder monkey who had sought cover) and a cache of grenades. The exploding grenades wounded or killed everyone on the quarterdeck—the captain was wounded in the neck—but a shot from the *Adventure* felled the mainmast of the *Two Lions and a Crown* and the pirates, unable to maneuver and unable to escape, surrendered at last. (The captives told their captors that they had wanted to surrender long before but a passenger, an elderly, retired Turkish pirate chief, who had come along for the pleasure of the ride, had inflamed their emotions with stories of the desperate engagements he had fought and won.)

In 1683 a French fleet bombarded Algiers. The bombardment killed 8,000 citizens. The survivors murdered their Dey and chose the commander of the galleys (a man known as "the Living Dead") to replace him. He threatened to shoot a Frenchman back at them if they did not break off the bombardment. When the French did not withdraw, he carried out his threat and when the first victim still did not convince the French he fired off others, twenty-nine in all. The French expended their whole arsenal of 6,000 shells before they departed. Five years later they returned and fired upon the town while forty-eight French prisoners were fired back at them.

A pattern of attack and reprisal developed. The European states just could not agree upon the concerted action necessary to eliminate the pirates. Various states at different times sold guns to the pirates, attacked them as enemies, and employed them as allies. All pirates respect force, and only force, and despise their ineffective opponents, but the Barbary pirates in particular had scant respect for the unbelievers, they depended upon piracy for their livelihood, and they were heroes in the Muslim world. As the entity of which they were a part became weaker, as the warring states of Europe advanced technologically, and as, gradually, European states outlawed slavery—they converted their ships to sail and had no use for galley slaves—and condemned piracy, the Barbary states became isolated and then condemned as "barbarous," but they continued their piracy into the nineteenth century.

— PART VI —
PIRATES OF THE SOUTH CHINA COAST

Lots of money makes the heart light!

—A Chinese pirate captain

─── 19 ───

Out of Poverty and Isolation

The Chinese divided the water world into the "outer sea" and the "inner sea"; the "inner sea" was a network of canals and channels connecting streams and rivers. This network (thousands of miles of waterways) was separated on its one side from the interior of China by mountain ranges and on its other side from the open ocean (the "outer sea") by hundreds of islands, which both augmented and defined the inner sea. This inner sea, protected as it was from the weather, provided a secure route for shipping, and shipping in the inner sea was plentiful.

The wealth of the center of shipping, Kwangtung Province, was proverbial. Goods flowed to Kwangtung from the interior of China and there were loaded onto ships that sailed from Kwangtung to the major ports, Canton and Macao, or farther south to Hanoi and Hue, and in these ports they sold or bartered, all at once, as much cargo as they could carry, or, if they chose, they could sail to the smaller villages along the way and sell or barter their cargo, item by item and village by village. Although Canton was the premiere port for trade (because the imperial government had decreed that all foreign ships had to process their goods in this port), other ports and Hainan Island also, were important trading centers. Hainan Island provided harbor facilities, warehouses, local products, and an easy passage.

Three distinct populations lived within this area: the people of the plains (rice-farmers and merchants), who believed that they lived on the land where their earliest ancestors had been brought to birth directly from the earth itself; the hill people, who were conscious that they had immigrated into a fully settled land and who, therefore, had occupied the hills and the islands; and, third, the water people. The land people, whether hill or plain, lived on the land where their parents had lived, they buried their dead in ancestral burial plots, traced their ancestry back to common ancestors—according to their family trees an entire village might be descended from one ancestor—celebrated their continuity, and despised the water people as a separate and inferior race of humans.

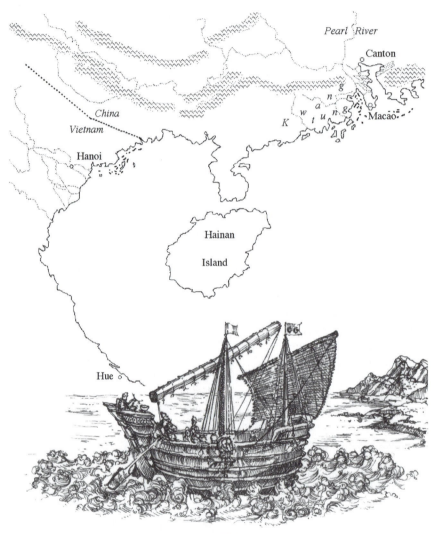

Pearl River

Canton

China

Vietnam

Hanoi

K w t u n g a n g

Macao

Hainan

Island

Hue

South China

The water people (hereafter called the *Tanka*) earned their living exclusively on the water. They lived in single-ship units—the Chinese "junk"—along the coast of Kwangtung Province in the inner sea among the countless waterways and more than 700 islands that formed that mix of land and water (much like the east coast of the Adriatic from which the Illyrian pirates operated). They were accustomed to a life of separation from other families in other ships and to the constraints imposed by life aboard ship—a family, for instance, could not expand unless it acquired another ship—and they were set apart from the land people, not only by their way of life and their means of livelihood, but also by their concepts of society and place.

The Tanka were expert boatmen and they had all the skills needed by pirates, but, prior to the end of the eighteenth century, they had only intermittently practiced piracy. (The imperial court that looked inward to the land, not outward to the sea ignored their activities because they seemed remote and trivial.) During the summer—the poorest season for fishing—the Tanka ranged north to seek supplements to their income by piracy, and then they returned south to resume fishing for the four or five months when fishing was profitable. Fishing and piracy together provided a scant enough living and the Tanka lived always on the edge of poverty.

The Tanka could not avoid interaction with some land people: they depended upon agents on land to buy their catch and to provide the loans they needed to repair and refit their boats or to buy a new boat, but, consequently, many of the Tanka fell into debt to unscrupulous agents and became, as it were, share-croppers of the sea. Their only alternative to using land agents was to participate in a fishermen's collective, in which they would pool their meager resources, donate their labor and a portion of their income, and help to repair, or refit, another's junk, or to build a new junk, all in the expectation that when their turn came and they needed help, they would get it. All Tanka shared at least this one conviction—no land person could be trusted.

By 1790 all the components of a terrible crisis were in place. First, the population of the whole of the Kwangtung region had outgrown its ability to feed itself by fishing and farming and the people there, including the Tanka, were forced to seek additional means of support. Second, the additional means of support seemed to have been thrust right before their eyes: rich commerce at the port of Canton, concentrated there because the Qing authorities (in 1760) had designated this port as the only port through which foreign goods could move; all this wealth could thus be found in the coastal waters that were the home of the Tanka, just at a time when the Tanka were being forced to seek additional means of support. And, third, the Tanka had been barred from pursuing the one legitimate possibility they had to improve their condition—trade with Vietnam.

China had iron, which the Vietnamese wanted, and Vietnam had surplus rice, which the Chinese wanted, but the Qing authorities forbade the export of iron and the Vietnamese authorities forbade the export of rice, so both sides resorted to a black market; and, as each side attempted to suppress its own smugglers, each side condoned, and even encouraged, smuggling from the other side. Thus the

Tanka, who smuggled both iron and rice, were declared outlaws by both sides and encouraged by both sides.

The Tanka grew accustomed to operating outside the law and they grew accustomed to the profits to be made by operating outside the law. They drew little distinction between the illegal activity of smuggling and the illegal activity of piracy, although, up to this time, piracy still remained the scattered and largely ineffectual operation of single ships. (Merchants felt so little threatened that some of them removed the cannon from their ships so they could carry more cargo.)

The last component in the crisis was the transformation of piracy from single-ship operations to fleet operations. The catalyst of the transformation was a twenty-year civil war in Vietnam, fought by three different factions, one supported by China. The Qing-backed faction captured a Tanka fisherman and his family and forced (or persuaded) the man to fight for them as a pirate. The former fisherman proved so successful a pirate that he was granted a title, *Totally Virtuous Marquis*, and as he continued to win victories, he was promoted to general, *General Pao, Virtuous Marquis*, given the command of 200 men and 6 war-junks, and authorized to recruit more pirates. His successes continued and he was reinforced with sixteen more junks and more men; in the end General Pao created a large and powerful fleet with which he was able to run supplies to his own faction and deny supplies to the enemy. In the end, the leader of his faction was recognized by the Qing court as the emperor of Vietnam, and General Pao, Virtuous—and now victorious—Marquis, had more honors and more responsibilities heaped upon him.

Chief among his responsibilities was the organization of the pirates—there were now hundreds of ships—into a stable and profitable enterprise. He created a system under which the Vietnamese court would pay the pirates a percentage (20 to 40 percent) of the value of their booty and, in exchange, would provide security and a safe harbor where the pirates could procure supplies and recruit new hands, before they sailed out to raid the borderlands and the south China coast. This system worked until the old emperor died and the court split into factions; the emperor's young son finally succeeded to the throne, but many of his erstwhile pirate allies defected to other factions and, as pirate fleets now commonly numbered over a hundred ships, his former allies had the power to hurt him.

Consequently, the new emperor promoted General Pao to *Great Governor General Who Controls Each Branch of the Naval Force* and invested him with the authority to create subordinate generals, to organize the "loyal" pirates into units commanded by the subordinate generals, and to eliminate (either by recruiting or defeating) the pirates who had defected; in effect, the emperor delegated to him all the powers the "Virtuous Marquis and Great Governor General" needed to whip the pirates into a semblance of a navy, albeit, a *pirate* navy. The Great Governor General granted titles, conferred political and social status, and transformed his pirates into a semilegitimate instrument of the Vietnamese state. As he, and his subordinates, trained the new navy to organize campaigns and to wage war on the sea, piracy became less chancy and more profitable.

The pirates who were not enrolled in General Pao's navy found that Vietnam was too dangerous a place to raid and they retreated to China, where several rebellions and other disturbances had diverted the government's attention away from the coast. When merchants complained to the Qing emperor about the depredations of the pirates—the pirates had even launched raids inland—they found that he was concerned only with the rebellions and that he had ordered the funds set aside for the suppression of piracy to be diverted to the suppression of the rebellions and disturbances.

The Qing emperor did present a formal complaint to the Vietnamese emperor that the Vietnamese court was encouraging pirates to attack China. The Vietnamese emperor promised that he would take immediate action and that he would order General Pao to subdue the pirates. Indeed, the Qing court was gratified to receive from General Pao—and to pay a bounty for—sixty-three pirate captives, but soon enough the Qing realized that they had been duped—General Pao had attacked only those pirates who were operating outside his own organization.

The Qing court then decided on an aggressive policy of interdiction and punishment: ships were stationed so as to attack the pirates as soon as they entered Chinese waters. All ships were to be stopped and the crews interrogated on the spot; if the crews were identified as pirates, they were to be summarily executed with the most ferocious methods known to the Chinese, including the infamous death of a thousand cuts, but, alas for the plan, the Chinese sailors were too afraid of the pirates to confront them and used their guns only to give the pirates warning of their presence and enough time to sail away.

The court, compelled to acknowledge that force had failed, next tried pacification. It offered amnesty and a reward to pirates who turned themselves in: they could return to their home villages, or join the army, or settle inland with a subsidy to get them started again in life. The court was encouraged by the first results—by the year 1800, 1,700 pirates had turned themselves in—but eventually the court was forced to acknowledge that the level of piracy was unaffected: either 1,700 pirates was a drop in the bucket or else the pirates, who had surrendered and accepted the subsidy, had returned to piracy. This policy, too, was a failure.

In the end a rebellion against the young Vietnamese emperor succeeded and the pirates were driven out of Vietnam by the victors. General Pao ("Virtuous Marquis, and Great Governor General Who Controls Each Branch of the Naval Force") saw which way the wind was blowing, deserted his own fleet, and surrendered himself to the Qing authorities. Without him his fleet was defeated and the men who had served in his navy were either killed or captured, except for those who had followed his example, deserted, and sought refuge in the inner sea of China. That area, however, which once had been their home, now was occupied by other and larger pirate bands.

While General Pao had been organizing the Vietnamese pirates, the pirates of the inner sea had waged a sort of civil war amongst themselves: they had fought each other and competed for recruits. They appealed to men from their own villages and offered them a bounty to join. Initially, they founded their organization on their family connections, and then, as they expanded, they organized their new forces as though they were branches of a larger family united under one "father." The "father" adopted some of the young men they captured, they gave "wives" to others, and they developed homosexual ties with recruits.

Eventually the different leaders came to the conclusion that they had expanded their factions as much as they could and that they would all lose if they did not work out some sort of accommodation that would bring peace to the warring factions. They met and they struck a formal agreement to divide all pirates into seven "families," each to fly a different colored flag and all to abide by a pirate code, which punished those who broke the code: it allowed no one to operate outside the seven families—if an independent operator were caught, his ship would be dismantled and distributed among the seven families—it proposed penalties for attacks upon each other or attacks by one faction upon merchants who had paid another faction for safe conduct, it punished (with flogging or beheading) those who held back booty and broke discipline, and it divided up the "hunting ground" so that the pirates would not compete against each other, but all could prosper and live in peace (with each other).

When the leader of the "red-flag fleet" (300 ships and 20,000–40,000 men) died, his wife—the original "dragon lady"—assumed the leadership and solidified her position through her family connections and through the use of her considerable sex appeal. She attracted as her mate a man named Chang Pao who had already transformed himself into a greater-than-human figure by converting his ship into a shrine attended by priests.

His priests bore witness to miracles: he had lifted a holy statue too heavy for ten men to lift and he, by himself, had carried it on to his ship; the gods guided his plans with the omens they sent and they helped him carry out the plans. Chang Pao was no fool: he studied European ships and tried to learn their tactics and acquire their armament. He had charisma: he captured a would-be assassin, interrogated him personally, convinced him that his grievance was ill-founded, gave him some money, and turned him into a loyal follower. In short, Chang Pao was a leader.

Pao's leadership kept his large fleet together and overawed the crews, who were mostly drawn from the lowest classes of Chinese, Tanka fishermen, or peasants who had been recruited or dragooned. Their daily life onboard ship was no worse than it would have been on land; they subsisted on rice and fish or rice and rats (which bred in the foul holds of the junks) and occasionally—when they captured ships with stores of food—they feasted. They did have to fear the discipline of the pirate captain and the conditions of the pirate code, but they were free from the exactions and taxes of the mandarins. They assuaged the harshness of their lives with opium. Many were inveterate gamblers, engrossed in their game even in the midst of battle, so engrossed once that not even the violent death of one of the players interrupted the game.

Their ships were indistinguishable from other ships—fishing boats, merchants, even Chinese naval vessels—and they had to lay alongside and board to seize their prey. They expected that their fearsome reputation—they were reputed to eat human hearts before battle—would quell resistance, though they were not afraid to fight. They fought with cutlass and knife and protected themselves from shot with magical charms, they were ruthless to those who resisted and they executed sailors of the imperial navy on the spot.

The pirates attained such a position of power at sea that commerce could not continue without some sort of accommodation with them; the different pirate families established offices on shore at which merchants—Chinese and foreign— bought passes to assure their ships' safe conduct; the passes, under the terms of the pirate code, were honored by all pirates regardless of which family had issued them. Soon every merchant ship carried a pass purchased from the local pirate family. The pirates developed a network of supporters on the mainland through whom they disposed of their booty, gathered intelligence, and acquired supplies. They bribed and intimidated government officials.

The owners of the salt fleet—the fleet that transported salt from the salt fields to the ports—were the last to capitulate to the pirates' demands: to pay a certain assessment per ship based on the amount of salt. The salt merchants too, after a few of their junks were burned, fell in line and paid the assessments. The pirates attacked settlements on land, first forts to acquire weapons, then villages, and finally they required each village to purchase its own, separate, immunity from attack. The pirates also took captives and ransomed them at regular rates, higher rates for Americans and Europeans (and because the pirates wanted only money and did not fear discovery, the captives, when ransomed, were released).

The pirates' ambition grew with their sense of power. Why should pirates limit themselves to booty, extortion, and ransom when they were powerful enough (1,800 ships and 70,000 men by the year 1809) to overthrow the imperial dynasty and establish themselves as rulers of China?

—— 20 ——

The Dragon Lady

The imperial court of China had fastened its attention upon the troubles of the interior of China, upon flooding and famine, rebellions, unrest, and the machinations within the imperial court, in short, upon what they considered *China*. The imperial staff received reports of sporadic, disorganized, and minor pirate raids, they heard complaints from merchants, and they instructed local authorities to act, but the sea was remote and to them largely irrelevant, until the pirates appeared to pose a threat to the throne itself. Then the emperor took notice and he appointed a new official, a governor-general to suppress the pirates.

The man chosen, Governor-General Na, had considerable experience and ability, but he was expected to accomplish a task that imperial policy made almost impossible: his area of operations comprised several major commands purposely kept separate and independent so as to prevent any one commander acquiring too much power or any coalition of commanders colluding against the imperial government. Thus Na had to convince the various commanders (who were jealous of their prerogatives, disinclined to cooperate—since cooperation could so easily be misinterpreted at court as treasonous collusion—and who personally had nothing to gain by his success) to cooperate with him. Na had to create an effective force out of an army divided between different jurisdictions and split among hundreds of forts (again on purpose to prevent one man gaining control of a sizable military unit) and out of a navy, which, while on paper was not inconsiderable, was like the army divided into different commands whose commanders saw no personal advantage in giving up their authority to make his job easier.

Governor-General Na, in short, had to transform a divisive system into a united and powerful force capable of defending the coast against a coordinated attack no one had ever planned for, nor even imagined, and all this without sufficient authority to command the different commanders. Consequently, he adopted two traditional Chinese methods, one bureaucratic and one extra-legal: first, to create a military force separate from the regular Chinese army and navy and outside the system and, second, to create a new bureaucracy.

He organized the people in his area of operations into units—units on land were organized by acreage, units on sea were organized by ship—and every person had to be registered in a unit, every unit had to have a leader, and the leaders had to report on the activities of each member of their units to identify any outlaw or any accomplice or any suspicious activity. Na used the land units as a basis from which to recruit a militia; he built fortified enclaves as places of refuge for the civilian population and also as centers of population control. All in all, he implemented a new system that, on paper at least, would deny pirates support on land, would protect civilians from pirate raids, and would provide the means to fight the pirates.

Na enlisted mercenaries and attempted to involve the Europeans in the struggle against the pirates but after mutual recriminations—by the Europeans that the Qing cooperated with the pirates, by the Qing that the Europeans wouldn't operate in the shallow waters where the pirates lurked—cooperation broke down. Na then set out with his own forces to exterminate the pirates. In his first attack on a pirate stronghold, Na's forces sank seven junks, captured three, and burned ten; they took prisoners and destroyed supplies and storehouses; and they fought off a counterattack. They won a fierce, desperate, engagement, but the fighting had been so severe and so many of the officers and men had been killed or wounded, and the survivors had run so many risks to win a victory that had not only not eliminated the pirates but had infuriated them and inflamed their thirst for vengeance, that their morale plummeted and they refused to fight the pirates again.

Na had to concede to himself that he had no hope of continuing an aggressive policy, but he thought that he might have made enough of an impression on the pirates that he could try "pardon and pacification" again. He offered to grant a pardon to any pirate who surrendered, and a reward too, if the pirate brought a token of his good faith, such as, perhaps, the head of a brother pirate. Three hundred men turned themselves in and brought with them a dozen ships. Their leaders were assigned military ranks; the crews were given money and sent home, or they were drafted into the army, navy, or labor battalions, or hired out as servants.

By the end of 1805 almost 2,000 pirates had come forward, but Na was all too aware that this number was only a fraction of the total number of pirates and so he shifted his energies from fighting pirates to convincing the court that his strategy was working: he exaggerated the number of pirates who had sought pardon and reported that the pirates at large were now weak and fragmented. In fact, the pirates had waited and watched, until they were certain that Na did not command resources enough to pursue and defeat them, and then they began operating on a grand scale again. Na's lies were exposed and he was sentenced to exile on the frontier.

In 1808 in a sea battle fought all one day and through the night the pirates killed China's foremost admiral and captured almost his entire fleet. The defeat was attributed to the lack of effective warships—the Chinese navy had no particular advantage over the pirates in type of ship they employed—and the emperor was petitioned to authorize a fleet of ships designed and built especially to fight pirates. While the emperor studied the situation, the pirates sailed up the Pearl River to attack Canton itself. Another Chinese admiral was appointed. He was caught in a trap. His flagship was boarded, but the admiral, then quite aged, refused to surrender and his crew fought hand-to-hand, until, the hold was choked with corpses and a single pirate broke through the ring of defenders around the admiral, struck him with a dagger, and killed him. The pirates were completely victorious.

The emperor appointed a new Governor-General. The new Governor-General convinced the emperor to commission the new fleet, hired local ships while the commissioned ships were being built, and, like Na, took immediate steps to stop money and supplies from reaching the pirates; he found that the merchants had suffered enough at the hands of the pirates, they were ready to cooperate with the authorities and agreed to three measures: to deliver salt overland, to stop buying passes, and to curtail the provisioning of the pirates, but the pirates, when they found their supplies cut short, invaded the mainland and took provisions by force.

Meanwhile, a third admiral, an energetic, bold, and experienced seaman, conducted a campaign that brought the pirates to the brink of defeat and annihilation, but then he was killed in the fighting, the tide of battle changed, and the pirates destroyed yet one more Chinese fleet.

The Governor-General then took the extraordinary step of enlisting the help of the gentry (who were always suspect and usually kept apart from any military operation to prevent their gaining control of a military force); he armed the villagers, allowed them to cast cannon, to acquire the arms, and to organize their own defense. Raid and counterraid followed, as the people tried to defend themselves and the pirates tried to terrorize and intimidate. Sometimes pirates were lured into ambushes and killed to a man. Sometimes villages cooperated, dispatched a combined force, and saved whichever village was under attack. Sometimes no help came or the help arrived too late, and the pirates had a free hand to pillage and destroy, kill the men, and carry off the women and children. Ten thousand people were said to have perished in one campaign.

As the pirates ranged up and down the Pearl River, they found, more and more often, that the villages were ready to fight them, but so long as the pirates remained on their ships, they were largely invulnerable. They could pick the time and place of their attacks and they overwhelmed the Governor-General's army. The pirate chieftain of that campaign offered a monetary reward for every head brought to him. He paid double to one pirate who approached him with two heads tied by their pigtails and slung around his neck.

Finally the imperial court was forced to admit that they would have to seek help from the Europeans (who were willing to help because their own trade was being affected). Pride kept the court from openly acknowledging that it wanted help and its oblique approach made it difficult to work out any deal. The Americans turned them down because the Qing would not insure their vessels, the British demanded a written request for help, and the Portuguese demanded trade concessions. As the Qing and the British bargained, the Portuguese concluded a deal—they would receive a payment, share the booty, and receive the right of extraterritoriality; in exchange they would provide six ships for six months.

The new combined Chinese and Portuguese fleet caught the Dragon Lady and her "family" by surprise and blockaded them. They hoped that all of her allies would be drawn into the battle to save her and that, consequently, the combined fleet would trap them and destroy them. The plan worked perfectly in its inception, but the pirate ships would not allow the Portuguese ships to close with them. (The pirates had learned a bitter lesson when they attempted to board an English ship and the English had swept the decks clear with grapeshot.) The pirates tried two counterattacks that were thwarted by the weather; the Chinese launched an assault with a fire ship and set two of their own ships on fire. In the end, the combined fleet could not finish off the pirates. The Chinese commanders were disgraced, the Portuguese lost face, and the pirates were encouraged to widen the scope of their ambitions. They sent an offer to the Portuguese to topple the emperor, rule China, and give the Portuguese two or three provinces, if the Portuguese would lend them some ships.

Before such fantasies could be realized, however, the pirates began to squabble over the division of the future spoils. The leader of the Black Fleet, rejected in love by the Dragon Lady (leader of the Red Fleet), and jealous anyway of her authority, decided that the time had come to cash in on the pirates' success. He asked the Portuguese governor of Macao to negotiate a deal for him with the Qing government: the government agreed to pardon him and his followers, grant him an official position, and pay him a large reward, if, in return, he would "prove his worth." He turned on the Red Fleet, after it had been battered in a battle, sank some of its ships, captured others, surrendered his captives as a proof of his sincerity, and brought in his own forces—5,500 men, 113 junks, 500 cannon, and 5,000 other weapons. He was awarded military rank, his fleet was added to the Chinese fleet, and the combined fleet won a victory over the remaining pirates.

The Qing authorities were convinced that they needed no more than the one pirate fleet on their side to be able to impose severe conditions on the other pirates, but the Dragon Lady had other ideas. First she cut a simple deal with the British— she would leave British ships alone and they would leave her alone—and then her Red Fleet conducted raids on the shore while the Dragon Lady negotiated with the authorities. She seemed unstoppable and the authorities capitulated to her every demand except only that the Red Fleet should remain in being. The Dragon Lady went in person to talk to the authorities and to insist on that condition; while she talked, the pirates continued their activities, and the authorities caved in. Once the Dragon Lady was satisfied, her Red Fleet cooperated with the Black Fleet and the Chinese navy in an expedition against the remaining pirates; they forced them to turn themselves in or be destroyed. Within a year organized piracy was over.

The pirate leaders were savvy enough to quit while they were ahead. They had personal reasons for quitting, it is true, but they also recognized that times had changed: resistance was growing, more places were fortified, more people were defending themselves, the Europeans were becoming involved—and despite the futility of the Portuguese the pirates did not stand much of a chance against European ships—the Qing government had been partially successful in denying the pirates supplies, and the authorities had shown themselves to be relentless, if ineffectual, in their pursuit of the pirates. Furthermore, the pirates were conscious that they were outsiders and outlaws, without any government behind them, and every hand raised against them. As a whole they could succeed only so long as they remained united, and the leaders realized all too well that their unity was fragile.

When they realized that they could work out an acceptable deal for their followers, and that they, themselves, could get just about everything they had ever wanted—acceptance, security, status—they concluded the deal. One of the reformed leaders entered the imperial system and attained high rank, another retired to a quiet, scholarly life, and the Dragon Lady ran a gambling club; less is known of the fate of their followers but there is no reason not to believe that they found a life consonant with their station in Chinese society and more secure than the life of a pirate.

In brief, social conditions created the pirates, the Qing imperial government addressed the social conditions and applied force, and piracy ended.

— PART VII —
TO THE SHORES OF TRIPOLI

First Lieutenant Stephen Decatur addressed his crew:

Comrades—we are about to embark upon an expedition, which may terminate in our sudden deaths, our perpetual slavery, or our immortal glory.

— 21 —

New Nation, New Victim

By the end of the eighteenth century the Barbary pirates had learned to avoid the ships of nations with powerful navies, but they still could find plenty of ships from weaker states and they continued their depredations—one ruler protested when asked to make peace, "I can not be at peace with all nations at once"—and, in turn, the victims proved all too ready to bargain with the pirates and settle on a payment to guarantee their ships safe passage and their territory immunity from attack. Companies that shipped in the Mediterranean accepted the necessity of the payments as the cost of doing business.

American companies were no different. One hundred American ships with total crews of 1,200 men and cargo of 20,000 tons turned to the Mediterranean from the West Indies, which had been closed to them by the British after the Revolution; in the Mediterranean they encountered the pirates for the first time. (Americans suspected that the new British consul in Algiers went out of his way to inform the Dey that America no longer enjoyed the protection of the British crown and that the British would not be sorry to see American ships captured.) When the pirates of Morocco seized the American merchant ship, the *Betsey*, and brought it into Tangier, American negotiators found that the Moroccan ruler was ready to make a deal to open trade with America and to guarantee the passage of American ships; in 1785 the Continental Congress authorized a payment to him of $10,000. (Morocco was the first neutral to recognize America as an independent nation.)

The Dey of Morocco preferred the steady and continuous profits from trade to the immediate but lesser profits from piracy, but Americans soon learned that an agreement with one of the Barbary states had no influence on the other states. In 1785 Algerian pirates seized the *Maria* out of Boston and the *Dauphine* out of Philadelphia, brought them into Algiers and imprisoned the crews. America, before the constitution created the United States, dealt from as weak a position as could be—it had no money, no navy, and few friends. Thomas Jefferson turned to American allies, France and Spain, to help him negotiate; their remonstrations did ameliorate the conditions for the prisoners, but the prisoners remained captive nonetheless. Algiers set a price of $60,000 for their American prisoners, Jefferson offered $4,000 (as much as, or maybe even more than, America could afford to pay).

Jefferson tried to organize an alliance of smaller nations to furnish ships to blockade the Barbary states for the eight sailing months in the year; the Barbary pirates mostly operated right out of the harbors; they had light ships, they depended upon boarding to capture merchant vessels, they acted alone, and they were not used to fighting ship actions, but since Jefferson could promise no American contribution to the effort, the alliance soon dissolved. In the Mediterranean, American ships joined convoys put together by the stronger naval powers and American captains bought or forged British ship passes, which the pirates respected. The pirates could not operate in the Atlantic, because the Portuguese, for their own reasons, had blockaded the straits of Gibraltar.

When the war between Britain and France broke out, and both sides attacked the ships of the other, neutrals stood to make huge profits by running the gauntlet and delivering goods, and the British were ready to protect those neutrals that brought *them* supplies. The Portuguese decided that it was no longer in their interests to keep a fleet guarding the strait of Gibraltar and they negotiated peace with Algiers. Without warning, the pirates sailed out into the Atlantic and began a war on American shipping. The new captives, stripped of everything, even their clothes, wrote letters begging to be ransomed.

In 1793 John Foss was a member of the crew of the *Polly* (a merchant ship out of Baltimore). While carrying cargo to Cadiz they were ordered to heave to by a ship carrying the British flag. The only person they could see on deck was dressed in European clothes and spoke English and they hove to and waited to be inspected and released as a neutral. Instead, when they stopped, a hundred Algerian pirates appeared on deck, dropped into boats, and boarded their ship. The Americans were herded to the bow of their ship and stripped of everything but trousers and shirt and Foss even was stripped of his shirt.

The pirates looted the ship. (Ship and cargo, once captured, were considered the property of the Dey of Algiers, but all personal items belonged to whoever got to them first.) Foss and the crew were transported to the pirate ship and interrogated by the captain. The captain informed them that they were now slaves of the Algerians and would be worked appropriately, starting by working his ship. When they complained that they could not work in just shirt and trousers, he told them that if he pleased he could strip them naked and work them naked.

When they landed in Algiers they were paraded down the street through a cheering throng to an audience with the Dey. The Dey told them that he had often tried to make peace with America and had been rebuffed and treated with disdain so that now he was resolved that he would never make peace with America and he added,

"Now I have got you, you Christian dogs; you shall eat stones."

At that time the crews of ten American ships were being held in captivity in Algiers. The prisoners were given one set of clothes and one blanket for the coming year, they were chained and set to work. Mostly the prisoners were set to quarrying rock, working from dawn to dusk, and encouraged in their work with whips and goads.

Many of the overseers used force strictly to compel the prisoners to work harder, but some, from reasons of sadism or piety, enjoyed inflicting pain on the Christian captives. One guard's sadism and eagerness to punish a Christian caused his death—he took a swing at a prisoner perched on a plank between two walls, missed, lost his balance, fell off the wall, and broke his neck—but the prisoners believed that he had fallen victim to the curse of a man he had just struck, a man who had whispered, "God grant, you may die, the first time you offer to abuse another man."

The prisoners were fed bread, and not much of it, and vinegar. They slept in an open courtyard on pavement with no bedding unless they had enough money to purchase admission to a room. The American government within a couple of months arranged with the Swedish consul to furnish the prisoners with clothes and a large enough allowance to enable them to pay for food and better accommodations. Many of the prisoners died in a smallpox epidemic. Of the nine crewmen of the *Polly* only four survived to be freed in 1796.

Foss published the journal of his sufferings in 1798. His account of his suffering—the Algerians' "tenderest mercies towards Christian captives are the most extreme cruelties"—and of the many tortures inflicted on the helpless captives and the numerous similar accounts and appeals with titles such as "A Solemn Call to the Citizens of the United States," played upon American sympathies and aided the shipping companies in their quest for support from the government.

The attacks prompted a debate in the newly created United States. A naval war would be expensive and a victory would not necessarily end the expense—ships would have to stay in the Mediterranean to watch the Barbary coast. Might not tribute be cheaper? Shipping interests demanded that Congress authorize and pay for a navy to protect American shipping, opponents expressed concern about the effects of a permanent armed force on the character of the new nation. On March 27, 1794, the U.S. Congress voted to authorize the president "to provide, by purchase or otherwise, equip, and employ, four frigates to carry forty-four guns each and two frigates to carry thirty-six guns each." (Congress allotted some $600,000 for the new navy, but attached a condition that if the war with Algiers was settled before the ships were completed, the project was to be abandoned.)

The frigates built by the United States incorporated the very latest technological advances in ship construction; they were fast enough both to catch those who might flee and to escape those who might pursue, to deliver a sizable blow in a battle, and to take a broadside and survive. The navy was also able to recruit a talented corps of officers and men and to maintain morale (without an issue of rum) and discipline (without recourse to the lash). In 1796 peace terms were agreed on between the United States and Algiers (at a cost of almost a million dollars, part of the sum being ransom for captives, part the cost of a frigate delivered to Algiers)—and terms were made with Tunis ($56,000) and Tripoli ($107,000)—and technically the construction of the ships for the new navy should have been halted but war with France—or Britain—seemed imminent and construction continued.

Despite the agreements the United States was presented with new demands every year, and every year it followed the practice of other countries and acceded to the demands because the trade with the Barbary states and in the Mediterranean was so lucrative that the United States could not afford to be shut out. In 1800, however, the United States sent a frigate, the *George Washington*, under the command of William Bainbridge to pay his respects to the Dey of Algiers and, it was hoped, impress him with American naval might. The Dey's understanding of the situation was quite otherwise—"You pay me tribute by which you become my slaves," and he insisted that Bainbridge use his ship to ferry women, children, and goods to Constantinople. Bainbridge, with his ship in harbor under the guns of the forts, decided that he had to accede to the demand.

In 1801 the Pasha of Tripoli, in a fit of pique that he was not being paid as much as the Dey of Algiers and that the profits from peace were less than the profits of war, chopped down the pole holding the flag of the United States and declared war. Jefferson was convinced that money paid to the Barbary states ". . . is money thrown away and that there is no end to the demand of these powers, nor any security in their promises. The real alternative before us is whether to abandon the Mediterranean or to keep up a cruise in it, perhaps in rotation with other powers, who would join us as soon as there is peace," but manning the fleet was difficult. Skilled sailors mostly preferred the better pay and living conditions of the merchant fleet and the officers trained in the Revolutionary War were now becoming too old for an active and lengthy campaign. Nonetheless, the ships were manned and the new United States navy was ordered to the Mediterranean.

The American commander, Richard Dale, wasted no time in getting his small fleet to sea, crossing the Atlantic, and entering the harbor of Gibraltar. The Spanish reaction to the new navy of a new nation was mixed. Shots were fired from a xebec at the captain of the *Essex* when he was returning from shore to ship. The next day his lieutenant, Stephen Decatur, visited the xebec that had done the shooting and asked to see the captain. The captain, he was informed, was already on shore. In that case, he said, "tell him that Lieutenant Decatur of the frigate *Essex* pronounces him a cowardly scoundrel and that when they meet on shore he will cut his ears off." The affair traveled all the way up to the king of Spain who settled the dispute with a command that the navy of the United States be afforded all courtesies.

Dale arrived in Gibraltar just as two enemy ships were about to put into the Atlantic to continue their raids on American shipping. Dale could not attack the enemy ships in the British harbor (one of them was the unfortunate *Betsey* converted into a man-of-war and renamed the *Meshuda*). The pirate captain was a Scotsman who had been taken prisoner long before and had converted to Islam and turned pirate. Dale told him that he intended to engage him and destroy him as soon as he cleared the harbor; the British refused to help the renegade Scot, refused to let the pirates resupply, or take on water. When Dale sailed on toward Tripoli, he left one ship, the *Philadelphia*, to watch the pirates. The pirates did not care for the odds, even so, and they left a maintenance crew on the ships and crossed from Gibraltar to North Africa by rowboat at night. The ships languished there for years.

Dale commanded three frigates and a schooner: *President, Philadelphia, Essex,* and *Enterprise*. With this fleet (except for the *Philadelphia* stationed at Gibraltar) he made a show of force at Algiers and Tunis to remind these states that they were at peace with the United States, and then continued on to Tripoli with one ship, the *President*. (The *Essex* was escorting a convoy and the *Enterprise* had had to sail away to replenish its water.) He found Tripoli alert and well defended and all shipping safe within its harbor.

He soon discovered that the war was fraught with difficulties. The first difficulty was simply to find a way to get at the Tripolitan pirates. While no single pirate ship was a match for the American ships, still they could maneuver by oar in shallow water where an American ship could not go, and they did not need to fight—they could remain safely within the harbor of Tripoli. The American fleet was not large enough to effect an entrance into a harbor that was well guarded by forts and cannon. In the end he adopted a strategy of blockading Tripoli and starving the Pasha into submission. (While, at that time, fewer individuals were concerned that a blockade would visit suffering upon everyone else before the Pasha suffered, nonetheless the American leaders hoped, for their own sake and for the sake of the people of Tripoli, that the campaign would be brief, inexpensive, and bloodless.)

The campaign proved to be far more difficult than expected. A north wind could blow the fleet upon the shore, a south wind would blow the fleet out to sea and remove it from the blockade as long as the wind continued to blow from the south, and, somehow, even with favorable winds, the blockade seemed incapable of preventing supplies from getting into the city—oared ships with low draught could navigate the shallows along the coast out of range of the fleet and enter the harbor with their cargo. Moreover the commanders did not have accurate charts of the coastal waters and they had to be supplied with food and water (eventually procured within the Mediterranean), powder and shot, rope and sail, across four thousand miles of ocean, a month's voyage, and their sailors had enlisted for one year and would have to be replaced or persuaded to remain.

Dale continued the blockade for several weeks in the hope that the ruler of Tripoli would offer terms, but when no terms were forthcoming, and the ship was running short of water, Dale lifted the blockade and sailed to Malta. He had decided that he needed a base, not in Africa because he did not have the men to defend it, but among the many nations sympathetic to the American effort (even if they were too involved in their own wars to offer any material support).

Dale continued to divide his effort, one ship to watch the straits of Gibraltar, one to protect American merchants, one to ferry supplies, and one to maintain the blockade, until the *Constitution* ran aground in the difficult waters off the north African coast and Dale was reduced to three ships. Although the objective had been crystal clear in America, exactly what would be required to attain the objective was not. The physical circumstances were much harsher than expected, the equipment did not work as well as expected, the enemy proved to be intransigent, and the initial plans went awry because they were unrealistic and impractical.

Not long after Dale had abandoned the blockade, the pirate man-of-war *Tripoli* entered the harbor after an encounter with the *Enterprise*. The commander of the *Enterprise*, Captain Sterrett, in a common ruse de guerre had been flying the British ensign and the pirate, suspecting nothing, had heaved to and had replied to inquiries about his actions that he was cruising the Mediterranean looking for American shipping. Captain Sterrett then raised the Stars and Stripes and ordered him to surrender. The pirates refused. The pirate captain tried to close and board, the American ship held off and fired broadsides. When the pirate ship managed to close, Marine musket fire cleared the pirate ship of boarders. Finally the pirate lowered his flag and Captain Sterrett brought his ship in to board the pirate ship and accept its surrender. The pirate raised its colors, fired on the American, and tried to board. Again the Marines broke up the boarding party and the American fired another broadside. Again the pirate lowered his colors and again tried to close and board, again Sterrett fired a broadside, again the Marines repelled the boarding attempt, and Sterrett gave the order to fire at the waterline and sink the pirate. Finally, after three hours, the pirate pulled down his colors, threw them overboard, and surrendered for real.

Captain Sterrett had managed the *Enterprise* so skillfully that the *Enterprise* had knocked over one mast on the enemy ship, inflicted fifty casualties (twenty killed), battered the ship, forced it to surrender, and all without loss of life on his ship. But President Thomas Jefferson did not believe that he had the power to prosecute a war without a declaration and naval instructions did not allow a ship to "take" another ship. Hence, once a ship surrendered, the victorious captain had no option but to release it. First, however, he ordered his men to dump the cannon, powder, and all small arms overboard, and chop down the masts, and then he released the pirate ship. When the ship limped into port the Pasha forced the defeated captain to ride down the streets of Tripoli backwards on a mule with sheep intestines around his neck and then had him bastinadoed (that is, he had the bottoms of his feet beaten with canes).

The ruler of Tripoli could make nothing of the Americans' bizarre act, to fight and defeat a ship of the enemy, and not to loot it, not to imprison its crew, but to release it. *What did this mean?* And then the American fleet intercepted a Greek ship on its way to Tripoli. The Greek captain claimed that he did not know there was a blockade and so he was turned back, but he was carrying twenty Tripolitan soldiers who could legitimately have been made prisoners. The ruler of Tripoli offered to exchange them for three American prisoners. The Americans agreed, landed their prisoners, and waited in vain for the three Americans to appear.

This unwarlike behavior and naiveté encouraged Tripoli and unsettled the other three Barbary states. If the Americans knew so little about war, what risk could there be in making demands on them? Why should their states be inconvenienced by the blockade. Richard Dale, faced with the difficult circumstances, the prospects of an expanding war, and the end of his men's enlistments, decided to sail his flagship home. He left his captains to conduct operations and they soon fell to arguing with each other, and with the other American officials in the region, as each of them pressed his own plan for a proper military campaign and conducted his own negotiations.

Back home Dale discovered that Congress (in February 1802) had finally authorized the president to take whatever action he saw fit to protect American shipping and that the navy had issued new instructions to its captains authorizing them to "take, sink, burn, or otherwise destroy" hostile ships. Dale also discovered that he had been superseded in command by Commodore Richard V. Morris.

Morris had been given a sizable command—twelve frigates and a schooner—and that was the last good news he had. His flagship, the *Chesapeake*, was damaged in a storm and had to be refitted at Gibraltar, a repair that took three weeks; part of his fleet was taken from him because it was thought that such a fleet would be too expensive and unnecessarily large; the emperor of Morocco wanted a series of concessions to prevent his entering the war, money, of course, and the *Meshuda*, still locked in the harbor at Gibraltar, and free passage for his ships into Tripoli. On the way to Tunis Morris took a prize, the *Paulina*, which the Bey insisted had cargo that belonged to one of his subjects and he demanded that Morris come ashore to negotiate payment for that part of the cargo. When Morris went ashore, the Bey arrested him and refused to let him leave until he had been paid $22,000. At Algiers the Dey was incensed because the Americans had sent him $30,000 in cash instead of promised naval goods and so he impounded the cash and insisted that the goods still be delivered.

The American negotiators insisted that Morris accept the demands. He refused. American merchant captains insisted that he protect them, but they refused to accept any limitations on their routes or timetables. Soon Morris heard that an American ship, the *Franklin* out of Philadelphia, had been captured and four Americans were prisoners in Tripoli. And he was having trouble controlling his subordinates. One of his captains, Murray, after a fight with Tripolitan gunboats wrote a long complaint to Morris that he saw no point in maintaining a blockade without a fleet of small boats to operate in the shallows, he was running out of provisions, he couldn't maintain his station with winter approaching, and he recommended that Morris negotiate peace; another captain removed his ship from the blockade and sailed around the Mediterranean, and the others were constantly complaining that they needed supplies. Morale was low. Tempers were short. Duels were common. Two of his ships were ordered home. And at the moment when he was most dependent on Malta for supplies, one of his midshipmen fought a duel with the British governor's secretary.

The British in Malta patronized the Americans, ridiculed their efforts against the pirates, suggested that Americans would never stand the smell of powder, and then emboldened by the Americans' lack of response, became more aggressive. A British officer three times tried to push an American midshipman out of his way.

The third time the midshipman knocked the Englishman down. The Englishman proved to be the secretary of the British governor of Malta and a famous duelist. He sent his second to the American ship to demand satisfaction. When Lt. Decatur learned what had happened he offered to act as a second to the young midshipman.

As the challenged party Decatur could set the conditions (so long as they were equally fair for both). He informed the British officer that the duel would be pistols at four paces. The officer replied, "That looks like murder, sir."

"No," Decatur replied, "like death."

The duelists met and Decatur called, "Ready," and then waited until the hand of the British duelist shook from the strain of holding his pistol steady, and called, "Fire." Both missed, but the American's shot touched his opponent's hat. Honor was technically satisfied, but the British officer refused to offer an apology, the two loaded, and took their stance. Decatur told his principal, "Aim lower," and again the two fired, and the British officer, shot in the face, fell dead. The governor demanded that the two American officers be handed over to him for trial, but their commander sent them back to the United States on the next ship.

Meanwhile Morris's flagship was wrecked by a gunpowder explosion, his ships deteriorated, and his few bright moments seemed to mock him. A new captain, Captain Rodgers of the frigate *John Adams*, captured a prize. The prize was the *Meshuda*, which had been released to the emperor of Morocco who then filled it with supplies and sent it to Tripoli. Rodgers captured it without a shot being fired. He joined Morris in Malta and Morris decided to return to Tripoli. He arrived just in time to surprise a grain convoy guarded by Tripolitan gunships. The convoy was close to the shoals in dangerous water. Morris hesitated to bring his ships in so close to shore, the gunboats got away into Tripoli, the grain boats beached, and Morris was urged to send in his ships' boats to burn the grain boats. He hesitated because of the uncertain coast. In the morning the Tripolitan army arrived and threw a breastwork around the boats, but Morris decided to make the attempt. He sent his force into a prepared position with predictable results—some of his men were killed, no boats were burned.

Morris was totally demoralized. He landed under a flag of truce and tried to negotiate a truce with the ruler of Tripoli. True, he had been authorized to spend up to $20,000 to gain peace, but such a sum could only be sufficient if offered from a position of strength. The ruler of Tripoli demanded ten times that and reimbursement for all his expenses during the war. Morris returned to Malta and left Rodgers of the *John Adams* in command. Rodgers had dash and he soon showed it. He maintained his station close to the port and his lookouts reported several gunboats emerging. Thus alerted, he soon spotted a ship trying to make the harbor. He cut it off, forced it to seek refuge in a bay, raced the gunboats by sea and the Barbary army on land, sailed into the treacherous shoals, and blasted the enemy ship. The enemy returned fire, but Rodgers continued to work his ship in through the dangerous waters, closer and closer, until the enemy abandoned ship. Rodgers was just about to run on the rocks and he had to wear his ship out and away from the shore without taking possession of his prize. The Tripolitans then returned to their ship, the army was almost there to help them, and Rodgers sailed into the shallows again and opened fire. The enemy ship exploded, throwing its masts a hundred feet into the air and covering the whole area in a cloud of smoke. When the smoke cleared, the Americans could see only fragments of a ship. The Tripolitan army and the gunboats returned to Tripoli.

Here, at last, was an occasion when Morris might have tried to negotiate. Instead he lifted the blockade, took a sailing tour through the straits of Messina, the Bay of Naples, the western Mediterranean, and out to Gibraltar. There he received a letter relieving him of command. In a subsequent board of inquiry he was censured and dismissed from the navy. In his defense he wrote,

Gentlemen can in their closets plan expeditions at their ease, make winds and seas to suit their purpose, and extend or contract the limits of time and space; but the poor seaman struggling with a tempest on a lee shore must have something to eat.

Two commanders now had failed, but President Jefferson and the Congress of the United States were no less determined to continue the war. Congress voted $96,000 to build two schooners and two brigs to aid in the blockade.

—— 22 ——

"Preble and His Boys"

Jefferson and his secretary of the navy chose Edward Preble to command the new expedition. Preble came from a prominent and influential New England family, reduced in circumstances because the British had burned their estate. After one season (1776) of farm work to help support the family, Preble ran away and found a job as the cabin boy on a privateer. He impressed the captain so much with his activity and his enthusiasm that the captain enrolled him as an ordinary seaman. In 1779 he was given the rank of midshipman and enrolled in a light frigate that had a running fight with an Indiaman and sank it, had another fight with an English frigate, and then was taken by a pair of British frigates in 1781.

Preble was sent to a prison hulk where he contracted typhus and almost died. He was exchanged and soon back in action. Preble became known for his energy, courage, seamanship, air of command, and hot temper. In 1782 he led a boarding party on a cutting-out expedition against a British brig that had been given the mission of hunting down the Americans; although his assault team was outnumbered, under his leadership they drove the English sailors over the side and brought the brig out of the harbor. After the war Preble was active as a ship captain and agent in commerce around the world and when it looked as though the United States might go to war with France over trade issues, Preble was appointed first lieutenant in the *Constitution*. He had not been aboard long before he decided that he could not serve under the captain, who (a citizen of Boston wrote) was as full of bluster as he was empty of courage.

This good citizen added that the second lieutenant was a young man "who is deficient in every point essential to a good officer, he is said to be intemperate and he looks it—the surgeon is the opposite of what he ought to be in morals and politics and in his profession; there is not a man in this town who would trust the life of a dog in his hands. His second is of the same cast of character, but not so highly finished—Mr. Preble [only], the first lieutenant, is a smart active popular man, judicious and well qualified for his station, or for the first command."

Preble's superiors shared these views and, in the end, they decided that he was so valuable to the new service that they must prevent his leaving the navy by promoting him to captain and giving him a ship. They convinced the secretary of the navy that Preble not only deserved promotion and a ship but that he was the man to place in command of the war in the Mediterranean. Preble, however, was junior even to Rodgers and if Preble were to command, Rodgers, and the other captains, who were senior to him, would have to be recalled and replaced with fresh, junior captains.

Although Preble had distinguished himself in the eyes of the president and secretary, he was not so well known in the navy and his appointment caused some resentment and some awkwardness. Jefferson and the secretary of the navy did believe in Preble, but they also suspected that the war was not being pressed as they wanted because the senior officers were motivated more by mutual jealousies than any desire to fight the enemy, and they preferred an outsider. In any case, their choice was brilliant. Preble infused his fleet (the *Constitution*, forty-four guns, the *Philadelphia*, thirty-eight guns, two brigs of sixteen guns, and three schooners of twelve guns) with his enthusiasm, energy, and purpose. He talked with men who knew the area and he studied the situation.

Still he was unknown to his subordinates and to the navy. He believed in discipline. Many officers believed a warship should be run like a merchantman. He exploded in anger and set his subordinates on edge. He was quick to censure and quick to fire off letters:

Your men on shore [he wrote to a subordinate officer] for the purpose of fitting your rigging, were this afternoon most of them drunk. This must undoubtedly have happened in consequence of the negligence of the officers in charge of them. I request you to make the necessary inquiry respecting this neglect on their part, as I shall most certainly take notice of it. One of your men is in irons on board this ship for impertinence to me.

He spoke aggressively and often of what his command would do and his subordinates suspected that he was all bluster and brag; then on a dark night out of Gibraltar one of his junior officers tried to hail a ship running parallel to them. The watch on the other ship seemed unwilling to identify themselves. Preble grabbed the speaking trumpet from his junior officer and demanded that the other ship identify itself. When he received a refusal he ordered them to respond or he would fire on them. They replied that they were the *H.M.S. Donegal*, 84 (that is, that they were armed with eighty-four guns), commanded by Sir Richard Strachan; they threatened to fire back and they shouted that their commander, Strachan, ordered the Americans to send a boat aboard. Preble replied,

"This is *U.S.S. Constitution*, 44, Edward Preble, an American commodore, and I'll be damned if I'll send a boat aboard any ship. Blow your matches, boys!"

"Blow your matches" was the last command before "fire!" The British ship sent a boat and proved to be a thirty-two-gun frigate. Preble's subordinate officers and the crew knew now for a certainty that Preble's talk was not bluster and, further, they knew that his watch, because of his insistence on discipline, had detected the other ship before it had detected them and that his crew was ready to fight while his opponent was not.

Preble arrived in Gibraltar in September of 1803, assumed command of his combined fleet, and learned that the emperor of Morocco was contemplating war upon the United States. Captain Bainbridge of the *Philadelphia* had stopped a Moroccan ship escorting a smaller vessel that he believed to be American. The Moroccan captain claimed to have no papers, thinking thus to thwart any questions about his possession of the ship, and he added that he had taken the ship in anticipation of war. Bainbridge then informed him that that was an act of piracy and he was within his rights to hang him immediately from the yardarm. The papers were discovered—they stated that the Governor of Tangier had commissioned the captain to make war. Preble without more ado proceeded to Tangier, caught the city by surprise, entered the harbor, seized their warships, imprisoned the crews, ran out his guns, and then offered to negotiate with the emperor.

The two men reached agreement quickly: Preble would not destroy Tangier and the emperor would not consider any thought of war, he would release all American captives, provision the American fleet, guarantee the safety of American ships (which, he claimed, had been attacked at the behest of the governor not himself), and would return to that peace and amity that the two nations had always enjoyed between them. The emperor assured Preble that he was a friend of America. The two sides parted with mutual understanding.

Preble then brought his fleet to Tripoli to join the two ships he had sent ahead to reestablish the blockade. While he was on his way disaster struck. Captain Bainbridge of the frigate *Philadelphia* had no sooner sent his schooner to check out a report of two pirate ships cruising to the west, than he had spotted a ship trying to slip into Tripoli. He pursued into such shallow waters that he had leadsmen on platforms on the sides of the ship casting the lead continually while he fired at long range at the escaping ship. He came to the mouth of the harbor before he broke off pursuit and turned. The leadsmen pulled in their leads and were prepared to cast them again when the ship ran full speed onto an unmarked reef. There was a crash, the ship rose and heeled over and stuck fast.

Bainbridge tried everything, using the sails to back off, lightening the ship by pumping out the fresh water, throwing overboard the anchors, the cannon, cutting away the foremast. All the while Tripolitan gunboats closed and fired into the wounded ship and Bainbridge was unable to return fire. The Tripolitan army marched up opposite the ship and prepared to board boats to rush the ship. Had Bainbridge not sent his schooner away the schooner would probably have been the ship that pursued the enemy into the harbor or, if not, the schooner could have protected the *Philadelphia* while the crew floated her off or in the last extremity could have taken off the crew. Instead Bainbridge had all military stores and weapons thrown overboard and then surrendered before night fell and the Tripolitan army boarded his ship.

Officers and men were stripped of their possessions and left only their shirts and trousers. The surgeon, Dr. Jonathan Cowdery, like the other officers, had to run a gauntlet of looters, one helping him on his way with one hand while the other rifled his pockets. He was marched between two lines of soldiers. One spit on him, another hit him in the head. Then he and the other officers were taken before the Pasha. The Pasha was quite satisfied to see them, he had a banquet prepared, and he found them (the officers) adequate quarters, the house that had belonged to the American consul. There the prisoners could walk upon the terrace at the top of the house and view the harbor. They received a visit from the Danish consul who did everything in his power to help them—he gave them a credit so they could buy clothes and supplies. (Their own possessions were offered back to them at an exorbitant price.)

The surgeon complained in his journal that his daily diet was a breakfast of two eggs and bread and a dinner of "poor beef, or camel's flesh and bread and sometimes boiled cabbage" and nothing to drink but rainwater. The surgeon was permitted to visit sick or injured members of the crew and the Pasha employed him as his personal physician and the physician for his family and courtiers. Consequently Dr. Cowdery was treated very well (although as his worth went up, so did the price of his ransom) and he was sometimes allowed, under escort, to go for walks outside the town and to visit the gardens of the Pasha and pick whatever fruit—figs, lemons, oranges, apricots, cucumbers—he wished. Ultimately, however, the officers' treatment depended upon the actions of the American fleet; sometimes the officers were housed in the consul's quarters and sometimes they were removed to the dungeons of the castle, but, all in all, they were treated well.

Quite otherwise was the fate of the enlisted men. The prisoners had been stripped of all but trousers and shirts, taken by boat close to shore, and cast off in the water, told to sink or swim, and marched between ranks of armed men, who spit on them, to a filthy dungeon where they waited while servants brought them clothes, tattered, but dry, to exchange for the wet; the sailors naively expected that their own clothes would be dried and returned to them. They spent the night in a piazza open to the weather. On their first morning a sorceress examined them, cried an incantation over them, chose the one black man among them to be a cook for the mamelukes, and boasted that her magic had brought the *Philadelphia* onto the rocks. Then they were marched to a filthy warehouse and driven by the lash to carry its contents to another site. This warehouse, twenty feet by fifty, was to be their prison.

In the evening each man was given a small loaf of bread, the first food they had been given since their captivity. They had only their tattered clothing, no bedding and no blankets. The following day the Pasha put them to hard labor. The members of the crew who were recalcitrant or who managed to get their hands on alcohol were trussed up so that the bottoms of their feet were exposed and then thrashed on the feet. They were issued a ration of two small loaves of bread a day and expected to purchase anything else they wanted. One of the sailors turned traitor, informed on the others, and eventually converted and openly joined the Pasha's troops. During the whole of their captivity they were worked, beaten, and threatened with torture.

Their first task (after they had prepared their own prison) was to help unload and repair their own ship. It was floated off the reef, the cannon were recovered, the ship was refitted, and it lay at anchor, ready to be manned and used against the American fleet. Preble's orders were to make war on Tripoli and negotiate peace. He did open negotiations (with no real hope of receiving an acceptable deal), but when the Pasha demanded that the damaged frigate be ransomed with a new schooner, Preble broke off negotiations and established his blockade.

Preble's first concern was to eliminate the captured *Philadelphia*. Ideally he would have liked to send a raiding party in the dead of night to board her, take her, and bring her out of the harbor, but the reality of the situation forbade such a solution—the ship might be guarded by 500 men and he had but a thousand in his whole fleet—so he concluded that he would have to destroy her. Wooden sailing ships were susceptible to fire because of the dry wood of the ship itself, the canvas sails, the tarred ropes, and the gunpowder. A careless light could destroy a ship; a determined attack should succeed, if it could only reach its target. *But how?*

Then Preble captured a two-masted ship being sent by the Pasha to Constantinople. He took it into service and renamed it the *Intrepid*. The *Intrepid* outwardly appeared to be a Tripolitan ship, the news of its capture might not yet have reached Tripoli, and Preble's mind turned naturally to the possibilities the capture afforded. He chose Stephen Decatur to command the ship, because Decatur had been the first to reach him with a proposal to take the *Philadelphia*.

On February 2nd he gave Decatur written orders "to proceed to Tripoli, in company with the *Siren*, Lieutenant Stewart, enter the harbor in the night, board the *Philadelphia*, burn her, and make good your retreat with the *Intrepid*, if possible, unless you can make her the means of destroying the enemy's vessels in the harbor, by converting her into a fire ship for that purpose, and retreating in your boats, and those of the *Siren*. You must take fixed ammunition and apparatus for the frigate's eighteen-pounders, and if you can, without risking too much, you may endeavor to make them the instruments of destruction to the shipping and Bashaw's Castle. You will provide all the necessary combustibles for burning and destroying ships. The destruction of the *Philadelphia* is an object of great importance, and I rely with confidence on your intrepidity and enterprise to effect it. Lieutenant Stewart will support you with the boats of the *Siren*, and cover your retreat with that vessel. Be sure and set fire in the gunroom berths, cockpit, storerooms forward, and berths on the berth deck."

Decatur took some seventy men, his officers, his midshipmen, and an experienced pilot, Salvadore Catalano, who knew the harbor at Tripoli and was fluent in the *lingua franca* of the Muslim Mediterranean. Decatur broke his command up into separate details, drilled the men in the harbor in Syracuse (Sicily), and then sailed for Tripoli. Their ship was only sixty feet long, loaded with vermin, crowded, and the rations were rotten, but the men were keyed up with the adventure and in only four days they were close enough to Tripoli to see the minarets. Then, as they waited for dark, a westerly gale blew up, blew them off station, and knocked them about for eight extra days of pounding, diarrhea, and vermin. On the ninth day the wind was fair for Tripoli, but the *Intrepid* outsailed its companion ship (which was supposed to supply them with boats and men to aid in the attack on the *Philadelphia* and on other targets, if possible) and arrived at the mouth of the harbor as night fell. Decatur could not delay without taking a chance that watchers on shore might become suspicious of a supposedly innocent vessel holding station outside the harbor and waiting for an enemy warship.

Decatur immediately abandoned part of the plan that he was to wait for boats from his companion ship, and sailed directly into the harbor. The storm had caused a nasty rip and Decatur had to maneuver his vessel around it, but once inside the harbor the moon lighted the water and he could easily pick out and steer for the *Philadelphia*. He and Catalano were dressed in Turkish clothing and when the guards on board the target hailed them and ordered them to fend off, the pilot spoke to them in the argot of the Muslim Mediterranean.

They had lost their anchors in a storm. Could they not tie up to the frigate and spend the night?

A Barbary guard replied,

What was that warship becalmed outside the harbor?

The pilot informed him that it was the *Transfer* (the ship purchased by the Pasha in Malta) and his knowledge of that detail convinced the guards that the *Intrepid* was just what she appeared.

Decatur intended to sail right into and collide with the *Philadelphia,* but the wind failed while he was still twenty yards short. Quickwitted, in a low voice he ordered the few of his men in Turkish costume to man a boat and carry a rope to the frigate. The Tripolitans were so convinced that the *Intrepid* was innocent that they also sent a boat with a rope. Once the ropes were attached, the American crew, lying out of sight, gently pulled their ship toward the frigate. Just as the ships were about to touch a guard shouted, "Americanos," and Decatur gave the order, "Board!"

The guards were caught by surprise. They did not have time to seize muskets or to form up. Some tried to defend themselves. Some ran to the side and jumped off the ship. A few rallied in the bow of the ship; Decatur charged them and they flung themselves into the sea. Only one American was wounded in the action. The Americans spread throughout the ship with rags soaked in turpentine, threw them down holds, scattered them throughout the ship, and set them ablaze. The fire spread so quickly that a few Americans barely escaped to their own ship. They cast off their rope and frantically tried to fend off the blazing *Philadelphia* but they could make no headway. Then they realized that the rope fixed by the enemy was still in place.

They chopped through that rope, but they were so close to the burning ship that they could not get the oars out on that side and they continued to try to fend off.

At last they cleared enough to put the oars in the water and row. They strained at the oars and seemed to make no headway, they could feel the heat from the fire, it threatened to jump to the *Intrepid*, but then the *Intrepid* moved a little and moved less sluggishly as they got under weigh. The blazing ship provided a target for the Turkish gunners who now at last were manning the guns, but the *Intrepid* pulled away and her companion ship sent in boats and crews to help as soon as Decatur fired the flare that was the signal that he had been successful, or, in this case, with the *Philadelphia* blazing brightly in the harbor, that he had survived. Before the *Intrepid* cleared the harbor the *Philadelphia* blew up. The expedition had been a complete and brilliant success and, because of it, Stephen Decatur was promoted to captain.

The Pasha, however, still held 300 Americans in his prisons and was in no hurry to accept any terms other than his own. Preble, then, had the hard part of the war ahead of him: to maintain the blockade month after month in all weather. He had to supply his ships, to refit and repair, and to keep his crews together when the sailors were on short-term enlistments and the harsh conditions convinced many to leave after their term of service was up (some left *before* their enlistment was up); he had to negotiate with the half-crazed king of Naples and Sicily for supplies and aid, to inspect the supplies that reached him from America, and condemn the half that had to be tipped over the side, and always he had paperwork: to requisition, to request, to explain.

Why had he let a Russian ship, captured while running the blockade, go.
Seven Russian battleships in the Mediterranean.
Why had he not let go . . .?

And he was ill. The harsh conditions exacerbated his illness. His hair had turned white. His patience was thin and he resolved on decisive action. He used all his resources, one frigate, six little brigs and schooners, and eight small gun vessels. He had borrowed the gun vessels and a hundred men from the king of Naples and Sicily. His own force was about 900 men. Tripoli had a hundred cannon, well manned, and dozens of small craft that in total could carry as many men as Preble had. His move was desperate—fragile wooden ships against stone fortresses—but he did not intend to destroy the fortresses, merely to cause the Pasha to count the cost of this war and agree to moderate his exorbitant demands.

While he conducted the bombardment, his little boats were to raid the shipping and destroy whatever they could. Stephen Decatur commanded a minor force of three little boats, but he employed them with élan, dashing into the shallows and attacking the pirates in their little boats, hand-to-hand, sixteen men against thirty, but an attack delivered with such ferocity that his force of sixteen overwhelmed the pirates. One lieutenant (Trippe) boarded an enemy boat and fought the captain hand-to-hand; Trippe received eleven cuts by the enemy's scimitar before he dispatched him. As Decatur was towing out a boat he had captured, he was informed that his brother had been mortally wounded by a pirate who had feigned surrender when James Decatur laid his boat aside and then, when the young Decatur had boarded the enemy boat, had shot him in the head.

Stephen Decatur immediately cast off the boat he was towing, turned on what he identified as the treacherous enemy, boarded, although he had only eleven men against the enemy's twenty-four; he fought his way through to the captain, a muscular man, and fought hand-to-hand against him. The enemy thrust at Decatur with a boarding pike. Decatur parried the thrust with his cutlass and the cutlass broke in two. The enemy struck again and wounded Decatur in the arm and chest. Decatur grasped the pike and wrenched it from his enemy's grasp, but before he could turn it on the captain, the captain threw himself on him and the two grappled. They fell and rolled on the deck. Another Turkish officer slashed at Decatur and an American sailor, wounded in both arms, threw himself between and took the blow intended for his commander. The enemy captain managed to draw his yataghan and stabbed at Decatur. Decatur caught his wrist with his left hand and scrambled in his pocket with his right for the pistol he had there; he cocked it, pressed it against the enemy, and fired. The enemy captain relaxed in death and his crew surrendered. Decatur towed out his two prizes.

Preble fired at the shore all afternoon. The shelling destroyed many of the houses, but caused few fires because the houses were of stone or mud brick. As the attacks began, the Turks bowed in prayer and then rushed to man the guns. The Pasha had a bomb-proof bunker where he stayed except for infrequent forays to check on the progress of the fighting. To protect himself at these times he had a slip of paper with a protective verse blessed by a holy man pasted to his forehead. Many of the soldiers had similar charms in velvet bags around their necks. While the battle was going on, priests chanted imprecations on the Americans and recited charms to bring the American ships onto the rocks.

Each time a ship's guns came to bear on a cannon emplacement the crew ducked for cover, but as soon as the ship turned away, they returned to their gun. Preble destroyed some pirate boats and his mortar vessels lobbed rounds into the city and terrified the inhabitants. Finally as night came on and the sea breeze blew toward land, Preble hoisted the signal for the fleet to withdraw. One final broadside brought down a minaret on a mosque. The fleet marshaled out at sea and in forty-eight hours repaired the damage done to the ships and manned and outfitted the three prizes for use in the next assault. Once again Preble engaged the enemy inshore. The resistance was fierce, one of his little ships blew up, and after three hours he withdrew.

Once more he marshaled at sea, determined to make another attack, but his fleet was joined by the frigate *John Adams*, which brought a dispatch informing Preble that he had been superseded in command by Samuel Barron (who was senior to him). Preble was not certain when Barron would arrive, but he decided in an act of moral courage to assume the responsibility of continuing the attack despite the deterioration of his ships and men. The sailors were beginning to show symptoms of scurvy, a disease brought on by vitamin deficiency and made worse by a high-salt diet, and Preble had to find a source of fresh vegetables and supply his fleet with them. His ships were running short of every supply and were themselves becoming unseaworthy because of the pounding they had been taking, but he attacked again and again, by day and night, even entering the harbor with his own ship, the *Constitution*, and sending his light boats in so close to shore that they received musket fire.

As the summer passed into the storms of autumn, Preble determined on one last spectacular attempt to force the pirates to negotiate. He decided to send an explosive ship into the harbor to wreak as much damage as possible. He had the *Intrepid* filled with tons of gunpowder and the gunpowder was layered with pieces of iron and flammable materials. His plan was that a volunteer crew would sail the ship, now a seven-ton grenade, into the harbor as close to the fortress as possible, set the fuses alight, and attempt to escape. He had no shortage of volunteers; his officers and men had long been infected with his aggressive spirit, and the *Intrepid* set out with its crew of thirteen to strike the decisive blow of the war. The sailors in the fleet could track the advance of the ship by the gun flashes directed at it and then, suddenly, outside the harbor, the *Intrepid* blew up. The catastrophic fate of the American ship raised morale in Tripoli and lowered morale in the fleet, but Preble did not lose his determination—he maintained the blockade and sent the light vessels back to Sicily. At this point his successor arrived.

Edward Preble left his mark on the United States Navy. He set a model of behavior as a commander in war, unrelenting in his determination to get at the enemy, a courageous leader who infused his subordinates with his same spirit, and also a teacher who taught them how to organize a naval campaign. His subordinates distinguished themselves as the leaders of the U.S. Navy in the War of 1812.

23

The Marines Go Ashore

The new commander, Samuel Barron, succeeded to the command of a fleet that had been held together and on station by the will of Edward Preble. Barron had new instructions. He was to bend every effort to negotiate a peace, but if he could not, then he was to keep a small fleet on station to effect a permanent blockade of Tripoli and to send the rest of the fleet home. All too often in the reporting of war the single brilliant action is described while the courage shown in enduring day after day is discounted. Samuel Barron kept his fleet on station during the winter storms, men tossed about on the waves, ships battered and in need of constant repair, incipient scurvy, the common injuries of muscle wrestling against machine, skin raw with salt, not enough fresh water to wash, clothes rotting, cramped quarters, inadequate food, the boredom of actions repeated over and over again, the moments of danger from the enemy, from the weather, from the uncharted shore, and the constant exposure to damp.

While the president, his secretary of the Navy, and Congress were steadfast in their determination to prosecute the war against Tripoli, they had to admit that the war had not gone at all as they had expected. They had thought the mere threat of blockade would be sufficient to compel the Pasha of Tripoli to negotiate. They were wrong. They had thought a small force could blockade the port. They were wrong. They thought that the blockade in and of itself would force the Pasha to negotiate. They were wrong. In short, they and their commanders had not known and had to learn how to conduct a naval war against a determined enemy.

As the weather improved, the health of Barron deteriorated and he was forced to make his headquarters on land and to ask Captain John Rodgers, who had distinguished himself in the early stages of the war, to assume command at sea. Rodgers was an active man, as careful with the lives of his men as he was willing to risk his own. On station off Tripoli, he went by night in his gig, so close to shore that he could hear the sentries talking. Back and forth he went, taking soundings, and making notes on the charts he had, so that in the future his ships would be able to operate close to shore with some confidence.

The blockade was to be maintained until Barron returned to sufficient health to resume command from his land headquarters, but Rodgers was not free to pursue the course that seemed best to him under the circumstances of the moment at Tripoli, and Barron did not have immediate intelligence of the situation on which to form the best judgment. Still, when two Americans approached Barron and laid before him a scheme by which to put pressure on the Pasha, and perhaps win the war, he approved it, and Rodgers supported it. The two Americans were William Eaton, the American consul in Egypt, and James L. Cathcart.

James L. Cathcart had been a slave in Algiers for ten years, the secretary to the Dey, and afterwards he had been appointed the American consul in Tripoli. When he was captured the Algerian captain told him and his fellow captives to be brave, fortune held many vicissitudes, the slave of one day may be the master of another, and no doubt "when you make your peace with your father, the King of England, the Dey of Algiers will liberate you immediately." As other prisoners had been, so was he stripped of everything and given verminous and tattered clothes, fed on poor food, and constantly reminded of his new state of existence in which he could be worked to death, sold as a galley slave, or sold into the interior of the country, punished at the whim of his captors or for their amusement. As they were the first Americans captured, they were paraded through the town and shown to the courtiers (one of whom expressed surprise that they looked so much like Englishmen).

Cathcart was first put to work in the gardens and then sent to the harbor to be chained and worked in a gang, until the loss of a large number of Neapolitans who were ransomed and the loss of other prisoners who died of the plague opened up positions for a literate man (by then he had learned Arabic): he employed his native wit, intelligence, and character to advance from gardener to coffee brewer to clerk of the harbor to clerk of the bagnio galeria. The clerk of the bagnio galeria was allowed to open a tavern in the prison and keep half his profits. With these profits Cathcart opened other taverns and made more money (although he was still put to hard labor from time to time). Finally he was appointed chief secretary of the Dey. As chief secretary Cathcart was involved in the negotiations for his own ransom and he was sent by the Dey to America to arrange payment. Cathcart sailed in a ship that he had purchased himself.

The other American, William Eaton, was one of thirteen children of a school master; his father introduced him to Plutarch's *Lives of the Noble Greeks and Romans* and he was determined to emulate them. At the age of fifteen he ran away from home to join the Continental Army but when he was set to washing dishes and doing chores, he deserted and went back home. Still the lure of adventure was strong and he reenlisted and rose to the rank of sergeant before the war ended. Later he attended college where he was known for his courage and athleticism; after college he taught, entered politics, and through favoritism received the rank of captain in the new army of the United States, joined the campaign of Mad

Anthony Wayne, feuded with his superior officers, just dodged a court-martial, and was appointed the American consul to Tunis.

Eaton was hardly the best choice to be consul. From the moment of his reception in Tunis—instead of gratitude for the gifts he brought, the Dey complained that Algiers had received much more and better stuff from America—he felt nothing but contempt for the rulers of the Barbary states and their people. As consul during the war he kept intriguing to eliminate, replace, or overthrow the Pasha of Tripoli. His first plan was for the U.S. Navy to capture Tripoli's admiral and then to use him to entice the Pasha onboard ship and kidnap him. Finding no enthusiasm for that plot, he tried to convince the government that 3,000 troops and a few cannon landed behind Tripoli could easily take that city—a Danish commodore had told him so—but the president had no desire to raise a force of 3,000 Marines and transport them across the Atlantic to fight in North Africa. Then he learned that the Pasha's older brother Hamet had fled to Tunis to escape what he suspected was an assassination plot in Tripoli.

Cathcart came up with the initial idea to use Hamet against his brother, and Eaton embraced the idea: how logical to replace Yusef with Hamet and then make peace with Hamet. He set out to convince others that Yusef was not so strong as they imagined and far more unpopular and that he could be toppled by a small expenditure of money and a small force. Eaton gave Hamet an allowance while he tried to put together the plan. Yusef learned of the plot and offered Hamet the governorship of Derna (a city to the east of Tripoli) and sent him a bodyguard of forty men to ensure his safe conduct from Tunis to Derna. Eaton convinced Hamet that his brother intended to murder him but he could not convince him to retaliate.

Meanwhile Eaton fell ill and had to leave Tunis. Without his constant intervention Hamet decided to accept his brother's offer. Eaton recovered and returned to Tunis, but Hamet had been expelled and Eaton soon was expelled himself. He returned to his early ideas of kidnapping, to intercept Hamet on his way by ship to Derna, take him off, and secure his person. The navy captains—"old women" as effective as "quaker meeting houses"—were not persuaded of the merits of his scheme.

Eaton and Cathcart proceeded to Washington to try to enlist support for their scheme while Hamet went to Derna. There he was greeted with such enthusiasm that for a time he considered marching on his brother, confident that he could raise a hundred thousand men! Eaton had to overcome the scruples of the president and Secretary of State James Madison to convince them that it was not unfair to use one brother against another, particularly when there was little to choose between them, except that one could aid the interests of the United States. Madison, finally, was convinced "although it does not accord with the general sentiments or views of the United States, to intermeddle in the domestic contests of other countries, it cannot be unfair, in the prosecution of a just war, or the accomplishment of a reasonable peace, to turn to their advantage, the enmity and pretensions of others against a common foe."

In addition, though all the other senior naval officers involved in the war were opposed to the plan, Edward Preble (then still on station in the Mediterranean) supported it and his support carried weight. Preble had already used the possibility to threaten Yusef. Yusef had responded by sending an army to rout his brother out of Derna and on the approach of the army Hamet fled to Egypt. Eaton returned to the Mediterranean and then had to convince the new commodore, Barron, to help him. Barron resisted, Eaton pressed, Barron grew ill, Eaton continued his suit, and finally Barron agreed to lend him the limited use of the *Argus* and a small number of Marines under the command of Lieutenant Presley O'Bannon. Lt. O'Bannon fell completely under the spell of Eaton; he called him "general" and declared that he was "the greatest military genius of our era."

Hamet could hardly have chosen a more dangerous refuge than Egypt, though one his brother was unlikely to penetrate. Napoleon had come to Egypt and then the British and then the Turks again, but they ruled only in Cairo. South of the city the Mamelukes were in rebellion, Arab raiders, or bandits, roamed the countryside, and a band of Albanian mercenaries were supporting themselves by plunder. Here Eaton came in two Nile riverboats, one flying the American flag, one the British, in search of Hamet. Eaton had to travel through lines of soldiers and marauders, convince the Mamelukes surrounded by the Turks not to kill him out of hand, convince Hamet to return through these manifold dangers to Cairo and to entrust himself to Eaton, to raise an army, and to fight a war against his brother. Eaton was confronted by the Turkish viceroy. The viceroy knew that his pose as a tourist was false. *Why had he come?* Eaton laid it on thick, to restore to his rightful place a Pasha wrongfully deposed by his brother, to right a wrong, and he so swayed the viceroy that the viceroy ordered his troops to break through the Mamelukes and bring Hamet back to Cairo. Eaton was appalled. The viceroy's plan was sure to get Hamet killed, by the Mamelukes if not by the Turks.

Then Eaton fell in with an adventurer of shady reputation, Eugene Leitensdorfer. "Leitensdorfer" was the *nom de guerre* of a man who had deserted from three different armies, held a series of menial jobs, and promoted himself assiduously. For fifty dollars he said that he could get through both the Turkish and Mameluke lines and fetch Hamet out. Eaton gave him the fifty and Leitensdorfer produced Hamet. (He had first to convince him that this was not just a plot by Eaton to deliver him over to Yusef in a trade for peace.)

Meanwhile the French consul told the Turks that Eaton was an American spy working for the British. On the way to Alexandria Eaton was detained by the Turks until he was able to convince them that he was not a spy and Hamet was refused entry to Alexandria because he had consorted with the Mamelukes, but at last Eaton was able to welcome Hamet in a luxurious pavilion outside Alexandria. Hamet was suspicious and Eaton made promises far beyond his instructions or his power—for instance, to let Hamet keep a pirate fleet and repay the United States from the loot it would take. Hamet finally agreed to make the attempt if Eaton could raise an army.

Eaton and Hamet settled on a plan to march overland to Derna. Although Hamet assured Eaton that all of Tripoli would rise in his favor, the two, nonetheless, decided to raise an army in Egypt. Eaton found no shortage of unemployed soldiers in Egypt, but he had no money and he had to recruit such men as would be attracted by the possibility of adventure and loot, should the expedition be successful. Somehow Eaton raised a force of 400 men from the disparate elements he found, a Greek artillery unit, mounted Arabian cavalry, Moors, a Frenchman who claimed to be Bourbon royalty, and, along the way, Bedouins, and a few Austrians and Italians. He had a personal guard of seven Marines under the command of Lt. O'Bannon and Midshipman Peck.

One of the two commanders of the cavalry and the owner of a train of camels, Sheik el Taiib, negotiated with Eaton for $11.00 per camel to carry the army's supplies. Eaton had $53 in cash, he had been authorized $40,000 by Washington, and he by this time had promised about $100,000 to be paid when the troops met the fleet and took Derna. The camp was divided between Christian and Muslim, each contingent camping apart from the other, and Hamet continued to be suspicious of Eaton. Eaton had made promises, Hamet expected those promises to be fulfilled immediately, and there were local officials who expected payments from the army.

One official refused to release some of the supplies because he had not been paid. This affair of the detained supplies quickly escalated into a Turkish army on the march to seize Hamet and turn him over to his brother. Hamet was ready to flee until Lt. O'Bannon assured him that the Marines were quite capable of defending his person. And then, while Eaton went to the *Argus* to inform the captain that he would not be carrying the army, but rather could return to Syracuse and pick up supplies and meet the army at Bomba (a landing place about three-days march to the east of Derna), a rumor reached Hamet that his brother was on the march with a great army. Hamet prepared to flee. Eaton reassured him, but he could never totally convince Hamet that his brother and a large army were not out there, lying in wait.

Eaton had arrived in Alexandria on November 26th, he got his army marshaled and prepared to move on March 4th, at which point el Taiib demanded more money for his camels. Eaton made him promises and on the 8th at about eleven o'clock and with the thermometer at ninety degrees the train of the army set out. They had to cross 500 miles of desert steppe, that is, not the sandy, dusty desert of the Sahara, but a more fertile land with decent footing for horse, camel, and man, and, at this time of the year, with well-spaced springs, wells, and cisterns to supply the army with water and pasture for the animals. That is not to say that there was no sand of the fine powdery type of the African and Asian desert that gets in the clothes and rubs the body raw, infiltrates the food, gets in the mouth and the nose and the eyes, and swirls at the slightest breeze, nor to say, if there was no breeze to stir the sand, that swarms of flies did not gather on every susceptible surface. The first day the army traveled a little more than ten miles and camped at an oasis. The next day they marched nine miles and in the evening the camel drivers demanded more pay; put off for the night, they returned to Eaton in the morning and repeated the demand. They wanted their money in advance, because, they had been told by el Taiib, they could not trust a Christian to keep his promises.

Hamet seemed to offer no help, so Eaton announced that if the camels would not move, the expedition was over, and they might as well return to Alexandria. The ploy worked but the day had been consumed in haggling. The next day the march resumed and the army covered forty miles in the next two days. At this point a false messenger arrived who claimed that he came from Derna and that the people there had risen and taken the town and were only waiting for Hamet to arrive to be installed as their ruler. The army around Hamet fired their weapons into the air to celebrate, but the camel train behind believed that the army was being attacked and they rushed forward to join with the attackers and get their share of the plunder. The Greeks aimed their artillery piece, sure that the Arabs had turned on them, and Eaton had to ride between the two sides, threaten them both, and finally get across to them what had happened. Peace was restored and they covered another seventy-five miles.

After they pitched camp a fierce rainstorm hit them and they had to move their flooded camp. They were forced to halt until the rain subsided, and then the camel drivers demanded more money. Put off again, the army soon resumed the march, buoyed by the ready supply of water and of the pasture that the rain had produced. The army reached the first settlement, a valley inhabited by Bedouins. Here el Taiib demanded that he and his men be paid as they had now fulfilled their contract. Hamet, they claimed, had hired them only to bring supplies to this point. Eaton confronted Hamet and discovered to his dismay that Hamet had indeed done just that. Hamet had assumed that as soon as he reached the border of Tripoli the people would flock to him with their draft animals and the army would not need el Taiib and his camels anymore. Eaton had to take up a collection among his officers to raise enough money to hire the camels for two more days. Once they were paid, the majority of the camel drivers slipped away into the desert with their animals. The rest refused to continue.

Hamet refused to move. He was convinced that his brother's army was on the march and he was afraid to go any farther until he had proof that the American fleet was at Bomba and that this was not all a plot on the part of Eaton to turn him over to Yusef in return for a general peace treaty. Eaton threatened and swore, but in the end he agreed to send a scout to check that the fleet awaited them, if, in turn, Hamet would agree to advance two days' march. Success now depended upon the *Argus*, packed with arms, ammunition, pay, and supplies.

The two-days' march brought the army to a large encampment of Bedouins. The Americans were the first Christians the Bedouins had ever seen and they were amazed that these devotees of Satan flourished as they apparently did. The army spent four days in the encampment, waiting for news of their ship at Bomba, but when a rider did appear, it was with news that the army of Yusef was three days' march from Derna. Hamet was ready to throw over the expedition, but again Eaton convinced him to continue and Hamet managed to recruit some one hundred of the Bedouins to join them, and, to bring with them, most importantly, a camel train of ninety animals. Now, when el Taiib refused to go any farther without more pay, Eaton could dismiss him and tell him to return to Egypt.

An ugly scene ensued, which terrified Hamet because he believed that el Taiib would turn on them and join Yusef. Eaton expressed no concern and el Taiib and his camels remained with the army for the day; that night the sheik convinced most of the Bedouins to desert. Eaton was forced to wait while Hamet negotiated. Eaton was exhausted after a month of marching and wrangling, forcing an unwilling pretender to come forward to claim his throne, holding an army together, negotiating with a wily sheik to whom the expedition was no more than an opportunity to enrich himself. Eaton gave up and spent five days wandering around the Bedouin encampments, taking ethnographic notes, and generally enjoying himself.

The sheiks scattered, Hamet disappeared—to find them, he said—and el Taiib demanded larger rations and threatened to leave, threatened worse, and Eaton told him to go. Hamet returned. El Taiib promised to behave and the army lurched forward, slowed by the Bedouins who had brought their families and saw no reason to hasten through an area known for its succulent dates. Still Eaton pressed them onward. And then, a few days' march from Bomba, Hamet ordered the army to pitch camp and he refused to budge. Eaton swore that he would lock up the rations and no one would eat until they got on the march again.

Hamet began to prepare to march back to Egypt. Meanwhile a group of the Arabian cavalry stormed the supply tent. Lieutenant O'Bannon drew up his Marines. The two sides confronted each other. A single shot, a single word—and their blood was up—would have started the melee that certainly would have ended in the death of all the Christians. Hamet joined the Arabs. Eaton rode between the two sides, dismounted, and approached Hamet. He asked him who his friends were, what his interests were, and persuaded Hamet to dismount and go with him into the tent. Hamet ordered the Arabs to disperse and Eaton promised to release the rations—which by now consisted of rice and only rice—if the Arabs would promise to march the next day. Eaton concluded that it was impossible to convince Muslims that Christians could be trusted.

After another short march Eaton learned that the Greek cannoneers had joined the Arabs and were determined to force Eaton to release the rations. Eaton sent an envoy to threaten them with execution, but, before he had to act, a scout returned to the camp with the news that the *Argus* and another ship were anchored at Bomba. The army celebrated and struggled on, still days away, marching until the rice gave out, eating a couple of sheep (purchased by bartering a camel)—the only solid food they had—consuming herbs along the way to sustain themselves, urged on by Eaton to cross the last ridge where Eaton looked out at the bay on the evening of April 15th and saw neither ships, nor any human being nor any food in Bomba. Fortunately Eaton and his army did not know how close Jefferson was at that very moment to giving up the entire war.

Hamet accused Eaton of bad faith. Meetings were held in his tent all night and Eaton feared that the *Argus* had decided that the army was lost and had sailed away. The next morning, while violence simmered below the surface, a sail was sighted and the *Argus* came into the bay. Eaton was able to distribute food, ammunition, and $7,000 among his men. The American fleet's local command of the sea allowed them to sail where they would and bring supplies, but the ships had no men to spare and Eaton had to make do with his few Marines and his ragtag army. He also received a letter from the commodore repudiating the agreement he had made with Hamet and stating without equivocation that the United States was free to withdraw its support from Hamet at any time.

Derna was just sixty miles away, a short and easy march compared to what they had just finished, but a rumor hit the army that Yusef was on his way to Derna with an army and he was intent upon revenge. The army was on the point of dissolution, Hamed was ready to flee back to Egypt, and Eaton once more had to use his persuasive powers, which were considerable—he had after all recruited an army with no more than promises—and he convinced his army that the rumor was false. In addition, this time he had cash to distribute. The army advanced. In three days they reached Derna and could contemplate its fortifications. Eaton dispatched a letter calling upon the governor to surrender.

"Let no difference of religion induce us to shed the blood of innocent men who think little and know nothing."

The governor sent the letter back. At the bottom of the letter he wrote, "My head or yours."

Eaton was lent a couple of guns by the American ships, manhandled one up an eminence above the city, and ordered the barrage to commence, while the ships sailed in close and bombarded the harbor and town. Eaton had divided his forces into the Marines, the Greeks, the few other Christian mercenaries, a few Arab foot infantry, all in all, about fifty men, under his personal command, and the Arab cavalry under the command of Hamet. He wanted to fire at least a few rounds from his cannon into the fortifications opposite him, where the enemy's fire had pinned down his men. (He thought that he was outnumbered about three to one.) His gunners were so excited that they forgot to remove the ramrod and fired it off at the enemy on the first shot—and so put the gun out of action.

Eaton kept his head and ordered his men to charge. The Marines led and the army followed. Meanwhile, all Hamet's doubts dissipated in the face of action and he led his cavalry around the town to attack from the south. When the enemy saw Eaton's little force charging at them with the Marines in the lead, they abandoned their fortifications and fled, except for one, who turned and fired one last shot. The bullet struck Eaton in the wrist, shattering the bones. The Marine lieutenant took charge, kept the army moving forward, and gave the enemy no chance to rally, until he had driven them from the town. Hamet and his cavalry captured the palace—the governor took refuge in a friend's harem—and Lt. O'Bannon raised the Stars and Stripes. Two Marines died in the attack.

Hamet was installed as the ruler of Derna. In this confused situation he had only one certainty: that his brother would act. Eleven days after they had taken Derna the army of Tripoli arrived. Again Eaton, despite the pain of his injury, had to rally his troops and organize the townspeople to hold the fortifications and not to abandon Derna. He was able to use the captured guns to good effect, and the fleet caught several flanking movements by the enemy and broke them up with cannon fire. An attack by 1,200 men broke through Hamet's Arabs and into the town, but the ships' cannon and the musket fire of the townspeople drove them off. The army of Tripoli settled into a siege. Eaton was convinced, if he was given enough money, he could induce the whole enemy army to desert.

Meanwhile the United States had made a further effort to build and dispatch small ships to operate in the shallows off Tripoli. Seven of these now joined the fleet. The blockade was intact and American ships continued to take prizes. While the blockade could not actually starve out Tripoli (the Pasha had said that if he had but three frigates he could blockade America as effectively as they were blockading him), it hurt, and now Yusef had to confront the fact that his brother and his brother's army was no farther away from Tripoli than he had been from Derna in the beginning. Further, he did not trust his commanders even though he held their closest relatives as hostages; he had been unable to raise troops in his own domain and had lost control of the sea to the Americans. *Might the Americans transport Hamet's army to Tripoli?* Rumor had it that the Americans had 4,000 Egyptians in Syracuse ready to invade Tripoli and 10,000 Marines available (so Dr. Cowdery had told the Pasha when he inquired of this force) and Eaton's army, which to Eaton, perhaps, seemed not so formidable, to Yusef was still an army formidable enough to cross 500 miles of desert, capture his fortress at Derna, and continue to hold it against a sizable force.

Yusef asked the Americans if they were willing to discuss peace terms. The Americans were more than willing. The two sides quickly agreed on terms. The American negotiators wanted the return of the captured Americans (whom the Pasha had promised to burn alive if his throne was threatened), they wanted guarantees that the Pasha would no longer raid American shipping, and they wanted peace. The Pasha readily agreed to end his war and he promised to keep the peace and, furthermore, if the two ever went to war again, then he promised that he would exchange prisoners without ransom. In the present case, however, since he already had the American captives, he asked and received $60,000 ransom and whatever prisoners the Americans held. Then he saluted the American flag and the war was over. Unspoken was the brutal fact that the Americans would now abandon the force in Derna. Yusef pledged to respect the persons of Hamet and his force, but no one really expected him to abide by his word.

On June 11, 1805 Eaton learned that the peace had been signed. He was furious. Our aim, he informed Barron, was "to chastise a perfidious foe, rather than to sacrifice a credulous friend." But facts were facts and he had to figure out how to extricate himself and Hamet from a dangerous situation. He brought Hamet and O'Bannon into a conference and told them, and only them, about the peace. Hamet had had a taste of power; had acquitted himself very well; had led a counterattack against the enemy, driven them to the foot of a cliff, forced them to dismount, and climb the cliff to get away from him; had received deserters from the army who brought offers to change sides if he could give guarantees. Now he accepted the change of fortune, but he told Eaton that if the news got out, they would all be killed by their own men.

Eaton announced to his troops that the *Constitution* (the ship that had delivered the news of the peace) had brought reinforcements and that he planned to attack the besiegers (who, uncertain of American intentions, had retreated fifteen miles into the desert); he issued ammunition and rations, and as night fell, Lt. O'Bannon had his men patrol the waterfront and ordered his Christian troops to leave fires burning and come to the pier. There he ordered them to get into the boats of the *Constitution*. They did in considerable puzzlement. Eaton sent word to Hamet that he needed to confer with him and Hamet came down to the harbor with his entourage. They boarded the boats and then the Marines and Eaton boarded. Suddenly the abandoned troops realized what had happened. They cursed Eaton and Hamet and then sought their horses, collected their possessions, and rode out of the city and away. Only the townspeople who had supported Hamet were left to face the wrath of his brother.

—— 24 ——

The End of Mediterranean Piracy...

The war was over, the United States maintained a presence in the Mediterranean, insurance rates dropped, shipping was protected, but in less than ten years the United States was at war with Britain and the British actively encouraged the Dey of Algiers to resume his attacks on American shipping. The assurances of the most powerful navy in the world joined to a natural rapacity convinced the Dey to join in the war. Yusef in Tripoli also returned to piracy and profited immensely from the war as did the other Barbary states. When the war ended in 1815, the United States had a substantial fleet, outstanding officers (who had gained their first introduction to war under Preble), and experienced crews; the president and Congress wasted no time in authorizing an expedition to neutralize the Barbary states.

The Department of the Navy appointed two fleets with two commanders on March 2nd. Whoever got his fleet ready to sail first would have the honor of commanding the first expedition. Decatur was still recovering from a wound, but he knew that the best sailing season in the Mediterranean was quickly approaching and he hurried to New York to take command of his fleet. On May 20, 1815, the fleet left New York harbor. Decatur had his flagship, *Guerrière* (fifty-three guns), the *Macedonian*, the *Constellation* (forty-eight guns), the sloop *Ontario* (twenty-two guns), the brig *Epervier* (eighteen guns), the brig *Firefly* (fourteen guns), the brig *Flambeau* (twelve guns), the brig *Spark* (twelve guns), the schooner *Spitfire* (eleven guns), and the schooner *Torch* (ten guns). Decatur was determined that the entire fleet would cross the Atlantic together and so come upon Algiers by surprise and in full force.

They set their sails day and night and lost only one ship to weather. (The *Firefly* had to return to New York). As Decatur approached Africa he asked every passing ship about the Algerine fleet (three frigates, three corvettes, two brigs, one xebec, and one schooner). At Cadiz he learned that the enemy fleet had already passed, in all likelihood headed home, and at Gibraltar he learned that they had put in only two days before. Decatur waited a day for the rest of the fleet to join him, set out again, and on July 17th his lookouts spotted a single ship. Decatur ordered his ships not to pursue openly, but to act like a British squadron, from which an Algerine ship would have nothing to fear.

The plan was too complex to communicate by flag and one of his ships broke out their colors. The suspect frigate immediately took to flight. By then it had been cut off from the African coast and it turned to seek refuge in Cartagena, but the game was up. The American ships closed until their yardarms almost brushed the enemy ship. Algerine marksmen were firing on the Americans and the captain of the Algerine ship could be seen, sitting in a lounge chair on the deck, directing his men, when Decatur gave the order to fire. A cannon ball cut the pirate captain in half, the broadsides cleared the decks and drove the gun crews below to safety, the marksmen in the yardarms were eliminated, but the Algerine ship would not surrender. The ships of the American fleet each had their turn, until the pirate no longer returned fire. Decatur ordered his guns to cease fire and he dispatched a boarding party. The Americans took 400 prisoners, put a prize crew on the battered frigate, and sent it off to Cartagena under the escort of the *Macedonian*.

Two days later the fleet spied an Algerine brig and pursued. The brig tried to escape in the shallows off the shore or entice the larger American ships into that dangerous water, but Decatur knew full well how dangerous the shore was and used his smaller ships in the pursuit. The brig ran aground, the crew took to the boats, the Americans manned their own boats and pursued, sank one of the enemy boats, chased the crew to land, took eighty prisoners, and boarded the brig. They towed it off and took it as a prize that was also sent to Cartagena. On July 28th Decatur sailed into the harbor of Algiers; he was prepared to bombard the town and sink the ships in the harbor. The Dey raised the white flag of negotiation.

The Swedish consul and the Algerine captain-of-the-harbor came on board the flagship to negotiate. The captain refused to believe that the Dey's frigate had been taken until Decatur brought forward that ship's lieutenant (who had been wounded in the action). Decatur then presented a letter from President Madison to the Dey:

A squadron of our ships of war is sent into the Mediterranean Sea, to give effect to this declaration. It will carry with it the alternative of peace or war. It rests with your government to choose between them.

Decatur and his chief negotiator had also set their own terms: negotiations would take place on board the flagship, any ship entering the harbor while negotiations were under way would be taken as a prize, all American captives would be returned without ransom, and no tribute would be paid to the Dey in any form. As the Dey was considering his options and possible delaying tactics, he was informed that a ship was approaching the harbor and Decatur was making preparations to attack it. To save his ships the Dey immediately sent his envoy to agree to everything; he freed the captives, signed the peace, received the American consul, returned all seized property, and paid an indemnity of $10,000 for the value of what could not be returned. Decatur had won a complete victory, albeit a victory only in Algiers and not binding on any other of the pirate states.

Decatur took his fleet to Sardinia for ten days' rest and recreation and then proceeded to Tunis. During the war with the British an American privateer had sent two prizes into Tunis, supposedly a neutral port. The Bey of Tunis had allowed, or had not resisted, a British cutting-out expedition and the prizes, valued at $46,000, had been taken. Decatur demanded that the Bey pay him the $46,000. The Bey, as he considered this proposal, could see the American ships beyond the entrance to his harbor and he could see a small boat crisscrossing the entrance to his harbor—the occupants of the boat were taking soundings in case the fleet needed to enter the harbor. The Bey threw the blame on the British for encouraging his hopes and then abandoning him, but he paid the indemnity with the complaint that Americans "send wild young men to treat for peace with old powers."

Decatur then proceeded to Tripoli, a place well known to him, to make the same demand for the same reason, prizes taken from the harbor by the British to the value of $30,000. In addition to the money Decatur also demanded that consular relations be restored and that the Pasha Yusef fire a salute when the American flag was raised. The Pasha refused at first but then he heard reports of the events at Algiers and Tunis, he realized that his memories of war with Americans were now outdated, and he reconsidered. Still the Pasha bargained with Decatur and in the end he paid $25,000 and ten Christians (valued at $500 per person). Peace was established and the flag raised over the American consulate and saluted on August 7th, 1815. In seventy-one days from leaving New York harbor Decatur had compelled the Barbary states to pay him indemnities and to recognize the United States, to conclude peace and to promise good behavior.

Decatur was well aware of the real substance of the victory—

It has been dictated at the mouths of our cannon, has been conceded to the losses which Algiers has sustained and to the dread of still great evil apprehended. And I beg leave to express to you my opinion that the presence of a respectable naval force in this sea will be the only certain guarantee for its observance.

American political and military leaders had learned how to conduct war, and their success protected American shipping, but the Barbary states still sent out pirates—and in 1818 carried plague to European ports. In 1820 the French sent an expedition to conquer Algeria. They had many reasons—the piracy, the plague spread by Algerian ships, the loss of prestige in the Napoleonic wars, the rivalry with Britain—but the result was the subjugation of Algeria. This conquest and the conquest of the rest of North Africa by other European powers ended Barbary piracy.

From the times of the Greeks and Romans down to the Algerians and Tunisians, the most profitable and desired form of booty had been a human being. The end of the Barbary states also ended a two thousand (and more) year history of slaving in the Mediterranean.

—— PART VIII ——
CONCLUSIONS AND REFLECTIONS

Strangers, who are you? Where are you from? Are you crossing the watery ways of the sea as merchants or are you just cruising here and there as pirates who risk their own lives to do harm to strangers?

—The Cyclops Polyphemus

—— 25 ——

How Pirates Are Made

There are still pirates today and they became pirates for much the same reasons men in the past became pirates.

POVERTY

The Greeks (who said of themselves that they did not eat all they wanted but all they had) and the Vikings lived under the same conditions—a growing population sustained by diminishing farmland. The pirates of the ancient Mediterranean all originated from lands that could not support them. The poorest of them may have been the savage men of the Balearic Islands. With no more weapons than their slings, they would rush down to hidden rafts and launch sudden attacks upon passing merchant ships. They naively believed that the sea, itself, was bringing to their barren island the means of survival. The buccaneers of the Caribbean saw their meager livelihood—hunting cattle—destroyed, leaving them no livelihood but the sea. Nor could the Barbary pirates be fed with the resources of the North African coast and the pirates of China, the Tanka, were forbidden to leave the ships on which they lived. All, at one time or another, faced deprivation if not starvation and all shared the second condition—sea-going expertise.

SEA-GOING EXPERTISE

The Athenians said that they needed no training before they took their places on the rowing benches of their triremes because they spent so much of their lives at sea. Greeks, in general, more than other men (before the Vikings), traded and fished and traveled on the sea, they explored and settled around the Mediterranean, and they loved and feared the sea. The Tanka lived only on their boats. The buccaneers needed sea craft just to travel to their hunting grounds and back. All the pirates came from environments where knowledge of the sea and of ships was second nature. And yet poor men with ships do not become pirates unless they have opportunity.

OPPORTUNITY

If there is no plunder available, there are no pirates. In the period from the fall of the Roman empire to the time of the Crusades, there were few merchants in the Mediterranean, and there were few pirates. The raids by the Vikings began only when the attack on Lindisfarne revealed a whole world laden with plunder. The buccaneers only threw themselves into piracy after the success of Peter the Great. And yet not all poor seamen succumb to temptation and become pirates.

In the ancient world both philosophers and generals debated whether piracy was a moral or an economic choice. In the *Odyssey* Odysseus, as hero, had no more qualms about plundering a place than a hiker has picking blackberries, but he considered himself of good, heroic character because he was motivated by the pursuit of glory, not profit. In his pirate guise he depicted himself as a man uninterested in glory, not a hero, but a man born to a pirate destiny. Likewise, the Romans, when dealing with pirates, though they certainly were prepared to execute every pirate they could get their hands on, nonetheless also provided the means for an honest living to pirates who renounced piracy and turned themselves in.

THE TIPPING POINT

Sometimes, it is true, seamen needed no more encouragement to piracy than the sight of a rich merchant ship passing by, but more often the tipping point from legitimate trader, fisherman, or explorer to pirate was brought about by war and its attendant chaos, confused loyalties, and moral ambiguities. Piracy in the modern Mediterranean arose as part of the conflict between Islam and Christianity, the Vikings turned the expertise they had acquired in their local wars against their hapless victims, the buccaneers retaliated against the Spanish who had attacked them and were used by English and French officials as an instrument by which to divert attention from themselves, defend their own colonies, expand their power, and weaken the Spanish, all without having to acknowledge this policy publicly and without having to spend a penny, and then they used the buccaneers in their war against each other.

In war pirates can freely raid the allies of one belligerent and find haven with the other, they can switch sides and be welcomed, can acquire a quasilegal status, be augmented, supported, and even paid by one side to attack the other. So the Barbary pirates were both independent entrepreneurs and agents of the states that gave them harbor and used them to attack Christian powers.

Up to a point piracy—though abhorred—is accepted as a normal risk of doing business on the sea, particularly by people like the Greeks, who believed that they lived in a dog-eat-dog world. Success, however, breeds success. The Illyrians, the Cilicians, the Vikings, and, particularly, the buccaneers, had spectacular successes, and their successes and the prospects of quick riches, attracted ever-increasing numbers of pirates. A larger number of pirates meant that pirates could carry out more ambitious raids. Pirates, plunder, and war mixed together can create a critical mass.

CRITICAL MASS

In the face of resistance pirates may become more brutal, may combine in larger fleets, may improve their techniques, and may become a threat to settlements, to governments, and even to nations. The Cilician pirates tried to enlist Roman dissidents, internal enemies (such as Spartacus), and external enemies to combine in coordinated attacks against the Romans; the buccaneers established their own semiautonomous communities; and the Tanka planned to overthrow the Qing dynasty.

The story of the Tanka pirates is in a sense the story of all pirates: a dispossessed people with expertise at sea and nothing to lose, turn to piracy, are employed in a war by one side against another; they organize under a dynamic leader, but the war ends, conditions change, the pirates are no longer welcome. They employ their newly acquired skills, cooperate, form a pirate nation, and seize territory where they can find secure havens and soft targets. The four Tanka pirate fleets comprised over a hundred ships in each fleet.

As with the Tanka, the Vikings' first raids were seldom conducted by more than one or two ships and 60–120 men, but, when they discovered their targets' vulnerability, they became more ambitious. The Vikings seized land, dominated or displaced the local inhabitants, and established permanent settlements in Ireland, England, and France. Resistance just increased the size of their attacking force, their ferocity, and their determination.

What, then, should their potential victims do?

DEFENSE

If there is no power strong enough or determined enough to suppress the pirates, then the victims have to muster their own defense—build cities inland where they would have some warning of pirate raids, set up watch towers and forts, make alliances, make arrangements to recover kidnapped or enslaved citizens, be constantly vigilant, ever suspicious of strangers and quick to act even at the risk of mistaken identity. Neighbors (Hesiod writes) are better than family because they don't have to pack a suitcase before they come. The French fortified bridges and improved their local defenses; the Chinese organized local defense forces and a system of mutual support; the Spanish relied on local fortifications and a reinforced defense, all with limited success. Communities can only be effective when they combine together in a league, or alliance, and cooperate to suppress piracy. The Athenians, when they dominated an alliance of Aegean states, could eliminate all the pirates' sanctuaries, but when they lost control of the Aegean, pirates rose again and operated freely there and throughout the Mediterranean.

The Romans delegated the problem to subordinate powers, so long as piracy in the Mediterranean seemed to be a local problem and no danger to Rome itself. They formulated no coordinated strategy to combat piracy in the Mediterranean because they could see no easy way to fight at one and the same time all the pirates scattered throughout the whole of the Mediterranean. The longer the Romans dithered, the greater the problem grew, until the pirates came to believe that they were more formidable than the Roman republic and could even kidnap Roman officials with impunity. The Romans had to be forced to act, but once they *were* forced to act, they delegated extraordinary powers to Pompey and he used the immense resources and the organizational abilities of the Romans to attack all pirates at one and the same time throughout the whole of the Mediterranean. He engaged them militarily and socially: pirates who resisted were destroyed, pirates who capitulated were resettled.

As in the Mediterranean, so, too, in the Caribbean, the pirates had the upper hand; the Spanish authorities could not protect all their settlements at one time, they almost never had time to prepare, or to gather troops, and when they retaliated against pirate strongholds, they seemed just to scatter the buccaneers over a wider area and make them more dangerous; in addition, the buccaneers had the support of the English and French crowns. When, at last (after the European powers had signed a treaty), the different powers agreed that it was in the interests of all parties to regularize and protect trade, they cooperated to eliminate the buccaneers. In an act of supreme irony the British crown appointed as assistant governor of Jamaica to suppress piracy no other than Sir Henry Morgan.

The task did not prove simple. The British crown tried various methods to end piracy—it offered pirates pardons and land, threatened them, closed ports to them, and ordered distant jurisdictions—as the Romans had—to handle the problem (without offering legal or material assistance). When all these methods failed, finally, it constructed and manned an effective navy, it dismissed governors who countenanced pirates, and established courts (officials of the crown and naval officers) to try pirates wherever they were apprehended and to execute them on the spot.

Like the Romans the Qing imperial government considered piracy a local, police matter, promoted policies that inadvertently encouraged the pirates to organize, and then allowed itself to be overtaken by events. Nonetheless, the Qing court, if largely ineffectual, disposed great resources, and proved relentless, so, in the end, when the imperial court addressed the pirates' social condition—the Tanka truly were on the outside of society—granted official rank to the leaders, and integrated the lower ranks into an appropriate level of society, it was able to break organized piracy.

These are hard lessons—if societies do not check piracy, when pirates are few, they may have to pay a fearsome price in cash, property, and lives, and possibly more, because sometimes the pirates win.

Independent America and the new nation of the United States faced all the problems the victims of piracy had faced before, with the attendant questions: would we be better off paying for a safe conduct or fighting; if we fought, would we find allies; how would we get at the Barbary states so far away; how would we fight a war with our slender resources; how would we manage public opinion at home; how would we rally support in a region uniformly hostile to, and suspicious of, Christians; and how would we do all this with an infant navy that had no tradition to call on and no experience in this kind of war?

While the president, his secretary of the Navy, and Congress were steadfast in their determination to prosecute the war against Tripoli, they harbored severe misconceptions of what would be required to win. After setbacks, failures, and reverses, they found some men who knew how to fight a pirate war and some who knew the area. American representatives were able to keep the other Barbary states out of the war and they were able to attract allies enough to furnish bases. A combination of blockade, bombardment, and invasion finally convinced the pasha to negotiate.

The United States had to prove that it could protect its ships and punish those who attacked them, and it did succeed in this objective, but its success was local and limited and the Barbary states continued to send out pirates against the shipping of other nations until European powers conquered and occupied North Africa.

26

Pirates and Terrorists

Pirates are not just an historical phenomenon. Still today they attack and seize ships, murder the crews, or maroon them, or cast them adrift, to live or die. Pirates still come from the same conditions that gave rise to pirates in the past—poverty, social isolation, active or tacit support on land, a lack of a controlling authority, a lack of cooperation among maritime powers, and a disinterest in committing the enormous resources necessary to put down piracy when it still appears to be a minor nuisance.

In his recent book, *The Outlaw Sea: A World of Freedom, Chaos, and Crime,* William Langewiesche describes a world not much different from the world of Odysseus. Today, as in the time of Odysseus, a general feeling prevails that at sea there is no law and, if nations are not exactly at war, neither do they exactly live in a cooperative peace. Today, too, no one power, or coalition of powers, maintains control of ports and no government regulates or controls the ships that transport goods from port to port. A United Nations agency—the International Maritime Organization—issues conventions on safe-practices, inspection schedules, rules of navigation, and crews, but the agency has no enforcement powers and each certifying nation is free to adopt the convention in whole, or part, or not at all. Ships are crewed by the very poorest of the poor and few of the men crewing the ships would choose to earn their livelihood at sea, if they could earn it at home. They are poor, alienated from their own societies, and familiar with the sea; exploited and ill paid, they are expected to protect the cargo of the very wealthy from men much like themselves, except that they have chosen to become pirates.

So far, in the modern world, pirates have remained independent entrepreneurs without an ideological bent, merely robbers in boats, not agents of any nation, although some nations profit from, and are complicit in, the criminal activities of the pirates. In the period 1998–2002, 1,228 pirate attacks were reported, about 300 on ships underway, and 68 by gangs of ten or more pirates. The most dangerous stretch of ocean today is the 550-mile-long Strait of Malacca between Malaysia and Sumatra in the south China Sea. There a "boss" picks the targets, makes the plan, and provides the pay; a "recruiter" assembles the captain, crew, and attack-ship. The pirate captain and crew coordinate their attack with cell phones and radios, hijack the target, get rid of the crew, rename and repaint the ship, and sail the ship to a port designated by the "boss." If the pirates are caught—and sometimes they are—they, alone, pay the price, because they do not know the boss and they fear retaliation if they identify the recruiter.

While modern pirates do not seem to pose any threat to the United States, nonetheless, with no controls on who owns ships—Al Qaeda is reputed to own some—and no fast and easy way to identify the owners of any particular ship, ships could not only be seized and used by pirates-turned-terrorists, but they could also be owned and operated by terrorists. Ships could enter an American port, dock, and remain unidentified until the moment of attack. It is true that the United States has expanded its program of interception and search at sea, but with limited success, because, if the United States undertook to identify and search every ship coming to an American port, that is, if the United States were actually to institute the practices necessary to provide a minimum level of security, then (as Langewiesche puts it) the shelves at Wal-Mart would be empty.

Might pirates become terrorists? Pirates and terrorists are not much different. The definition of terrorism, "the intentional use of violence against civilian and military targets generally outside of an acknowledged war zone by private groups or groups that appear to be private but have some measure of covert state sponsorship," also defines piracy. The laws of war are quite clear—wars are to be fought between the armed forces of the belligerent states, and those armed forces are to respect the rights of noncombatants. Not only is any attack that targets noncombatants prohibited but any operation that uses noncombatants as shields is also prohibited. Both terrorists and pirates specifically target noncombatants.

True, the motives of pirates and terrorists are different. Pirates, while they have employed terror to soften their targets and to discourage resistance, ultimately are driven by profit. Terrorists use terror to effect political or social or ideological change. Pirate crews have shown themselves willing to run any risk for plunder, ready to go to sea in leaky boats, to launch attacks against superior forces, to bear hardship and starvation and the risk of drowning, ready even to divide themselves into two parties to fight each other to the death, survivors take the plunder. Would men like these turn to terror? The answer can only be—if the money were right and they thought they had a chance to survive long enough to spend it.

If modern pirates did turn to terrorism, or terrorists took to ships, we would find ourselves faced with a monumental task, a task great enough to change the way we live, as so many societies in the past have had to change when confronted by masses of pirates. The difference is that one ship today could do more damage than the largest of pirate fleets in the past. We would have to learn again the bitter lessons of the past, that our best defense would have been to kill piracy, or terrorism, at birth, but having failed to do that, then we would have to learn to be vigilant—every ship would be suspect—and we would have to form a cooperative defense, to attack the pirates, or terrorists, wherever they are, and, last, to address the sponsoring states who encourage pirates and terrorists and we would have to force these sponsors to disavow the pirates and terrorists.

These are the hard lessons learned by those who throughout history have fought pirates.

Notes

Preface

"... no commission or delegated authority from any sovereign ..."—Ormerud, p. 60.

PART I: GREEK PIRACY

If you wish to sail to the isle of Rhodes—*Anthologia Palatina* xi 162.
The drawing (from a vase painting) depicts a pirate forcing a merchant (under threat of
ramming) to heave to.

1. Odysseus: Hero and Pirate

The Persians claimed that Phoenician pirates ... —Herodotus I 1–4.
"We killed the men"—*Odyssey* IX 39ff.
"... who know justice and are kind to strangers and reverent to the gods"—*Odyssey* IX
172ff.
We kindled a fire—*Odyssey* IX 231ff.
"In the evening the Cyclops."—*Odyssey* IX 336–414.
And the devious Odysseus told him the tale—*Odyssey* XIV 185–320 (= XVII 424–433).
"They hatched a criminal plot"—*Odyssey* XIV 337–352.

2. Greeks and Barbarians

to gain some warning against the incursions of pirates—Thucydides I 5 and 7.
That is not to say—*Apollodorus Bibliotheca* II 1, 5.
"... By the harbor was a spring with fresh, cool water."—*Odyssey* IX 106–115.
"to ring the town about with a wall"—*Odyssey* VI 9–10.
"... so the Phocaeans gathered their women and children"—Herodotus I 166.
distributed in equal shares to all citizens—Diodorus Siculus V 9, XIV 97; Livy V 28.

Another pirate state (with no pretensions to being a utopia)—Herodotus III 39–60.

public celebrations outside cities—Herodotus VI 138: the Pelasgians of Lemnos raided the feast of Artemis at Brauron.

the barking of the dogs—Apollodorus *Bibliotheca* III 2, 2.

conducted an intense manhunt for rebels everywhere (except, of course, in Samos)—Herodotus V 97–101.

Miltiades traded upon his prestige—Herodotus VI 132–135.

The drawing on the map ("Greece and the Aegean Sea") comes from an archaic vase painting. It has been interpreted in various ways. The author believes that it may well depict the abduction of Io.

3. Greek vs. Greek

and close off the approaches into the Aegean—Thucydides II 32, II 69.

Democracy, one Athenian wrote—[Xenophon] *Athenaion Politeia.*

so effective that they caused a severe famine—Thucydides III 85.

pirates took advantage of their weakness—Thucydides III 51.

since the Athenian side shipped more cargo—Thucydides IV 41, VII 26, VIII 34.

One of the pirates, Theopompos of Miletus—Xenophon *Hellenica* II 1.30.

the current government to reinstate them or to reimburse them—Thucydides V 115.

States separately attempted to suppress piracy by setting penalties—*Sylloge Inscriptionum Graecarum* 37, 38.

collectively states concluded reciprocal agreements to protect each other's citizens—Tod 34, cf. Thucydides I 5–6: Oiantheia and Chaleion.

to pay their soldiers and sailors during the war—Plutarch *Alcibiades* 29.3; Diodorus Siculus XIII 69.5 and 73.

and the home territory of Athens itself—Lysias XXX 22; Xenophon *Hellenica* V 1.1–5, 14–24 and VI 2.1.

driven by the necessity to raise money to pay their troops—Xenophon *Hellenica* IV 8.35; Pritchett, pp. 82–85, 85–89; Demosthenes XXIII 60.1.

booty belonged to Athens: the ambassadors had to cough it up—Demosthenes *Against Timocrates* XXIV 11–12, 120.

Athenian rapaciousness affected so much of the Greek world—Demosthenes LIII 6–7.

a rogue named Theron—Chariton *Callirhoe* I 7.

until a Syracusan warship found it—Chariton III 3.14.

"I never did anything wrong in my whole life."—Chariton III 4.9.

Even Plato, the great philosopher—Diodorus XV 7; Plutarch *Dion* 5.

4. Greek vs. Macedonian

"waging peace as though it were war"—Bradford, p. 104.

They lived the licentious life of a pirate—Bradford, p. 128.

and raised the Macedonian kingdom to the pinnacle of power—Bradford, pp. 27–28.

Philip lavished his wealth on the most influential—Bradford, pp. 64–65.

Philip commented that he would much rather increase—Bradford, pp. 64–65.

Philip turned to piracy as one way—Bradford, pp. 52–53, 119–120, 126–127.

"It was not the Athenian people"—Bradford, p. 126.

until they had amassed enough money—Bradford, pp. 26–27.

A pirate named Sostratus—Bradford, pp. 92, 101–105.

The Athenians were just as desperate—Bradford, pp. 26–27, 126–127.

a significant portion of Athens' annual income—Bradford, pp. 52–53.

The Athenians appeared to their allies—Bradford, pp. 101–105.

"he is to be the enemy of all participating in this peace"—Bradford, p. 153.

then they captured another ten pirate ships—Curtius IV 5.18–21.

One of the successors, Demetrius the "Besieger"—Diodorus Siculus XX 97.5 cf. 110.4;
    Polyaenus V 19, IV 18.

source of their power—the promotion and protection of trade—Diodorus Siculus XX 81.3–
    82.2; Lycurgus *Against Leocrates* 18; Polybius IV 47.1.

Cities made reciprocal agreements with each other—*Supplementum Epigraphicum Grae-
    cum* XXIV 154, 19–23; *Sylloge Inscriptionum Graecarum* 535, 1–20; de Souza,
    p. 62.

". . . has a good reputation and he is rich, too"—Menander *The Sicyonian* 3–15.

their favorite joke was to bind a living captive—Valerius Maximus IX 2, 10.

Who has ever heard of an honest man in Crete?—*Anthologia Palatina* VII 654.

Arrive and unload, Depart with the gold—Strabo XIV 5.2.

PART II: THE ROMANS

"Pirates are the most hated enemies of Rome, and not just of Rome"—Cicero *Verrines* 76.

Drawing: Harbor scene (of Trajan's harbor?) from a marble relief (ca. AD 200).

5. The Romans Take Decisive Action

threw them in their ships—Pausanias IV 35.

"Queen Teuta, the Romans have an excellent tradition . . ."—Polybius II 8.

the Romans had no ambitions in that part of the world—cf. Appian *Illyrice* 7.

The drawing on the map ("The Eastern Mediterranean with an Inset Map of the Adriatic")
    depicts a Roman lembus (from a Pompeian wall painting).

6. The Pirates of Cilicia

"send letters to all those people . . ."—Riccobono *Lex De Piratis Persequendis* 122.

quench their thirst for gold—Diodorus Siculus XXXVI 20-23; Appian *Mithridatic Wars*
    92; Plutarch *Pompey* 24.

". . . captured more pirates."—Cicero *II Verrines V* 66.

a Turkish pirate chief taken by Greeks was turned slowly on a spit—Ormerud, p. 55.

"resist violently and be ready to fight."—Bean and Mitford, pp. 21–23.

7. The Scourge of the Mediterranean

"farmed the sea."—Appian *Mithridatic Wars* XIV (XII 14).

Men who preferred "to commit a crime rather than be a victim"—Appian *Mithridatic Wars*
    XIV 92.

"soldiers' pay."—Appian *Mithridatic Wars* XIV.

One crew of Cilician pirates—Plutarch *Caesar* 2; Suetonius *Julius* 4.1; Valerius Maximus
VI 9.15.
the Roman orator Cicero would say . . .—*de officiis* III 107.
". . . their harbors celebrating a kind of triumph."—Florus I 42 (iii 7) *Cretan War*.
When Verres, as rapacious a man as ever—Cicero *II Verrines I* 86–90, *II Verrines V* passim.
"exacting the rights of the victor over the defeated."—Florus I 42 (iii 7).
The Romans landed and hunted them down—Florus I 43 (iii 8).

8. The End of Mediterranean Piracy

Did anyone take to the sea . . . ?—Cicero *de imperio Cn. Pompei oratio* 31–33.
What an incredible man!—Cicero *de imperio* 33–35.
". . . declared dead and a funeral had been held for them"—Appian *Mithridatic Wars* XIV.
"The son of the man you executed, seeking revenge."—Plutarch *Marc Antony* 67.2–5.
The drawings on the maps (West and East) come from two Roman coins.

PART III: THE VIKINGS

"I cannot understand why I have kept away from the sea for so long . . ."—Frans G.
Bengtsson, *The Long Ships: A Saga of the Viking Age*, New York: The New American
Library (A Signet Book), 1954, p. 359 (a Viking named Toke speaks).
The drawing depicts a Viking ship under sail.

9. "From Merciless Invaders . . ."

"Out of the North an evil shall break forth upon all the inhabitants of the land."—*Jeremiah*
1.14.
let them feel your blade. . . . —Jones, p. 147.
an unrelieved diet of fish and more fish. . . . —Magnus Magnusson, p. 68.
"The number of ships increases. . . . "—Jones, p. 215, the account of Ermentarius, a monk
of Noirmoutier.
To taste the Frenchman's flesh.—*Heimskringla*, p. 794.
Out from the Nid our brave Harald steers.—*Heimskringla*, pp. 752–753.
The drawing on the map ("The Viking Raid in Western Europe") depicts a Viking
figurehead.

10. The Rus

"We seek a prince to rule over us and judge us according to the law."—Jones, p. 245.
Then the bier was set on fire and in an hour totally consumed.—Jones, pp. 426–429.
". . . you have seen the fetch that follows you . . ."—*The Story of Burnt Njal*, pp. 55–56.
". . . because I make more of taking life?"—*The Story of Burnt Njal*, p. 71.
. . . then they continued on their way to the city of Constantinople.—Constantine Porphy-
rogenitus (911–959) in Riha, 1969.
the Greeks had harnessed the fires of heaven.—*Russian Primary Chronicle*, p. 72.
". . . Death lies in wait for us all."—*Russian Primary Chronicle*, p. 73.
". . . Go forth with us after tribute, o Prince, that both you and we . . ."—Riha, p. 4 (AD 945).
The drawings on the map ("Rusland") show a Viking helmet and Byzantines employing
"Greek fire" (from a Byzantine manuscript).

11. Conversion and Containment

as the following story from the sagas—*The Story of Burnt Njal*
"Adopt our faith and revere Mohammad."—*Primary Russian Chronicle*, pp. 96–98.
"The sea spewed forth . . ."—Jones, *annals of Ulster*, p. 204.
in 965 Harald Bluetooth "made the Danes Christians"—Jones, p. 73.
Thus did King Olaf convert the people of Trondhjem.—*Heimskringla*, pp. 413–418.
and a church was built on the spot.—*Heimskringla*, pp. 420–427.

PART IV: THE WORLDWIDE STRUGGLE AGAINST PIRACY

"Yo-ho-ho and a bottle of rum!"—Robert Louis Stevenson, *Treasure Island*, Philadelphia
and New York: J. B. Lippincott Co., 1948, p. 8.
Drawing: "Captain Kidd's Ship"

12. The Buccaneers

". . . to be tortured by flies and other insects."—Gosse, p. 142.
and their roof the hot and sparkling heavens of the Antilles.—Gosse, p. 143, quoting Clark
Russell "Life of William Dampier."
beaten to death more than a hundred servants.—Exquemelin, p. 55.
". . . six days shalt thou collect hides, and the seventh shalt thou bring them to the beach."—
Exquemelin, p. 46.
"Jesus!" the Spanish cried, "They are demons!"—Exquemelin, p. 57.
". . . in the greatest wretchedness in the world."—Exquemelin, p. 66.
The drawing on the map ("The Caribbean with an Inset Map of Maracaibo") shows a
buccaneer ship under sail.

13. Tortuga and the Pirate Utopia

"No, they have all run away"—Exquemelin, p. 74.
"I will lead and I will shoot the first man who shows cowardice."—Exquemelin, p. 82.
"Those Spanish buggers will pay for this!"—Exquemelin, p. 88.
pieces of eight would rain down on them—Exquemelin, p. 93.

14. Henry Morgan

"I would rather die a brave man than be hanged for cowardice."—Exquemelin, p. 113.
"I will show you my house and money."—Exquemelin, p. 123.
". . . unrighteous acts you have committed against the Spanish nation in America."—
Exquemelin, p. 128.

15. The Raid on Panama

"God permitted the unrighteousness of the buccaneers to flourish for the chastisement of
the Spaniards."—Exquemelin, p. 139.
"Come on, you English dogs, you shall not get to Panama."—Exquemelin, p. 151.
A Spanish guard shouted to them, "Tomorrow, dogs, we shall see."—Exquemelin, p. 161.
a convent, hospital, cathedral—Exquemelin, p. 164.

that he had not come to listen to moans but to get money.—Exquemelin, p. 170.

"... retained nothing of his first profession except his seraglio."—Gosse, p. 171 (Walpole, Last Ten Years of George II, 1822, I, 75).

"Do not be troubled, father," the captain said to the priest, "the rascal just needed to be taught a lesson."—Gosse, pp. 172–173.

16. The Infamous Captain Kidd

"That is their mistake, not my crime"—Ritchie, p. 38.

"would have [his] soul fry in Hell-fire"—Ritchie, p. 117.

pirates who had on their persons several hundred, or thousand, pounds—Ritchie, pp. 120–121.

Not many leagues from shore, as I sailed.—Lane, p. 178.

"... and to obtain a new grant of my cargo from the king."—Ritchie, p. 209.

"... so kept the Company hot, damned hot, then all things went well again."—Gosse, p. 194.

PART V: THE BARBARY PIRATES

"Christians, be consoled ..."—Baepler, p. 108.

Drawing: A galley from the doors of St. Peters

17. Crescent and Cross in the Mediterranean

"a huge beast which silly folk ride like worms on logs."—Gosse, p. 12.

one Christian slave was "not worth an onion."—Gosse, p. 27.

Dragut replied, "Fortune is changeable."—Anthony, p. 95.

won the title "drawn sword of Islam."—Gosse, p. 32.

"Do not trouble yourself about anything but fighting."—Gosse, p. 39.

The drawing on the map ("The Western Mediterranean") depicts a galleass under sail and oar.

18. War by Other Means

"... to serve our beautiful prophet Mohammed?"—Gosse, p. 46 (paraphrase).

the Barbary pirates captured 466 British ships—Gosse, p. 54.

The fame of the action was celebrated in a ditty—Gosse, p. 59.

PART VI: PIRATES OF THE SOUTH CHINA COAST

Lots of money makes the heart light!—Aleko Lilius. I Sailed with Chinese Pirates. New York: Appleton, 1931, pp. 38–57.

Drawing: A Chinese junk

19. Out of Poverty and Isolation

to Great Governor General Who Controls Each Branch of the Naval Force—Murray, p. 38.

powerful enough (1,800 ships and 70,000 men by the year 1809)—Murray, p. 76.

The drawing on the map ("South China") is a Chinese junk.

20. The Dragon Lady

two heads tied by their pigtails and slung around his neck.—Murray, p. 131.
5,500 men, 113 junks, 500 cannon, and 5,000 other weapons.—Murray, p. 139.

PART VII: TO THE SHORES OF TRIPOLI

First Lieutenant Stephen Decatur addressed his crew. . .—Anthony, p. 71.
The drawing depicts the burning of the *Philadelphia*.

21. New Nation, New Victim

"I can not be at peace with all nations at once"—Baepler, p. 95.
the British would not be sorry to see American ships captured.—Baepler, p. 107.
"Now I have got you, you Christian dogs; you shall eat stones."—Baepler, p. 78.
fell off the wall, and broke his neck.—Baepler, p. 81.
"tenderest mercies towards Christian captives are the most extreme cruelties."—Baepler,
    p. 73.
"A Solemn Call to the Citizens of the United States,"—Baepler, p. 102.
". . . and two frigates to carry thirty-six guns each."—Watson, pp. 4–5.
"You pay me tribute by which you become my slaves"—Anthony, p. 68.
under the guns of the forts, decided that—Watson, pp. 6–7.
". . . who would join us as soon as there is peace."—Watson, pp. 8–9.
". . . when they meet on shore he will cut his ears off."—Anthony, p. 76.
the Bey arrested him and refused to let him leave.—Paullin, p. 104.
their commander sent them back to the United States on the next ship.—Anthony,
    pp. 80–82.
". . . the poor seaman struggling with a tempest on a lee shore must have something to
    eat."—Paullin, p. 103.

22. "Preble and His Boys"

". . . judicious and well qualified for his station, or for the first command."—Pratt, p. 15.
"Your men on shore . . ."—Anthony, p. 120.
". . . Blow your matches, boys!"—Pratt, p. 29.
". . . camel's flesh and bread and sometimes boiled cabbage"—Baepler, p. 167.
Quite otherwise was the fate of the enlisted men.—Baepler, pp. 188–203.
On February 2nd he gave Decatur written orders—Anthony, pp. 124–125.
a guard shouted, "Americanos," and Decatur gave the order, "Board!"—Watson, pp. 14–15.
recited charms to bring the American ships onto the rocks.—Baepler, p. 171.

23. The Marines Go Ashore

". . . the Dey of Algiers will liberate you immediately."—Baepler, p. 108.
as effective as "quaker meeting houses."—Whipple, p. 182.
". . . the enmity and pretensions of others against a common foe."—Whipple, 1991, p. 184.
he was "the greatest military genius of our era."—Whipple, 1991, p. 187.
At the bottom of the letter he wrote, "My head or yours."—Whipple, p. 228.

could blockade America as effectively as they were blockading him!—Baepler, p. 177.
had told the Pasha when he inquired of this force—Baepler, p. 180.
if his throne was threatened—Baepler, p. 181.
"chastise a perfidious foe, rather than to sacrifice a credulous friend."—Whipple, p. 235.

24. The End of Mediterranean Piracy

"... It rests with your government to choose between them."—Anthony, p. 248.
"send wild young men to treat for peace with old powers."—Anthony, p. 253.
"... a respectable naval force in this sea will be the only certain guarantee for its observance."—Anthony, p. 251.

PART VIII: CONCLUSIONS AND REFLECTIONS

Strangers, who are you?—*Odyssey* IX 252–255.
The drawing is a Viking coin.

26. Pirates and Terrorists

In the period 1998–2002—Langewiesche, William. *The Outlaw Sea: A World of Freedom, Chaos, and Crime*. New York: North Point Press, 2004, p. 46.
"the intentional use of violence against civilian and military targets ..."—Reisman and Antoniou, *The Laws of War*, p. 292.

Bibliography

PRIMARY SOURCES (FOR PARTS I–II)

(Translations were done by the author.)
Anthologia Palatina
Apollodorus *Bibliotheca*
Appian *Illyrice, Mithridatic Wars*
Aristotle *Politics*
Chariton *Callirhoe*
Cicero *de imperio Cn. Pompei oratio, Verrines*
Curtius *vita Alexandri*
Demosthenes *Orationes XXIII, XXIV, LIII*
Diodorus Siculus
Florus *epitome*
Herodotus
Homer *Odyssey*
Hymn to Dionysus
Livy
Lycurgus *Against Leocrates*
Lysias *Oratio XXX*
Menander *The Sikyonian*
Pausanias *descriptio Graecae*
Plutarch *Alcibiades, Caesar, Pompey*
Polyaenus *Strategematikon*
Polybius
Strabo
Suetonius *Julius*
Thucydides
Tod, Marcus N. *Greek Historical Inscriptions*. Chicago: Ares Publishers, Inc., 1985.
Valerius Maximus

Woodhead, A. G. (ed.). *Supplementum Epigraphicum Graecum*, Vol. XXIV. Amsterdam: J. C. Gieben, 1969.

Xenophon *Hellenica*

SECONDARY SOURCES

Anthony, Irvin. *Decatur*. New York: Charles Scribner's Sons, 1931.

Baepler, Paul (ed). *White Slaves, African Masters*. Chicago, IL: University of Chicago Press, 1999.

Bean, G. and T. B. Mitford. *Journeys in Rough Cilicia in 1962 and 1963*. Österreichische Akademie der Wissenschaften. Philosophisch-Historische Klasse. Denkschriften, vol. 102. Erganzungsbande to Tituli Asiae Minoris 3. Vienna, 1965.

Beeching, Jack. *The Galleys at Lepanto*. New York: Scribner, 1982.

Blöndal, Sigfús. *The Varangians of Byzantium: An Aspect of Byzantine Military History*. Translated, revised, and rewritten by Benedikt S. Benedikz. Cambridge: Cambridge University Press, 1978.

Bradford, Alfred S. *Philip II of Macedon*. Westport, CT: Praeger, 1992.

Braudel, Fernand. *The Mediterranean and the Mediterranean World in the Age of Phillip II*. 3 vols. London: The Folio Society, 2000. (Vol. 2, 865–891)

Breverton, Terry. *Admiral Sir Henry Morgan: "King of the Buccaneers."* Gretna, LA: Pelican Publishing Company, 2005.

Cordingly, David. *Under the Black Flag: The Romance and the Reality of Life among the Pirates*. San Diego, CA: Harcourt, Brace and Company, 1995.

Cross, Samuel Hazzard and Olgerd P. Sherbowitz-Wetzor (ed. and trans.). *The Russian Primary Chronicle* (Laurentian Text). Cambridge, MA: The Medieval Academy of America, 1953.

Crouse, Nellis M. *French Pioneers in the West Indies, 1624–1664*. New York: Columbia University Press, 1940.

Dasent, Sir George Webbe (trans.). *The Story of Burnt Njal*. New York: The Norroena Society, 1907.

de Souza, Philip. *Piracy in the Greco-Roman World*. Cambridge: Cambridge University Press, 1999.

Dittenberger, W. *Sylloge Inscriptionum Graecarum*. 3rd ed. Leipzig: S. Hirzelium, 1915–1924.

Earle, Peter. *Corsairs of Malta and Barbary*. London: Sidgwick and Jackson, 1970.

Exquemelin, A. O. (Alexis Brown, trans.). *The Buccaneers of America*. London: The Folio Society, 1972.

Fitzhugh, William W. and Elisabeth I. Ward (eds.). *Vikings: The North Atlantic Saga*. Washington, DC: Smithsonian, 2000.

Forester, C. S. *The Barbary Pirates*. New York: Landmark Books, Random House, 1953.

Guilmartin, John F. *Gunpowder and Galleys: Changing Technology and Mediterranean Warfare at Sea in the Sixteen Century*. Cambridge: Cambridge University Press, 1974.

Gosse, Philip. *The History of Piracy*. London: Longmans, Green, and Co., 1932.

Hacke, William. *A Collection of Original Voyages* (a facsimile reproduction with an introduction by Glyndwr Williams). 4 vols. Delmar, NY: John Carter Brown Library, 1993.

Hess, Andrew C. *The Forgotten Frontier: A History of the Ibero-American Frontier.* Chicago, IL: University of Chicago Press, 1978.

Hudson, Benjamin. *Viking Pirates and Christian Princes: Dynasty, Religion, and Empire in the North Atlantic.* Oxford, New York: Oxford University Press, 2005.

Jones, Gwyn. *Vikings.* Oxford: Oxford University Press, 2001 [1984].

Klindt-Jensen, Ole. *The World of the Vikings.* Washington: Robert B. Luce, Inc., 1970.

Lambert, Frank. *The Barbary Wars: American Independence in the Atlantic World.* New York: Hill and Wang, 2005.

Lane, Kris E. *Pillaging the Empire: Piracy in the Americas, 1500–1700.* Armonk, NY: M. E. Sharpe, 1998.

Langewiesche, William. *The Outlaw Sea: A World of Freedom, Chaos, and Crime.* New York: North Point Press, 2004.

London, Joshua E. *Victory in Tripoli: How America's Wars with the Barbary Pirates Established the U.S. Navy and Built a Nation.* Hoboken, NJ: John Wiley and Sons, Inc., 2005.

Magnusson, Magnus. *Vikings!* New York: E. P. Dutton, 1980.

Murray, Dian H. *Pirates of the South China Coast, 1790–1810.* Stanford, CA: Stanford University Press, 1987.

Naval Documents Related to the United States Wars with the Barbary Powers. 6 vols. Washington, DC: Government Printing Office, 1942.

Ormerod, Henry Arderne. *Piracy in the Ancient World: An Essay in Mediterranean History.* Liverpool: The University Press of Liverpool Ltd., 1924.

Oxenstierna, Eric Graf. *Die Wikinger.* Stuttgart: W. Kohlhammer Verlag, 1959.

Parker, Richard B. *Uncle Sam in Barbary: A Diplomatic History.* Gainesville, FL: University Press of Florida, 2004.

Paullin, Charles Oscar. *Commodore John Rodgers, Captain, Commodore, and Senior Officer of the American Navy, 1773–1838.* Cleveland, OH: Arthur H. Clark Co., 1910.

Pratt, Fletcher. *Preble's Boys: Commodore Preble and the Birth of American Seapower.* New York: William Sloan Associates, 1959.

Pritchett, W. Kendrick. *The Greek State at War.* Part II. Berkeley, CA: University of California Press, 1974.

Reisman, W. Michael and Chris T. Antoniou. *The Laws of War.* New York: Vintage Books (Random House), 1994.

Riccobono, Salvator (ed.). *Fontes Iuris Romani Anteiustiniani, Pars Prima: Leges.* Florence: S.A.G. Barbèra, 1968.

Riha, Thomas. *Readings in Russian Civilization.* Vol I, 2nd ed. Chicago, IL: University of Chicago Press, 1969.

Ritchie, Robert C. *Captain Kidd and the War against the Pirates.* Cambridge, MA: Harvard University Press, 1986.

Roesdahl, Else. *The Vikings.* 2nd ed. New York: Penguin Books, 1998.

Senior, Clive. *A Nation of Pirates: English Piracy in Its Heyday.* New York: Crane, Russak, 1976.

Stevenson, Robert Louis. *Treasure Island.* Philadelphia, PA: J. B. Lippincott Co., 1948.

Sturlason, Snorre. *The Heimskringla.* 3 vols. Edited and translated by Samuel Laing. New York: Norroena Society, 1907.

Vernadsky, George. *Ancient Russia*, Vols. I–II. New Haven, CT: Yale University Press, 1943.

Watson, Paul Barron. *The Tragic Career of Commodore James Barron, U.S. Navy*. New York: Coward-McCann, Inc., 1942.

Whipple, A. B. C. *To the Shores of Tripoli*. New York: William Morrow and Co., 1991.

Wilkinson, Clennell. *Dampier: Explorer and Buccaneer*. New York: Harper and Brothers Publishers, 1929.

Williams, Neville. *Captains Outrageous: Seven Centuries of Piracy*. London: Barrie and Rockliffe, 1961.

Wolf, John B. *The Barbary Coast: Algiers under the Turks, 1500–1830*. New York: Norton, 1979.

Wolf, Kirsten. *Daily Life of the Vikings*. Westport, CT: Greenwood Press, 2004.

Zacks, Richard. *The Pirate Coast: Thomas Jefferson, the First Marines, and the Secret Mission of 1805*. New York: Hyperion, 2005.

Index

About the Author

ALFRED S. BRADFORD is the John Saxon Professor of Ancient History at the University of Oklahoma. He earned his Ph.D. in Classical Languages and Literature from the University of Chicago. He served with the 1/27th Infantry in Vietnam. He has been a research assistant and a member at the Institute for Advanced Study, Princeton.